DESERT ROCK

ROCK CLIMBS IN
THE NATIONAL PARKS

Eric Bjørnstad

Graphics by Chris Becker

CHOCKSTONE

FALCON®

Desert Rock: Rock Climbs in The National Parks

Send all corrections and new route information to Eric Bjørnstad, PO Box 790, Moab, UT 84532 or call (801)259-7516. For information on the Colorado Plateau not covered in these volumes, you may contact the author at the above address.

Desert Rock Series ISBN 1-57540-010-3
Desert Rock: Rock Climbs in The National Parks ISBN 0-934641-92-7

Developed by:
Chockstone Press

Falcon Publishing, Inc
P.O. Box 1718
Helena, MT 59601

www.falconguide.com
email: falcon@falconguide.com

Front cover photo: From left to right: Washer Women Tower and Monster Tower, Canyonlands National Park. Photo courtesy of Tom Till Photography PO Box 337, Moab, UT 84532 (801)259-5327.

Back cover photo: The Marching Men, Arches National Park. Photo courtesy of Frank Mendonca, Perpetual Images, PO Box 366, Moab, UT 84532.

DEDICATION

Rob Slater 1960–1995

In tribute to his legendary Fisher Tower climbs, his shared love of the desert, and in fond memory of our visits in Moab. Rob died in an avalanche August 1995 after summiting via the Abruzzi Ridge of K2.

TABLE OF CONTENTS

FOREWORD

The vast sandstone canyons and desert climbing areas of the American Southwest have for several generations played host to adventurous climbers. Best known for extremes of weather, friable rock and other "character-building" qualities, with few exceptions, the desert is not a sport climber's paradise.

To say you fell in the desert because a hold broke is to say you weren't prepared for the obvious. Desert holds often break or are covered with sand. Self-placed protection is often questionable: Friends rip grooves in the stone, hard-driven pitons pull with disconcerting ease. Free climbing in the desert is an exercise in mind control, demanding a subtler understanding of the rock medium than does the more solid stuff like granite, limestone, and quartzite.

Then why are so many climbers flocking to the cracks of Indian Creek, the hoodoos of the Fischer Towers and the uncompromising walls of Zion, where a pitch or two of execrable rock is encountered on even the cleanest routes?

For one thing, there's the beauty and the special light in a combination found nowhere else on Earth. The elegant architecture of the ruddy spires against a pure blue sky, the Earth's ancient autobiography etched on pastel sandstone walls–this synergy of elements inspired painters like Georgia O'Keefe to focus on form, color, space, and light in their interpretations of the desert's stark serenity. Latter-day artists of ascent, from the Sierra Club members on Ship Rock in the 1930s, to Coloradans on the cracks of Indian Creek in the '70s, to big wall climbers from around the world in Zion in the '90s, have been equally inspired by the simple drama of the summits and walls and their sweeping lines.

Besides the beauty, there's the adventure inherent in climbing in such a vast region of variable geology. Although this guide highlights many of the better climbs, there are thousands of other routes that have yet to see an ascent, and even the classics will never be as secure as their counterparts in areas of greater crystalline integrity. For some climbers, the intrinsic insecurity of desert climbing is the primary reason for climbing there, while others simply tolerate or overlook it, drawn as they are to the purity of the monolithic geometry of the Wingate or Navajo sandstone.

Personally, the desert has stimulated my senses and climber's imagination since the mid-'60s, when many of the most prominent towers were climbed for the first time. Eric Bjørnstad was one of the great pioneers of that period and has remained involved through the years. This book is proof of his continued spiritual involvement. In concert with the Native American tribes who have inhabited the Four Corners area for centuries, Eric espouses a philosophy of living in balance with the land–mandatory for climbers visiting this exceptionally fragile region. Besides documenting the climbs in an excellent fashion, Eric tells fascinating stories of the natural and human history, putting climbing in its proper context.

At the climber's campfire, Eric Bjørnstad is a tribal elder. His wealth of life experience, unquenchable curiosity and vision, make him a formidable treasure trove of climbing lore, and the perfect author of this important series.

Jeff Lowe
October 1995

ACKNOWLEDGMENTS

The monumental task of collecting, sorting, and researching the countless details of sandstone climbs on the Colorado Plateau–a vast area nearly the size of California–has been possible only through collaboration with hundreds of climbers. Many contributed not only topos and details of their climbs but also gave slides and reviewed information on other areas they had climbed.

Those providing slides are credited with their photographs. Size limitations for these new *Desert Rock* volumes has prevented the use of many photos I would like to have included. The following are gratefully thanked for their time, support and contribution:

Jeff Achey, Tom Addison, John Allen, Steve Allen, Dave Anderson, Jay Anderson, Steve Anderton, Chris Andrews, Steve Angelini, Jim Angione, Mark Austin, Benny Bach, Fran Bagenal, Mike Baker, Fran Barnes, Alan "Crusher" Bartlett, Alen Bartlette, Fred Beckey, Christine Beekman, Chris Begue, George Bell, Mark Bennett, Bobbi Bensman, Jim Beyer, Josh Blumental, Jim Bodenhamer, Brad Bond, Jake Bos, George Bracksieck, Cameron Burns, Ralph Burns, Jon Butler, Keen Butterworth, Doug Byerly, John Byrnes, Kitty Calhoun, Chip Chace, Les Choy, Erick Christianson, Ben Clower, Tim Coats, Darren Cope, Kyle Copeland, Marco Comacchione, Tom Cotter, Jeff Crystal, John Culberson, Carolyn Dailey, Perry Davis, Carl Diedrich, Topher Donahue, Rick Donnelly, Bill Duncan, Jimmy Dunn, Teri Ebel, Warren Egbert, Greg Epperson, Blaine Erickson, Dave Evans, Paul Evans, Jeff Fassett, Randy Falk, Joe Fitschan, Bill Flemming, Mike Fredrick, Graham Frontella, Doug Frost, Andrew Fry, James Funsten, Cindy Furman, Paul Gagner, Peter Gallagher, Bego Gerhart, David Gloudemans, Jim Goldberg, David Goldstein, Paul Gonzales, Todd Gordon, Stewart Green, Tony Grenko, Ken Guza, Chris Haaland, Doug Hall, Lisa Hathaway, Jorma Hayes, Mark Hesse, Kris Hjelle, Jeff Hollenbaugh, Steve Hong, Paul Horton, Jim Howe, Rodger "Strappo" Hughs, Bruce Hunter, Ray Huntzinger, George Hurley, Dave Insley, Eric Johnson, Steve Johnson, Chris Kalous, Teri Kane, Todd Kearns, Jason Keith, Tobin Kelley, Max Kendall, Craig Kenyon, Fred Knapp, Robert Kooken, Jon Krakauer, Chuck Kroger, Luke Laeser, Matt Laggis, Mark Lassiter, John Lewis, Young Hee Lowrie, Craig Luebben, Dougald MacDonald, Glen Mann, John Markel, Andrew Marquardt, Keith Mass, Bonnie McElhinny, Betsi McKittrich, Doug McQueen, Steve Mesdough, Chris "Renegade" Meyer, Paul Midkiff, David Mondeau, Sasha Montagu, Matt Moore, Melisa Morrow, Patrick Morrow, John Mudd, Dave Nessia, Jim Newberry, Rene Newman, Bob Novellino, Mike O'Donnel, Bob Palais, Simon Peck, Mike Pennings, Rich Perch, Andy Petefish, Andy Pitas, Wendy Pitas, Linus Platt, Ferdl Ploerer, Hanni Ploerer, David Pallari, Jack Pope, Steve Porcella, Jason Predock, Brad Quinn, Steve Quinlin, Duane Raleigh, Glenn Randall, Alf Randell, Eric Rasmussen, Keith Reynolds, Stu Ritchie, Ann Robertson, Chuck Santagati, Antoino Savelli, Joede Schoeberlein, Sallie Shatz, Joseph Sheader, Tom Sherman, Walt Shipley, John Shireman, Rick Showalter, Paul Sibley, Paul Seibert, Eric Siefer, Ken Sims, Jeff Singer, Rob Slater, Rick Smith, Doug Snively, Merlin Spiller, Carrie Sood, Tracy Sternburg, Andrea Stoughton, Pete Takeda, Brian Takei, Eve Tallman, Tom Thomas, Mel Thorsen, Reed Tindall, Tim Toula, Jake Tratiak, Paul Turecki, Ray Vought, Barry Ward, Robert Warren, Randall Weekley, Ed Webster, Frosty Weller, David Whidden, Mark Whiton, Earl Wiggins, Chad Wiggle, Ron Wiggle, Tony Wilson, Mike Woods.

I have been very fortunate in using the photos of nationally acclaimed photographers Ed Cooper (my climbing partner in the early 1960s), Bill Hatcher, Frank Mendonca (for trusting me with his priceless shots), and Tom Till. Michelle Goldstein was liberal with her professional photo work. Bill Godschalx has given freely of time and expense for telephotographing Wall Street and developing and enlarging the shots used into an 8x10 format. These volumes would lack much in quality without his generous contribution.

Chris Becker took time from teaching and house building to accompany me on weekends to Zion National Park with John Middendorf, Colorado National Monument with K.C. Baum, Indian Creek with Steve Petro and Bret Ruckman, the San Rafael Swell with Cris Coffey and Rene and Warren Newman, as well as numerous other infield jaunts. Chris' meticulously drawn topos have set a standard for detail, accuracy and artistic excellence. I am profoundly indebted to him.

James Garrett camped with me in the San Rafael and was tireless in his collaboration on routes there. Jeff Lowe gave his time and his knowlege of Zion and Capitol Reef National Parks and kindly wrote the Foreword to Volume 1. John Middendorf made possible the selection of climbs in Zion and also contributed the Zion climbing history profile. K.C. Baum made the Colorado National Monument chapter possible, with his time and principle contributions, as well as the climbs in the Unaweep area. Steve Petro made available his file on Indian Creek and drove a couple hundred miles to meet me there and hike to the climbs. Bret Ruckman's support and help with Indian Creek climbs was invaluable.

Kevin Chase, Dave Medara and Peter Verchick of Moab Adventure Outfitters were generous in providing information on many climbs in the Moab area. Jay Smith accompanied Chris Becker and me on research outings, and Tom Gilje made valuable contributions to new climbs on the River Road and Kane Creek areas.

Bob Van Belle, park administrator at Capitol Reef, and his wife Joslin, provided bed and vittles and guidance to the routes.

Canyonlands Natural History Association, together with a host of park personnel, edited or in one way or another were helpful with the Canyonlands chapter. They are Jim Braggs, Nancy Coulam, Paul Cowan, Larry Fredricks, Galen Howell, Wendy Hurlbert, Mary Beth Maynard, Char Oberg, Sonja Paspal, Steve Swanke, Cynthia Williams, Tara Williams. Noel Poe, superintendent at Arches, together with Paul Cowan and Diane Allen reviewed the Arches chapter.

Jeff Widen wrote the "Environmental Considerations" section of the Introduction, as well as contributing numerous slides for consideration and reviewed many chapters with an eye for detail and accuracy.

Finally, the keystone to bringing these volumes to fruition, Cris Coffey, who contributed the majority of the editing on the original *Desert Rock* (Chockstone, 1988) has, with her critical eye, sharpened and helped clarify these new *Desert Rock* volumes, bringing them from the dark ages to literacy.

Eric Bjørnstad
Moab, 1996

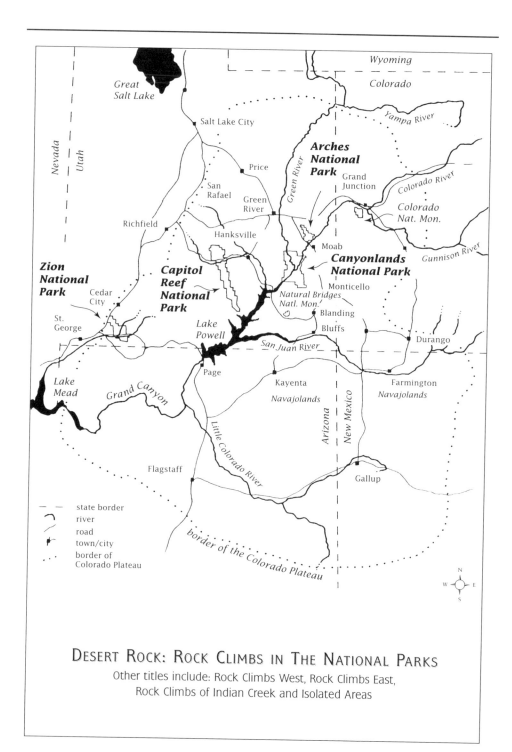

Desert Rock: Rock Climbs in The National Parks
Other titles include: Rock Climbs West, Rock Climbs East,
Rock Climbs of Indian Creek and Isolated Areas

DESERT ROCK

The sandstone canyon walls, mesas, buttes and spires of the Colorado Plateau are the focus of this new Desert Rock series.

The Colorado Plateau is a physiographic province lying north and east of the Basin and Range province and south and west of the Rocky Mountain province. It covers about 160,000 square miles (nearly the size of California) in Utah, Arizona, New Mexico, and Colorado. Within its vast reaches of sedimentary sandstone lie the greatest potential for crack climbing in the world. It is a sector of North America with thousands of miles of vertically fractured Wingate sandstone walls. Although hundreds of climbs have been established, this is only a fraction of the potential on the Plateau. The majority of routes lie within the higher registry of difficulty, but there remains a large selection of excellent climbs below the 5.10 level, and all within the incomparable canyon country of the high southwest desert.

Stephen Trimble in *The Bright Edge* says, "Time ticks slowly for the Canyon Country. A year means nothing, a human lifetime sees arroyos deepened a bit, the collapse of an arch or cliff here and there, the creation of a new window or two. A millennium scarcely changes the landscape. Only in tens of thousands of years does the land see much change. And even then, a hundred thousand years is a fraction of an instant in the millions and billions of years of the earth's history. On this time scale the Plateau itself becomes a temporary phenomenon, a passing fancy of an earth with a restless skin of drifting, dynamic continents."

The Plateau contains eight national parks–Zion, Bryce, Capitol Reef, Arches, and Canyonlands in Utah; Mesa Verde, Grand Canyon, and Petrified Forest outside Utah, in addition to 19 other regions managed by the National Park Service–the greatest concentration of national parks and wilderness areas outside Alaska.

The Colorado River is the principle artery of the Plateau, giving its name and draining 90% of canyon country. Each year the river transports about three cubic miles of sandstone sediment to the impounded waters behind Glen Canyon Dam. Like the branches of a tree, the Colorado is fed by a network of tributaries, with countless arroyos further contributing during periods of storm. It is a land of haunting beauty, a region without parallel on earth, and its fragile ecosystem is in grave danger.

What has changed in the years since *Desert Rock* was first published early in 1988 is the escalating numbers discovering and frequenting the desert. Each season attendance records are routinely broken at Canyonlands National Park, Natural Bridges National Monument, and Dead Horse Point State Park. Visitation at Zion National Park exceeds two million and Arches National Park now approaches one million per year. Recreationists of every disposition now make the desert their vacation destination. The gamut runs from mountain bikers, river runners, climbers, four-wheel drivers, to hikers, campers, artists, photographers, mystics, and nature enthusiasts. The challenge becomes balancing their enjoyment with preserving what they have come to enjoy.

It has long been assumed that the desert is a tough, indestructible land, indifferent to human impact. In other regions of the country moisture promotes a bacterial breakdown. Trees rot, litter (with time) dissolves, new growth covers scars. But here the desert is so dry and growth so slow that the land is like another planet where time has stopped. Our appearance has been dramatic and caustic. The dry air mummifies our castaways. Orange peels, egg shells, and other material tossed to the land do not biodegrade. Discards become permanent monuments to our sloth.

Cryptobiotic soil is eminent to the health of the desert. Without the aid of this vulnerable crust the majority of indigenous flowers and other shrubs would simply not exist. Once the soil is impacted by tire or foot, such prints remain visible for decades. Recovery is estimated to take up to 250 years. If we are to preserve this island of earth, it is most important that we walk only on slickrock (rock devoid of soil or vegetation), in drainages, or on a trail. Direct cross-country travel is unconscionable.

The indelible print of our seemingly benign inroads to the desert are not readily apparent from our state of the art vehicles equipped with the emblems of our sybaritic society. With us we bring not only quick draws, space ship alloy light cams, freeze dried foods, and satellite maps but also an invincible confidence in our superiority as a species. We have a long history of annihilating the land as we reshape it to suit us. I implore all who visit the unique canyon country to be responsible not only for our present love of the desert, but for the generations yet to be thrilled by this magical place.

Perhaps now with the kindling of a new consciousness, we are on the threshold of a new direction not previously traveled. We may now value and protect the wild regions of the planet not for the short term plunder of the past, but as the very root of our survival.

Please visit with prudence, responsibility and love.

Eric Bjørnstad
January 1996
Moab, Utah

About the new Desert Rock series

Desert Rock (1988) attempted to document the known climbs established throughout the sandstone formations of the Colorado Plateau. Not included were hundreds of ascents up the buttes, towers, and walls of the Grand Canyon and Zion National Parks. The present volume includes a subjective selection of the best of Zion but leaves the 280-mile-long Grand Canyon to future writers.

A technical rock climbing guide is necessarily an assemblage of material from a great many sources. This is especially true regarding the vast deserts of the Colorado Plateau. Unlike most areas, where routes are established mainly by resident climbers and route detail is easily accessible, here resident climbers are comparatively few and the majority of sources for route information are scattered across the country and overseas. Although the three years and 8,000 hours of research which went into *Desert Rock* (1988) has provided a solid foundation for the present series of guides, the past couple of years have brought additional contacts with hundreds of climbers and racked up an astonishing number of research hours. I have climbed on the desert for over 30 years and for many years made canyon country my home. This series of guides is the product of a long love affair with the desert.

This new *Desert Rock* series covers the Colorado Plateau from Colorado National Monument east to Zion National Park west, from Valley of the Gods and Indian Creek south to Moab and San Rafael Swell north.

Desert Rock Climbs in the National Parks includes a subjective selection of routes in Arches and Zion National Parks and the known routes of Capitol Reef and Canyonlands National Parks. It also includes the adjacent Glen Canyon National Recreational Area and Green River area just outside the park boundary of Canyonlands.

Desert Rock Climbs West covers the region west of the Colorado River in the Moab area, and includes Wall Street, Day Canyon, Long Canyon, and the majority of routes established in the San Rafael Swell.

Desert Rock Climbs East covers climbs east of the Colorado River in the Moab area. Included are Kane Creek, the River Road (highway 128), Castle Valley, Fisher Towers, and the Colorado National Monument.

Desert Rock Climbs of Indian Creek and Isolated Areas is a definitive coverage of Indian Creek, Valley of the Gods, Tooth Rock, Arch and Texas Canyons, and other isolated regions of the Colorado Plateau.

Though the Navajoland was documented in *Desert Rock* (1988) from a historic point of view (equipment lists and other pertinent ascent information excluded), the present volumes do not include the climbs located on the reservation. There is still a climbing ban imposed by the Navajo Tribal Council although there have been numerous new routes clandestinely established since Desert Rock. There have been reports of windshields broken on anglo-owned vehicles left unattended, as well as climbing equipment confiscated and stiff fines imposed on those disregarding the climbing ban. On the other hand, reports have also surfaced regarding numerous climbs accomplished on the reservation with the permission of the neighboring Navajo residents. If permission cannot be obtained, please respect tribal limits. After all, there is more than a lifetime of legal and spectacular buttes, towers, spires, and canyon walls to climb on the Colorado Plateau.

E. B.

Environmental Considerations of Desert Rock Climbing by *Jeff* Widen

The Colorado Plateau is a stunning and magical arena in which to climb. After experiencing the desert world, many climbers have written about the need to slow down, take in the desert's aura and walk more softly. Indeed, just being within this incredible landscape is a major part of any climbing trip. The starkness of the earth's bare bones, along with the extremes of heat, cold, wind, and weather–are all part of the desert climbing experience. As harsh as the desert may be in many ways, though, it is also an extremely fragile place. Plants and animals carry out a tentative existence and are easily disturbed. The visual scars left by careless activity are extremely slow to heal. The desert needs extra care, a lighter touch.

There is another compelling reason to tread lightly in the desert. The extractive industries of mining, timber cutting, ranching and water development have long been criticized for their abuse of public lands. Damaging climbing practices threaten to put climbers in the same category, at least in the eyes of environmental organizations if not the general public. Land managing agencies increasingly view climbing as an activity with real impacts and also one that can be dealt with fairly easily, meaning increased regulation. One has only to look at recent attempts at bolt bans by various agencies to understand the seriousness of the threat. Climbers can go a long way toward staving off overly harsh regulation by acting responsibly. Although the debates over climbing styles rage endlessly, nearly all climbers agree on the importance of protecting the climbing environment. The desert contains some of the most radical and outrageous crack climbs on Earth. It's up to everyone climbing there to help protect access to these climbs—and to protect the rock and land itself.

Climbing impacts in the desert center around all aspects of a climb, from multiple trails to rock damage to trash. The desert environment requires extra care at each turn.

Approaches: Check out approach routes in advance. For the driving portion of the approach— a major part of many desert climbs—stay on established roads. If you are unlike most desert

climbers and own some beefy four-wheel drive with real clearance, resist the urge to get a few hundred yards closer to the route by driving off road. On foot, follow established approach paths wherever possible. Take an extra minute to see if there is a common route up to a climb. Take special care not to walk over areas of Cryptobiotic soil (you can recognize this unique desert plant assemblage by its appearance as black, crusty soil). It is critical for prevention of erosion in the desert, takes hundreds of years to form and is destroyed instantly when crushed. To avoid cryptobiotic soil and other plants and animals, walk in washes and over slickrock and boulders whenever possible. Approaching climbs in this way will also prevent the all-too-visible trashing of the desert's surface.

Protection: Using clean pro is perhaps more important in the desert—the rock simply can't take the abuse of piton placement. Free routes don't present

Photo: Jeff Widen

Pin scars

much of a problem, since desert cracks are tailor-made for camming devices. On aid routes, however, there are too many examples where cracks have been nailed that could have been climbed with clean hardware (see pitons below). It's true that you need a huge stock of caaming devices to climb desert routes, but that's part of the game. People often go in groups and pool their gear to do these routes. When retreating or rapping off, leave gear, webbing, etc. of neutral colors–brown, black, or tan are the best.

Bolts: Nothing raises the ire of land managers more than over-bolting, whether real or perceived. If there is one thing climbers can do to prevent excessive regulation, it is to minimize bolt use. This doesn't mean bolt placement elimination, for indeed the nature of desert climbing–vertical walls and towers without natural rappel anchors–makes bolt placement a necessity. But climbers should keep the number to a minimum. The days of long bolt ladders in the desert are long gone. Short ladders are sometimes necessary to reach the crackless summits of towers, but when the route is a predominantly bolt-clipping ascent, the formation is better left unclimbed.

Bolts placed next to cracks would seem anathema to most climbers, yet a disturbing number of bolts can be found next to bomber cam placements. If you don't have the gear, go hit up your friends and come back later. When bolts are placed, they should be placed well, whether to give you the extra courage to do a few more free moves or to prevent the eventual formation of an ugly and unusable hole when the bolt comes out.

The standard desert bolt has long been a $\frac{1}{2}$" angle piton pounded into a $\frac{3}{8}$" hole drilled at a slight downward angle. Some of the newer $\frac{1}{2}$" expansion bolts are now being used–check out recent reviews in various climbing publications to see which ones are best for soft rock.

Power drills have no place in the desert. Not only can holes be quickly hand-drilled in sandstone, but a major part of the desert climbing experience is the feeling of quiet and vast open spaces, and the sense of high adventure. The use of power drills not only runs counter to this sense, but leads quickly to over-bolting.

Pitons: Climbers should adopt an attitude of minimization when nailing in the desert. Pin scars are more visible in sandstone and nailing routes here get beat out faster than on any other rock type. Minimizing piton damage includes reducing the number of pin placements as much as possible, looking for alternative routes and perhaps stopping to ask yourself whether a formation with existing routes really needs a new nail-up. Devices such as Lowe ball nuts and Tri-cams, Rock and Rollers and small camming devices can often substitute for pins down to Lost Arrow size. Using clean gear can also have the desirable effect of upping the fear factor of an aid route.

If you must nail, use constructive scarring techniques. This involves favoring upward blows to the pin when cleaning so the eventual hole will accept a nut or other clean pro.

Chipping/Gluing: These are destructive practices that are indefensible anywhere, especially in the desert.

Chalk: Many desert pioneers and early locals climbed without it, but most modern climbers use chalk. White chalk is especially visible and obnoxious on red rock. If you use chalk, use colored chalk–dark brown or dark red are the best colors. Most of the national parks already require colored chalk.

Archaeological Sites: The Colorado Plateau is rich in Native American archaeological resources. Special care must be taken to avoid these areas, whether ruins, rock art panels or areas with pot shards, tool fragments or other ancient artifacts. Stealing artifacts is a federal crime. Avoid climbing near any of these archaeological sites–you can bet there is another perfect crack around the corner.

Human Waste: Desert areas are booming in popularity and human waste is becoming an increasing problem. It is critical to take the extra couple of minutes to do it right. Go at least 300 feet (91m) from major washes and other watercourses. Although land managers are looking at the viability of surface disposal, the currently accepted method for dealing with excrement is still to dig a small hole six-to-eight inches deep and bury the waste. Used toilet paper should be packed out in Ziploc-like bags and disposed of. There are also reports of increasing human waste near the bases of popular towers–climbers should treat the base of towers as a stream and go several hundred feet away to do their business. It goes without saying that all other trash, tape, old slings, etc. should be carried out.

Wildlife: It is important to respect wildlife closures, usually imposed to protect nesting raptors or other species. Closures are posted at visitor centers or land manager's headquarters.

Attitude: No climbing is totally without impact. But in this desert land–with its special qualities of fragility, beauty and silence–it is essential to adopt an attitude of reducing our impact. We must walk and climb a bit more lightly. The self-interest issue of preventing over-regulation is crucial. But there is also a much bigger issue–it is the right thing to do and makes the incredible experience of climbing in this place all the richer.

Mount Majestic

EMERALD STAR MAJESTICUS V, 5.8X, A3, 5 pitches technical plus much 3rd class

First Ascent: Doug Byerly, James Funsten, 7-10 October 1993.

Location and Access: First Ascent party suggests a special rating of BC5 (bush, cactus rating). The route climbs the mountain via its south buttress. This is the first prow to the right of Behunin Canyon. Approach via Emerald Pools Trail. [....]

Paraphernalia: (2) sets of Friends #2.5 through #3.5 and (1) #4; Camalot #7; small TCUs to #2; (2) sets of hooks; (1) set of ball nuts; (3) sets of cams; (4-5) Leepers; (2) each ½" and ⅜" angles; (2-3) #5 and #6 Lost Arrows; (1-2) #7; (4-5) Bugaboos; (4) knifeblades; (3-4) Birdbeaks; (2) Fish Hooks.

Descent: Reverse the route.

About this book

Each chapter has the same format. Shaded areas title the general location of the climbs and are followed with a written description of the area's location. Routes are listed from left to right on any particular formation. Route names are followed by grade, free climbing difficulty, aid rating, number of pitches, length of route or height of the landform measured from its longest side, followed by a star rating where available. First ascent particulars are followed by location and access of the climb. Paraphernalia is followed by descent information.

Rating System

Each climb is given a grade of I through VI

Grade I   One to two hours of climbing

Grade II   Less than half a day

Grade III   Half a day climb

Grade IV   Full day climb

Grade V   Two day climb

Grade VI   Multi-day ascent

Free climbing difficulty on a scale 1 through 6 with 5 broken down from 5.0 through 5.13+ free climbing and 6 broken down to A1 through A5 of aid climbing.

1   Trail

2   Cross-country hiking

3   Scrambling

4   Exposed scrambling usually with rope for protection

5   Free climbing

6   Aid climbing

Free climbing difficulty 5.0 through 5.9

5.0 through 5.9

5.9+

5.10-(a)

5.10-(b)

5.10+(c)

5.10+(d)

5.11-(a) through 5.13+

R = runout

S = hurt on fall

X = killed on fall

Aid climbing difficulty A1 through A5– C1, C2, A0

A0   Aid points fixed.

A1   Easy secure placements

A2   More awkward placement which will hold less weight than A1.

A3   Still more difficult placement and less secure. Will hold only short fall.

A4   Difficult placement, not secure enough for a fall. Will hold body weight only.

A5   Multiple A4 placements. A fall would result in injury or death.

C1, C2   Ratings for clean hammerless aid of increasing difficulty

Paraphernalia

Quantities are set off in parentheses, items are separated by semicolons.

Standard Desert Rack Two sets of Friends with a selection of wired stoppers, Tri-cams and quickdraws.

A Zion Free Climbing Rack consists of 2-3 sets of cams, hexes and stoppers, plus a load of full-length slings and carabiners.

A Zion Aid Rack consists of 3 or more sets of cams, many stoppers and brass-nuts, carabiners, slings, hooks, plus 3-4 birdbeaks, 3-5 knifeblades, 3-5 horizontals (Lost Arrows), 2-3 each baby angles ($\frac{1}{2}$", $\frac{5}{8}$") and 1-2 each of the bigger pitons.

Star Rating

Ratings are based on a scale of 1 to 5 stars of increasing aesthetics and with few exceptions are the consensus of those who have climbed the routes.

Paraphernalia Size Comparison Chart

This chart is designed to assist the climber in assembling and borrowing gear necessary for desert climbing. It gives a general idea of size comparisons between brands. Measurements are from the manufacturer or distributor but in no way are guaranteed to be accurate. Provided courtesy of Moab Adventure Outfitters, 600 North Main, Moab, Utah 84532, (801)259-2725.

Colorado Custom Hardware Aliens: Measurements are manufacturers fully closed to fully open. Cams are not strong fully open.

⅜	½	¾	1	1½	2	2½
.38–.65	.53–.87	.6–1.06	.76–1.34	1.03–1.63	1.2–1.95	1.4–2.35

Wired Bliss TCU and FCU: Measurements and manufacturers list of "range."

.4	.5	.75	1.0	1.5	2.0	2.5	3.0
.4–.6	.5–.8	.6–.9	.8–1.3	9–1.4	1.2–1.9	1.4–2.2	1.8–2.8

Wild Country Friends and Flexible Friends: Measurements and manufacturers list of "range."

0	½	1	1½	2	2½	3	3½	4
.52–.76	.60–.96	.76–1.16	.92–1.40	1.16–1.76	1.32–2.20	1.72–2.64	2.08–3.24	2.56–4.00

Metolius TCU and FCU: Measurements and manufacturers list of "range."

0	1	2	3	4	5	6	7	8	9	10
.40–.60	.50–.75	.60–.90	.75–1.10	.90–1.35	1.10–1.70	1.28–1.90	1.65–2.25	2.00–2.75	2.20–3.30	2.80–4.20

Hugh Banner (HB) Quadcams and Micromates: Manufacturers measurements of "crack size."

00	0	.5	1	1.5	2.0	2.5	3.0	3.8	5.0
.42–.66	.52–.76	.60–.92	.76–1.16	.88–1.40	1.12–1.76	1.40–2.20	1.80–2.76	2.36–3.72	3.40–5.08

Black Diamond Camalot and Camalot Jr.: Manufacturers measurements of "size range." Old style Camalots are slightly larger in sizes 1 through 4.

.5	.75	1	2	3	4	5
.8–1.3	1.0–1.6	1.2–2.0	1.5–2.5	2.0–3.4	2.9–4.8	4.2–7.0

Sidewinder Protection Big Bros: Manufacturers measurements of "expansion range."

1	2	3	4
3.2–4.4	4.0–5.8	5.2–8.0	7.3–12.0

Lowe Balls: Actual minimum and maximum size "functional range is less."

1	2	3
3mm–6mm	4.5mm–9mm	6mm–12mm

Yates Big Dudes: Manufacturers stated "camming range."

1	2
3.74–6.0	4.5–7.0

Photo: Ed Cooper

Sentinel Rock

ZION NATIONAL PARK

If you are old, go by all means; but if you are young, stay away until you grow older.... It is not well to dull one's capacity for enjoyment by seeing the finest first.

Henry Gannett, U.S. Geological Survey

Beautiful and impressive contrasts meet you everywhere: the colors of tree and flower, rock and sky, light and shade, strength and frailty, endurance and evanescence.

John Muir

Zion National Park covers an area of 230 square miles (147,000 acres) containing eight geologic formations and four major vegetation zones. There are now national parks in over 100 nations throughout our tiny planet, yet not one, I would venture to submit from a hardcore rock climber's point of view, could equal Zion National Park. This oldest and most famous of Utah's five national parks has long been a sleeper among the climbing world. In places the walls of Zion Canyon rise half a mile into the sky. Its majestic rockscapes have inspired names of beauty, reverence, awe and exaltation found in no other land: The Watchman, Altar of Sacrifice, East Temple, West Temple, Great White Throne, Angels Landing, Three Patriarchs, The Pulpit and Temple of Sinawava. The great climbing mentor Chuck Pratt, in an *Ascent* article, spoke of the walls of Zion as "more intimidating than those of Yosemite." John Middendorf, the well-known big wall climber, speaks of Zion as, "the most awesome series of canyons and formations in the world." A very splendid place!

Location and access

The park lies at the juncture of the Great Basin, Mojave Desert and the vast Colorado Plateau in the southwest corner of Utah. As a result all these regions influence the park. It is reached by auto 4.5 hours from Las Vegas, 2 hours from Bryce Canyon, 2.5 hours from Grand Canyon (north rim), 4 hours from Capitol Reef and 7-8 hours from Arches and Canyonlands National Parks. Except for Las Vegas, all of these regions are part of the incredible 1100 mile Grand Circle, the largest concentration of National Parks (eight), National Monuments (seven) and State Parks and Historic Sites anywhere on earth. Zion Canyon is reached from the south through the town of Springdale or from the east, a descent via the Zion-Mount Carmel entrance. There are 35 miles (56km) of improved roads in the park, including 11.5 miles (18.5km) of the Zion Mount Carmel Highway and 26 miles (42km) of well-kept trails. Zion's roads are surfaced with scoria, rock mined from volcanic cinders, which provide an abrasive non-slip surface. These abrasive edges result from bubbles created as trapped gas escaped from the cooling rock. The cinders' red blends well with the surrounding landscape.

Kolob Canyon In 1937, the Kolob area (northwest of Zion Canyon), came under protection when it was designated Zion National Monument. It was elevated to the National Park system in 1956. This satellite region of Zion is located 45 miles (72km) northwest of Zion Canyon, 19 miles (30km) south of Cedar City, 33 miles (53km) north of St. George. To reach from Interstate 15, take Exit 40 and drive to the visitor center in view a short distance ahead. Although the Kolob Canyon visitor center is small, it is worth stopping before entering this remote sector of the park. At the center information on weather, road conditions, trails and overnight backcountry permits are available. There is also a limited selection of books, topographic maps, posters and postcards, slides and film for sale. Also available is a Kolob Canyon road guide keyed to numbered stops along the canyon road. Hours are 8 A.M.–4:30 P.M. daily with extended hours between Memorial Day and Labor Day weekends, telephone (801)586-9548.

From the visitor center the park road climbs 1300 feet (396m) in 5.7 miles (9km) up moderately steep grades and sharp curves as it ascends along the Hurricane Fault, a 200 mile (322km) fracture in the earth's crust that forms the western edge of the Markagunt Plateau. To the east is a jagged escarpment of tilted rock layers (deformed by friction) where the Colorado Plateau rose nearly a mile in geologic time.

The drive leads alongside Taylor Creek, over Lee Pass and into the Timber Creek drainage. The road ends at a spectacular viewpoint with an overlook, exhibit and picnic area atop the fault. Looming to the east are the dramatic Kolob Finger Canyons with narrow 1600-foot-deep (488m) canyons in between vertical Navajo Sandstone walls. It is some of the most beautiful and awe inspiring country in all of Zion National Park if not the entire Colorado Plateau. Kolob Canyon was named by Mormon pioneers when they settled in nearby Harmony in the fall of 1852. Kolob: "the great one...nearest the throne of God," in Mormon literature refers to the star that shines brightly.

Snow Canyon State Park is a sculptured canyon 500-700 feet (152-213m) high. Open all year, it offers excellent one- to two-pitch routes and is a recommended visit while in the Zion area. The canyon was named for Lorenzo and Erastus Snow (not for the rare snowfalls of the area). Like Zion, many names in the park honor Mormon pioneers. The park is located west of Zion, about 12 miles (19km) north of St. George. State Highway 18 circles the upper edge of the canyon and is the most direct way to reach the park from the Interstate. A loop road between State 18 and Old US 19 near Santa Clara also gives access. Snow Canyon State Park is about 3 miles (4.8km) long and offers, besides recommended climbs, intricately sculptured sandstone cliffs, remnants of black lava streams which cascaded over sedimentary cliffs to solidify into formidable falls, Indian rock art, an improved campground, a picnic area with tables, drinking water and toilets. For further information contact Snow Canyon State Park at Box 140, Santa Clara, Utah 84765. Telephone (801)628-2255.

History

Like much of the Colorado Plateau, Zion was home to the Anasazi. There is physical evidence of their presence from about 500 A.D.–1200 A.D. As elsewhere, they hunted game, foraged for plant food and tended small garden plots. After the Anasazi left (from drought, from overuse of the land–no one knows) the Paiute Indians were known to come and go, although they were fearful of spending the night in the canyon. It is likely the first non-natives to visit Zion were 16 mountain men led by Jedediah Smith in 1826 in search of beaver pelts. It was a brief visit. Next came Nephi Johnson who was sent by Brigham Young of the powerful Mormon Church. He was directed to explore the upper Virgin River Valley for a potential settlement. And in 1871 Major John Wesley Powell visited the region of Zion. The land became known and protected.

Zion was first set aside for protection as Mukuntuweap National Monument in 1909 by President Taft. Just nine years later the Monument was enlarged by President Wilson and the unpopular name was changed to Zion. Zion was named by its first settler, Isaac Behunin, a Mormon pioneer. One evening, the story is told, while Isaac was sitting on his front porch in the "lingering golden twilight," he was so moved by the grandeur before him that he thought of the canyon as Zion, from a passage in the Bible (Isaiah 2:2-3) describing such a place "in the top of the mountains" where "the Lord's house shall be established." A year later (1919) the status of the land was changed again by an act of Congress to that of a National Park, then enlarged again in 1931.

A Brief History of Climbing in Zion by John Middendorf

Rock climbing in Zion began in the '20s with the ascent of the Great White Throne by William H. Evans. Evans, described in a Superintendent's memo dated July 13,1927 as a "distinctly daredevil type and a mountaineer," arrived in the park on June 20, 1927 and heard that the *Great White Throne* had not been ascended. On June 24, he made an attempt to climb the north side but was thwarted by steep walls and returned to the valley floor realizing that it was not the right way to go. On June 27, armed with but 15 feet of rope and a small canteen of water, Evans climbed to the saddle on the south side and made his way up slabs to the summit where he made several signal fires that night to prove his accomplishment to the people in the Grotto auto camp below. The next morning, he began his descent and fell. A historic rescue effort, led by Chief Ranger Ruesch, was organized the following day after his absence. After several days of searching, the rescuers found Evans motionless among the bushes at the saddle. He was delirious from shock, covered with severe bruises and sporting a cracked skull and remembered little of the preceding days after his fall. His rescuers carried him to the East Rim Trail where he was placed on a horse and carried down, chastised for his recklessness.

On June 30, 1931, Dan Orcutt made the second ascent via Evan's route. (Evans reported finding a human skull on the summit, perhaps the remains of some venturesome native.) Both Evans and Orcutt's ascents were condemned by the park, as they were "improperly executed and done in a manner that is strongly disapproved by all alpinists having recognized reputations" (from a 1931 Park Service memo).

The second major formation climbed in Zion was The Cathedral, presumably from the Angels Landing Trail, by Walter Becker, Fritz Becker and Rudolph Weidner on August 31, 1931. This was a technical climb for the day (climbed with ropes) and involved a difficult chimney and an overhanging rock which "taxed all their powers of ingenuity and endurance to pass."

In 1933 the West Temple was climbed by an eight-man team, with the brothers Norman and Newell Crawford reaching the summit. The East Temple was climbed in 1937 by Glen Dawson,

Dick Jones, Homer Fuller, Wayland Gilbert and Jo Momyer, followed by an ascent of The Sentinel by Bob Brinton and Glen Dawson in 1938. All of these routes are described as treacherous climbing on loose white rock, with insecure footings and holds. Today the historic ascents are still considered difficult with sections of 5th class climbing–not for the casual hiker.

The Great White Throne, subject of a commemorative stamp of the 1934 National Park series, received only a few ascents over the next 20 years, including the fourth ascent by the legendary husband and wife team of Herb and Jan Conn in 1949.

Modern climbing in Zion began in 1967 with the ascent of the Great White Throne via the Northwest Face, the first of Zion's big walls to be climbed. Prior to this ascent, the Park Service had long refused to give permission for climbing the long and steep canyon faces. Fred Beckey gained permission after sending a letter to the park guaranteeing a Seattle based rescue team on call and particulars of each of the original team member's experience: Warren Harding, Galen Rowell, Eric Bjørnstad and Fred Beckey. By the time permission was granted however, the team had changed to Fred Beckey, Galen Rowell and Pat Callis, who spent several days preparing the lower section and made the first ascent on May 5-7, 1967.

George Lowe, Karl Dunn, Dick Bell, Robert Sears, Peter Gibbs and others were also active in the mid- to late-1960s with technical ascents of many formations, including the west face of Bridge Mountain in 1965, the east face of *Sentinel* in 1966, the Twin Brothers in 1968 and Mt. Spry in 1970.

In the early '70s, Jeff Lowe, with various partners including Cactus Byran, Mike Weis, Bruce Roghaar, John Weiland and Wick Beavers, established a number of difficult modern wall routes, awesome achievements especially considering the tools of the day (passive chocks and pitons). These routes included the north and east faces of Angels Landing, *The Toad* on the north face of Sentinel, the southeast buttress of *Isaac* and the mega classic *Moonlight Buttress*.

Bill Forrest and Bill March dominated the mid-'70s with outstanding first ascents of Grade VIs in Kolob and the main canyon. Jimmy Dunn bagged a few outstanding lines, including a new route with no bolts on the north face of Angels Landing (*Angel Hair*) with Dean Tschappat.

In the late '70s and early '80s, Ron Olevsky and Dave Jones were responsible for a new wave of quality routes, as they developed a new clean ethic largely made possible by the advent of Friends, revolutionizing climbing smooth parallel cracks in the desert. Two separate trends that enabled many of the longer routes to be climbed clean developed: Ron Olevsky began a trend of modifying placements on routes to enable subsequent ascents to be completely clean, while Dave Jones found natural lines and pushed free climbing standards so fewer non-clean placements were necessary. Routes of this period include *The Thunderbird Wall* and *Catharsis* in Kolob and *Monkey Finger Wall, Spaceshot, Touchstone Wall, Shune's Buttress* and the *Fang Wall* in the main canyon.

Throughout Zion's history, many short routes have been established in the park, but the big attraction has always been the walls. Several trends developed in the 1990s: Attempts to climb the harder aid lines on the walls resulted in the first ascent of *Streaked Wall* by Mugs Stump and Conrad Anker in four days (VI, 5.10, A4+), followed shortly thereafter by the first ascent of Abraham in the Court of the Patriarchs by John Middendorf and Walt Shipley up the overhanging southwest buttress *The Radiator* (VI, 5.10+, A4). Trying to free climb the aid pitches on the walls led to free ascents of routes like *Monkeyfinger Wall* (V, 5.11+) in 1989 by Mike O'Donnel and Craig Kenyon and *Shune's Buttress* (IV, 5.11c) on Red Arch Mountain by Conrad Anker and Dave Jones. In 1992, Peter Croft and Johnny Woodward climbed *Moonlight Buttress* free (V, 5.13b), thus establishing the most sustained and highest standard free climbing route on sandstone in the world.

Multiple-route speed ascents have been another trend. In 1991, Conrad Anker and John Middendorf climbed the first link-up when they climbed *Touchstone Wall* and the northeast buttress of *Angels Landing* in eight hours. In 1992, Doug Heinrich and Seth Shaw climbed *Space Shot*, *Monkeyfinger* and *Touchstone* in an 18 hour period. With the addition of *Moonlight Buttress*, this combination was later upped to four walls in a 24-hour period by Heinrich and Anker.

Climbing traffic in Zion has increased considerably in the '90s. In 1991, 105 climbers spent a total of 190 nights bivouacked on Zion's walls, either on small ledges or in portaledges. Today this number has increased dramatically. It is imperative that conservation be the number one rule for climbers in Zion, as it is a precious unrenewable natural resource.

Zion Canyon Visitor Center

Located just within the southern entrance to the park, the Visitor Center is open daily all year: 9 A.M.-5 P.M. in the winter, extended to 8 A.M.-9 P.M. in the summer. A large museum/exhibit room introduces the visitor to the plants and animals of the park, as well as the geology of the region. Early Mormon pioneer farmers are commemorated in another exhibit. There is also a variety of handouts ranging from information on hiking, to history, flora and fauna checklists and numerous other aspects of the park. For more information contact the park at Springdale, Utah, 84767, telephone (801)772-3256.

Zion Natural History Association: There are 64 non-profit Natural History Associations working in partnership with National Park Service areas throughout the U.S. At the Zion Visitor Center the Natural History Association offers an excellent selection of books, maps, slides, postcards, et cetera–just as at Colorado National Monument and Canyonlands Natural History Associations. Their professional staff publishes brochures, books and maps (many are free to visitors), and produces numerous educational programs. At Zion the Kolob Visitor Center was financed by the Zion Natural History Association.

A must see for climbers visting Zion is the dramatic 37-minute movie *Zion Canyon Treasure of the Gods* shown on an IMAX six-story-high screen at the Zion Canyon Theatre located just outside the entrance kiosk to the park. The climbing in the film was done by Nancy Feagin and Doug Heinrich.

Geology

The following is a very brief review of geologic features represented in Zion and is provided solely for indentification purposes on the rock. More complete information can be found at the Visitor Center where there are numberous excellent books on Zion's geology and a large relief model of the park giving a bird's eye overview. There are also a number of excellent books on the park's geology at the Visitor Center. My favorite for the desert in general has long been *The Colorado Plateau, A Geologic History* by Donald L. Baars (New Mexico Press) but each Visitor Center concession will have a wide selection of books specific to the area.

Streaking and Desert Varnish: The dark colored streaking on most of Zion's canyon walls is a stain caused by organic material as water flows through decomposing vegetative matter. Black coloration is a result of carbonization. White areas on the walls are usually a salt stain resulting from evaporating water.

Recent research has found that desert varnish stain is the product of bacteria living on the surface of rock faces usually facing sunlight and exposed to rain and wind. The bacteria consume windborne dust from which manganese, iron and clay minerals are absorbed. Color of the varnish results from the mineral composition of the airborne dust. If it is composed predominantly of manganese the varnish will be a purple-black; if composed mostly of iron, the varnish will be a reddish-brown.

Rock Layers: The rock layers found at Zion had their origin 53-225 million years ago and are the product of ocean, river and lake sediments or wind deposition. They are identified here from the oldest to youngest.

Moenkopi Formation: Moenkopi is the oldest layer exposed at Zion, measuring 1800 feet (549m) thick along the Virgin River. It comprises thousands of thin layers of siltstone and shale with beds of limestone and gypsum, generally maroon in color.

Chinle Formation: The Chinle is divided into two members, the Shinarump Conglomerate and the Petrified Forest.

The Shinarump Conglomerate is the lowest member of the Chinle Formation and is less than 100 feet (30m) thick. This prominent cliffmaker is white, gray or brown in color and composed of cemented thin, short lenses of fine sandy shale embedded with pebbles of flood water deposition. The Petrified Forest, the upper member of the Chinle Formation, is more than 350 feet (107m) thick and is composed of muds, silts, oozes and volcanic ash. It was stream deposited in shallow bodies of fresh water.

Moenave Formation: Composed of three divisions. The lower slope forms the Dinosaur Canyon Sandstone Member, the middle is the Whitmore Point Member and the upper unit is the Springdale Sandstone Member. Dinosaur Canyon Sandstone: the lower member member of the Moenave Formation, is 140-375 feet (43-114m) thick. This sandstone is lake deposited and consists of thin, interbedded siltstone, mudstone and fine sandstone.

Whitmore Point Member is about 100 feet (30m) thick and grayish and reddish in color. Siltstone, claystone and sandstone composition.

Springdale Sandstone, the upper member of the Moenave Formation, is a river channel deposit forming vertical cliffs 75-150 feet (23-46m) high.

Kayenta: The Kayenta is river deposited and composed of sandstone, shale and clay. It is the soft, red layer which consists of shelving slopes 200-600 feet (61m-183m) thick. The sandstone is cemented together by calcite and iron oxides. At the Temple of Sinawava the river has cut completely through the Navajo reaching the Kayenta. Erosion has increased in this soft layer, undermining the vertical Navajo cliffs. Eventually the undermined wall collapses along pre-existing fractures and the cliffs perpetuate as the canyon widens downstream. This layer is impervious to water and responsible for the many famous spring lines or seeps found in Zion. Water seeps through the Navajo above and when it reaches the Kayenta is forced to move horizontally and emerge as a spring line at the cliff's edge. These seeps support hanging gardens of wild orchids, monkeyflowers, columbines, maidenhair fern and soft mosses.

Navajo Sandstone: The Navajo Sandstone is a formation occurring from Wyoming to California. In Wyoming it is known as Nugget Sandstone and in Nevada as Aztec Sandstone. Its greatest thickness is in Zion at the Temple of Sinawava, where it reaches a mass of 2400 feet (732m). It was deposited by wind-blown sand dunes which developed about 170 million years ago in a desert environment greater in size than today's Sahara. It is a huge mass of homogeneous fine-grained sand, notably friable especially when wet. The grains of sand composing the Navajo are weakly cemented by lime, iron oxides and to some degree calcium carbonate.

Temple Cap: Flood waters entered the desert, which produced the Temple Cap Sandstone. These waters carried red muds and formed thin layers of clay and silt. The accumulating sediments thickened to a depth of 260 feet (79m) and produced what we now call the Temple Cap Formation. Streaking from this layer stains the upper faces of Navajo Sandstone in many places. In the same way, the blue-gray Redwall Limestone at the Grand Canyon is named for the red stain it has received from the Hermit Shale and Supai Sandstone above it. The Temple Cap is named after Zion's rock temples which it caps, such as The Great White Throne, West Temple and East Temple.

Carmel: This resistant layer was formed when seas once again encroached over the land that is Zion resulting in the Carmel, 100-300 foot (30-91m) thick compact limestone. It appears at the top of the highest domed cliffs of the park, many areas on the Kolob Terrace and is prominently exposed along the Zion-Mount Carmel Highway.

Flora and fauna

Elevations from 3650 feet (1113m) to 8740 feet (2664m) range from desert to alpine. Within the park's numerous deep canyons and high plateaus small niches provide a wide variety of habitats for both flora and fauna. Conditions exist here to support species that could not survive elsewhere in the world. An example is the tiny Zion Snail, only about ⅛" in diameter, dark brown to black in color. This Lilliputian primordial creature, found at seeps in Zion Canyon, is one of many species whose existence is endangered. There are 68 species of mammals, 36 species of reptiles, 7 species of amphibians, 285 species of birds and 899 plant species identified within Zion.

Cryptobiotic soil

Zion National Park is a unique ecosystem toured by over two million visitors annually. Six to seven thousand visitors hike the park's backcountry each year. As a result, there has been a dramatic increase in the degradation of the critically important cryptobiotic surface soil. For further information on cryptobiotic soil, see page 3 of the "Introduction.".

Climate

Temperatures are the most pleasant in spring and autumn, the choice seasons to climb in Zion. Spring is the time of year best for viewing wildlife and wildflowers. In the fall, colors are beautiful as those of New England, when deciduous trees and shrubs paint the canyon floor in rainbow colors. Stunning box elder trees line the Virgin River with brilliant yellow and scrub oak provides a blend of reds and rust.

In the winter, Farenheit temperatures average 60 degrees (15.6C) during the day and near freezing at night. They can range from 5 degrees to 105 degrees (-15 to 40.5C) during summertime. Rainfall is 10-20 inches (2.5 to 5cm). Winters are generally short and mild– summers hot and long. One can expect two wet seasons: winter/early spring and late summer. There are also two dry seasons: one in late spring/early summer and one in the late fall.

Campgrounds

There are two campgrounds in Zion Canyon. South Campground, elevation 4000 feet (1219m) is 1 mile (1.6km), beyond the South Entrance of the park, located in a grassy and shaded area next to the Virgin River. It has 140 sites and is open all year. Facilities include water, flush toilets, telephones, an amphitheater with evening programs and a dump station. Watchman Campground, elevation 4000 feet (1219m), is also located in a shady area next to the Virgin River and is often closed in the winter. It includes the same amenities as the South Campground. In the Watchman Campground, pioneer Mormons planted an apple orchard which still produces and is enjoyed by those who camp there in the spring.

Zion Lodge: Open year-round. In addition to a motel and western cabins (reservations usually necessary), the lodge offers a snack bar (fast food), restaurant (closed in the winter), post office (open Monday-Saturday), a gift shop, shuttle service for hikers, horseback rides along the Virgin River (one hour), a three-hour Sand Bench Trail ride and an all day Cable Mountain ride. Tours in an open-air vehicle provide narrated sightseeing trips in Zion Canyon between Memorial Day and Labor Day weekends and the lodge offers a variety of evening programs. Reservations for Zion Lodge is made through the parks concessionaire, TW Services, Box 400, Cedar City, Utah 84720, telephone (801)586-7686.

Observation Point: Observation Point is reached by a 3.7 mile (6km) trail which climbs from the Weeping Rock Parking Area 2200 feet (671m). The Kaibab Forest is visible on the north rim of the Grand Canyon far to the southwest.

Pine Creek Tunnels: Pine Creek tunnels penetrate the canyon wall for 5607 feet (1709m) and are bored parallel to the cliff edge. Windows were cut into the walls for access and ventilation. The project was dedicated on 4 July 1930, touted as an engineering marvel and celebrating the completion of the longest tunnel in the United States. Six switchbacks in an area 1 mile (1.6km) long by 0.25 mile (0.6m) wide climb the 800 feet (244m) from valley floor to the tunnels.

Precautions and regulations

There are numerous steep big wall climbs at Zion ranging from 600 feet (183m) to 2200 feet (670m) with many free routes not requiring pitons or a bolt kit. It is fundamental that all visitors practice low impact on off-trail travel and while wilderness camping. This of course includes no littering (tossing bags of human waste off big wall climbs), no graffiti and a general respect for the fragile nature of the park. In addition, please respect the style in which a route has been climbed. Approach and descents are often as serious as the climbs themselves. Zion Canyon runs north/south giving it few south-facing climbs for periods of cooler weather. When Zion's sandstone is wet it loses two-thirds of its strength and should not be climbed. (A chunk of rock dipped in the river for a few seconds and then broken will dramatically demonstrate this loss of strength.) In recent years 12 areas (80% of the climbing locations) have been closed from spring to mid-August to protect the nesting of peregrine falcons. Please check at the visitor center for dates and locations. All overnight climbs must be accompanied by a free backcountry permit. Water bottles may be filled at the visitor center or Zion Lodge.

Paraphernalia

A Zion Free Climbing Rack consists of 2-3 sets of cams, hexes and stoppers, plus a load of full-length slings and carabiners. A Zion Aid Rack consists of 3 or more sets of cams, many stoppers and brass-nuts, carabiners, slings, hooks, plus 3-4 birdbeaks, 3-5 knifeblades, 3-5 horizontals (Lost Arrows), 2-3 each baby angles (½", ⅝") and 1-2 each of the bigger pitons.

Order of climbs

In this chapter routes are listed in an ascending order, west from Springdale up through Zion Canyon to the Temple of Sinawava, then down the east walls and finally Kolob climbs in the satellite region of Zion National Park.

John Middendorf on headwall of **Tricks of the Trade**   Photo: Bill Hatcher

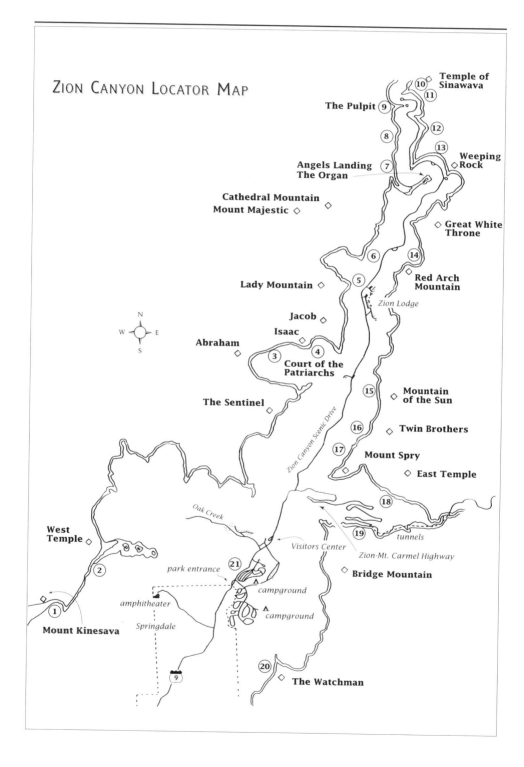

ZION CANYON LOCATOR MAP

Temple of Sinawava
The Pulpit ⑨
⑩
⑪
⑧
⑫
⑬
Angels Landing ⑦
The Organ
Weeping Rock
Cathedral Mountain
Mount Majestic ◇
Great White Throne
⑥
⑭
Lady Mountain ◇
⑤
Red Arch Mountain
Zion Lodge
Jacob ◇
Isaac
Abraham ◇
④
③
Court of the Patriarchs
The Sentinel ◇
⑮
Mountain of the Sun
⑯
Twin Brothers
⑰
Mount Spry
East Temple
⑱
Oak Creek
West Temple ◇
⑲
tunnels
Visitors Center
Zion-Mt. Carmel Highway
②
park entrance
㉑
campground
amphitheater
campground
①
Springdale
Bridge Mountain
Mount Kinesava
9
⑳
The Watchman

N
W — E
S

Zion Canyon Scenic Drive

(1) Mt. Kinesava:
King Corner, Plumbline

(2) West Temple: *Gettin' Western*

(3) Middle Canyon West:
The Radiator

(4) Issac: *Southeast Buttress, Tricks of the Trade,*

(5) Lady Mountain: *North Spur*;
Mount Majestic: *Emerald Star Majesticus*

(6) The Spearhead: *Iron Messiah*

(7) The Organ and
Angels Landing Area:
The Organ: *Organ Grinder*
Angels Landing Area:
Jokers and Theives, Northeast Buttress, Swiss-American Route, Angel Hair, Empty Pages, Archangel, Prodigal Sun, Southeast Buttress, Ball and Chain, G-Money, Days of No Future, Sheer Lunacy

(8) *Lunar Ecstasy, Moonlight Buttress, March-Forrest Chimney*

(9) The Pulpit: *The Pulpit, The Pulpette*

(10) Temple of Sinawava Area:
Tourist Crack

(11) *Monkey Finger*

(12) Leaning Wall Area:
Equinox, Spaceshot

(13) Cereberus Gendarme Area:
Touchstone Wall,
Cerberus Crags

(14) Red Arch Mountain: *Rights of Passage, Shune's Buttress*

(15) Mountain of the Sun:
The Tao of Light

(16) Twin Brothers–Right Twin:
Peyote Dreams

(17) Mount Spry–Northwest Face:
Sandblaster, Moria, Black Crack

(18) East Temple:
Lovelace, The Fang, Cowboy Bob Goes to Zion, Uncertain Fate, Freezer Burn, 10th Division

(19) Tunnel Crags Area

(20) The Watchman:
S & M, The Vigil

(21) South Entrance Bouldering Area

Photo: Mike Baker

King Corner

Mount Kinesava

Mount Kinesava is the massive sandstone monolith south of West Temple as viewed when looking west from the town of Springdale. To the Paiute Indians Kinesava was the moody and unpredictable god who started mysterious fires–lightning–on heights no human could reach.

King Corner is the huge smooth right-facing dihedral intermittently visible from Rockville but not visible once within the city limits of Springdale. *Plumbline* is located just in from the long prominent southern-most buttress of the peak (right of King Corner). To reach, drive to the Chinle Trailhead (formerly Petrified Forest Trail) located at a pulloff on the west side of the Springdale/Rockville highway across from Mile Marker 29 and the Springdale city limits sign (located at the town's southern edge). High clearance vehicles will be able to continue through a gate and drive 1.3 miles (2km) to the park boundary. At the 1 mile (1.6km) point the dirt road branches left to private property. Continue straight another 0.3 mile (0.5km) to the park boundary and information kiosk for the Chinle Trail leading to the Petrified Forest. Please leave gates as you find them. At the park boundary is a locked vehicle gate with an adjacent horse/hiker gate. From here hike about 2 miles (3.2km) to the drainage directly under the prominent King Corner dihedral.

KING CORNER V, 5.10, A3+, 9 pitches

First Ascent: Mike Baker, Bob Wade, March 1994.
Location and Access: Hike up the drainage to th base of the massive smooth dihedral of King Corner. The first pitch begins up a 5.6 right-facing chimney.
Paraphernalia: Technical Friends #.0, #.5; Camalots (2) #.5 to #4, with extra #1, #2, #3; TCUs 1, 2, 3; Tri-cams #.4 to #2; Big Dude #6, #7; stoppers #1 to #9; (2) knifeblades; (2) Birdbeaks; (3) Lost Arrows; (3) ½" baby angles.
Descent: See descent for *Plumbline*.

PLUMBLINE V, 5.9, A3

First Ascent: Larry Derby, Mike Weiss, Billy Westbay, March 1975.
Location and Access: This west-facing route climbs just in from the south ridge up the obvious splitter crack on the southern-most buttress of the peak. It is 80% free with no bolts placed on the first ascent. The bottom 350 feet (107m) is brushy with the rest of the route clean. *Plumbline* has a southern exposure but the route is a good warm weather climb since most of it is in the shade much of the day.
Paraphernalia: Standard Zion free rack with selection of pitons and (4) 2.5 " and (1) 4" bong.
Descent: Move north via a small hanging park which affords several easterly exit slots, permitting easy descent without rappels if the correct slot is found.

West Temple

West Temple at 7810 feet (2380m) in elevation, is the highest point in the southern portion of the park. It towers 4100 feet (1250m) above the valley floor, about 700 feet (213m) higher than East Temple. It has been noted that "Its sheer east face is like a smooth wall of veined marble." Both West and East Temples were named by Clarence E. Dutton in an 1882 geologic report. West Temple towers above the town of Springdale on the western ramparts of the

Virgin River Valley in much the same way as The Watchman towers above the town from the east. Frederick S. Dellenbaugh described West Temple in 1903 as a "titanic mountain of bare rock" that "lifted its opalescent shoulders alluringly against the eastern sky."

GETTIN' WESTERN V, 5.11+, 17 pitches using 200-foot (60m) rope, 2000 feet (610m)

First Ascent: Originally VI, 5.10, A2 by Brad Quinn, Darren Cope, October 1990, three days, two bivouacs. First Free Ascent: Doug Byerly, Doug Hall, 1-2 October 1993, two days, one bivouac, no pitons and no drilling on the ascent.

Location and Access: The approach is made from Springdale 0.7 mile (1.1km) south from the entrance kiosk at Zion. Turn west (right) up Lion Blvd. at the sign reading "Dixie College–Obert C. Tanner Amphitheater" and park at the gate 0.6 mile (0.9km) beyond. The route ascends the prominent right-facing dihedral system reaching from bottom to top in the center of the face directly below the summit. There are shaded picnic tables but no overnight camping on the approach road. A one-to-two-hour bushwack is required through manzanita, cliff bands and washes to reach the base of the climb. The route is one of the longest all-free sandstone routes in the lower-48 states and had been attempted by a team from Arizona in the early 1990s and by Bill Forrest and party at an earlier date. The Forrest party reached the halfway point.

Paraphernalia: Double set of Friends to #3 plus a #6; Camalots #3, #4; (1) set of TCUs; Tri-cams .5 through 1.5; (14) quick draws mostly with two-foot (0.6m) slings; small selection of small and medium nuts. No hammer or bolt kit is needed.

Descent: Ridgeline trending down and south to reach the notch between West Temple and Mount Kinesava, ultimately dropping into the largest notch to reach the ground. Continue straight out from the wall through scrub oak and manzanita. After reaching a cliff band, traverse around until able to downclimb via fifth class. Continue out until spur roads to Springdale are reached. The descent requires intricate route finding and involves exposed downclimbing.

Zion Canyon West

These routes are located on the west side of the North Fork of the Virgin River, the opposite side of the river from the Zion Canyon Scenic Drive. The great west wall is 3 miles (4.8km) long and from 3000 to nearly 4000 feet (914m to 1219m) high.

NOTE: River crossing can be extremely dangerous or impossible during spring runoffs or at high water levels resulting from seasonal thundershowers. Hiking the Narrows located above the Temple of Sinawava can be fatal. It is essential to check the dangers of flash flooding at the visitor center. Isaac and the Angels Landing area are closed in the spring to protect nesting peregrine falcons. Please check at the visitor center for exact dates.

The Three Patriarchs: Abraham

THE RADIATOR (Direct Southwest Buttress) VI, 5.10, A4, 15 pitches

First Ascent: John Middendorf, Walt Shipley, 2-6 May 1990.

Location and Access: To date this route is one of the longest and probably of the highest difficulty of Grade VI climbs in the park. The first ascent was made over four days involving two ledge and two hanging bivouacs with only ten belay bolts and seven aid bolts placed. This was also in all likelihood the first ascent to the summit of Abraham, the highest of the Three Patriarchs at 6990 feet (2131m). Isaac is 6831 feet (2082m). Begin up the first crack system to the right of the central gully. From the top of the buttress (Pitch 15) the summit is reached via 5.5 climbing.

Paraphernalia: (2.5) sets of Friends with #5 and #7; (3) sets of TCUs; Mondo Tri-cams; hexes #5 to #11; Seismo brass nuts and stoppers; Monkey Paws; pitons (12) blades, (10-12) Lost Arrows, (3-4) ½", (2-3) ⅝", (2-3) ¾", (1) 1", (1) 1¼", (1) 1½" sawed-off okay, (2) Leepers, (6-8) Birdbeaks.

Descent: From the top of the buttress traverse right several hundred yards on a ledge system to the edge of a major drainage. Eleven rappels will take one to the top of a hanging waterfall. Three more rappels to the ground.

The Three Patriarchs: Isaac

Isaac, 6831 feet (2082m), is the center of the Three Patriarchs, located on the opposite (west) side of the valley from Mountain of the Sun. It was named in 1916 by Methodist minister, Frederick Vining Fisher who was so inspired by Zion Canyon he gave religious names to the monoliths he viewed.

SOUTHEAST BUTTRESS V, 5.10, A2-3, 1800 feet (549m), 15 pitches plus 300 feet (91m) of 3rd class to the summit

First Ascent: Jeff Lowe, John Weiland, Mike Weiss, Wick Beavers, February 1972.

Location and Access: The route is located south of *Tricks of the Trade*. The upper seven pitches ascend two dihedrals left of *Tricks of the Trade*. Approach from the Court of the Patriarchs parking area 1.7 miles (2.7km) up Zion Canyon and hike to the left edge of the southeast buttress.

Paraphernalia: Standard Zion free rack with a few thin pitons for short aid sections.

Descent: Walk north to a low-angle gully. Make four rappels into the gully system, rappel into a hanging valley, go through the valley, then three rappels down a waterfall area.

TRICKS OF THE TRADE (aka Tricks of the Tramp) V, 5.11, A2+ (two piton placements), 1900 feet (578m), 19 pitches

First Ascent: Brad Quinn, Bill Hatcher, John Middendorf, 1 April 1993, lower pitches with Calvin Herbert. Second ascent Doug Byerly, Calvin Hebert, October 1994.

Location and Access: Right of the *Southeast Buttress* route on Isaac. The climb is one of the longest free routes in the park with only 60 feet (18m) of aid in over 1900 feet (578m) of climbing, including a 500 foot (152m) handcrack. Approach from the Court of the Patriarchs parking area 1.7 miles (2.7km) up Zion Canyon. Hike to the foot of the outermost buttress, the center of the Three Patriarchs. The route begins up a 2" (5cm) crack system 50 feet (15m) right of a major chimney system on the outside of the buttress.

Paraphernalia: (2.5) sets cams; (1) set nuts; (1) set Big Dudes; (2) each Lost Arrows, Birdbeaks and long blades; (1) wall hauler (for packs). Helmet recommended. See topo, pages 26-27.

Descent: Continue to the summit and then descend slabs to the east. Nine rappels from trees and bushes in a deep, steep canyon are needed to reach the drainage between Isaac and Jacob (to the north of Isaac). Descend the drainage to a hanging valley where it is necessary to rappel three to four times down a waterfall. Descent time is about six hours.

The Three Patriarchs: Isaac

Tricks of the Trade

V, 5.11, A2+ (bottom)

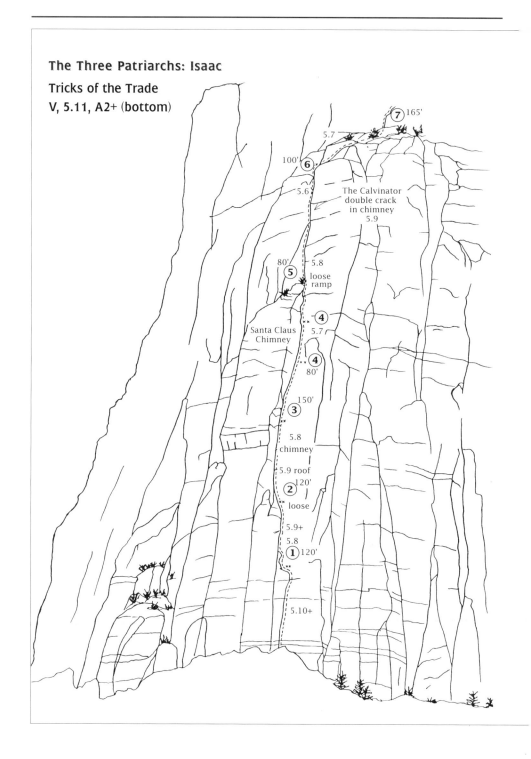

165' ⑦

5.7

100' ⑥

5.6

The Calvinator
double crack
in chimney
5.9

80' ⑤   5.8

loose
ramp

④

Santa Claus   5.7
Chimney

④
80'

150'
③

5.8
chimney

5.9 roof
② 120'

loose

5.9+

5.8
① 120'

5.10+

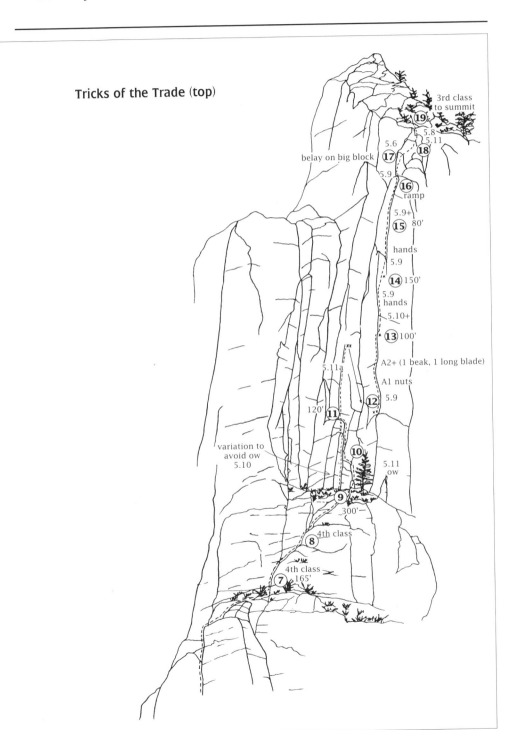

Tricks of the Trade (top)

3rd class
to summit

⑲

5.8
5.11

5.6 ⑰   ⑱

belay on big block

5.9

⑯
ramp

5.9+
⑮ 80'

hands
5.9

⑭ 150'

5.9
hands

5.10+

⑬ 100'

A2+ (1 beak, 1 long blade)

A1 nuts

5.9

⑫

5.11a

120' ⑪

variation to
avoid ow
5.10

⑩

5.11
ow

⑨

300'

4th class

⑧

4th class

⑦ 165'

Lady Mountain

Lady Mountain, 6940 feet (2115m) in elevation, is located south of The Spearhead and north of the Three Patriarchs on the west (left) side of the Virgin River as one travels up the Zion Canyon Scenic Drive.

NORTH SPUR III, 5.7, 11 pitches, 1100 feet (335m)

First Ascent: Curt Haire, Wes Hall, July 1975.

Location and Access: The route climbs the east face of the north spur of the monolith. It is identified from the Zion Lodge as the tower immediately right of Lady Mountain itself. The upper half of the landform from below appears as a large collection of columns. The chimney system which the route ascends is identifiable at the north (right) side of the tower's east face. Approach is about an hour via scrambling and bushwhacking from the Zion Lodge located about 3 miles (4.8km) from the visitor center. The old Lady Mountain Trail is now closed and should not be used. Approach cross-country. At a point where the old trail swings near the base of the spur of rock, bushwhack uphill to the north in the direction of the prominent chimney system identifiable from below. Belay from trees at the base of the chimney system.

Pitch 1: Climb the left of two cracks up a close bushy chimney to a good belay ledge, 50 feet (15m), 5.4.

Pitch 2: Continue up the right of two obvious cracks via hand jams for about 15 feet (5m) ending in an easy chimney. A tree provides a good anchor for belay at the top of the pitch, 60 feet (18m), 5.6.

Pitch 3: Ascend the obvious chimney behind the belay, 4th class, 50 feet (15m).

Pitch 4: Continue via the left of two crack systems for 60 feet (18m) until it is possible to make a traverse to a right-hand crack. Continue up the crack to a broad ledge with another tree anchor, 120 feet (37m), 5.7.

Pitch 5: Scramble around to the right, then angle back toward the spur for 300 feet (91m) where a chimney is met.

Pitch 6: Ascend the chimney to a large ledge with several boulders atop it, 50 feet (15m), 5.6.

Pitch 7: From the belay ledge the route would appear to continue straight up via another chimney, but rather make an unlikely-looking traverse left, step across the chimney just climbed and lieback up a small crack to a bush. Traverse above the bush to the base of another chimney, 120 feet (37m), 5.7.

Pitch 8: Climb the chimney and exit left (south) onto a large ledge with boulders and a crack at the back of the ledge, 60 feet (18m), 5.5.

Pitch 9: Continue up and right (north) around a corner via a small jamcrack and a very narrow ledge to the base of the final wide chimney, 50 feet (15m), 5.6.

Pitch 10: Climb the chimney about three-quarters of the way to its top to a narrow crack in the right-hand wall which affords a belay from chocks, 130 feet (40m), 5.2.

Pitch 11: Continue up the chimney to a belay from trees on the summit knob, 100 feet (30m), 5.2.

Paraphernalia: Standard Zion free rack.

Mount Majestic

EMERALD STAR MAJESTICUS V, 5.8 X, A3, 5 pitches technical plus much 3rd class

First Ascent: Doug Byerly, James Funsten, 7-10 October 1993.

Location and Access: First ascent party suggests a special rating of BC5 (bush, cactus rating). The route climbs the mountain via its south buttress. This is the first prow to the right of Behunin Canyon. Approach via Emerald Pools Trail. The summit takes about two hours third class from the last technical pitch, via mostly uphill or ridge climbing. Final summit is reached after dropping down past a false summit and climbing the line of least resistance on the southwest side at 5.8X. An 180-foot (55m) rope was used on the first ascent.

Paraphernalia: (2) sets of Friends #2.5 through #3.5 and (1) #4; Camalot #7; small TCUs to #2; (2) sets of hooks; (1) set of ball nuts; (3) sets of cams; (4-5) Leepers; (2) each ½" and ⅗" angles; (2-3) #5 and #6 Lost Arrows; (1-2) #7; (4-5) Bugaboos; (4) knifeblades; (3-4) Birdbeaks; (2) Fish Hooks.

Descent: Reverse the route.

Cathedral Mountain

The Spearhead

A pullout at the Grotto Picnic Area and West Rim Trailhead on the left side of the park road at 3.5 miles (5.6km) up Zion Canyon gives a view across the river to The Spearhead at the southern end of Cathedral Mountain.

NOTE: The Spearhead is closed in the spring to protect nesting peregrine falcons. Please check at the visitor center for exact dates.

IRON MESSIAH III, 5.10 R, 12 pitches, ★★★★

First Ascent: Ron Olevsky, solo, 1988. First Free Ascent: Darren Cope, Jeff Rickerl, 1988.

Location and Access: The route ascends to the shoulder left of The Spearhead. The obvious upper corner of the route and beginning of Pitch 3 require some route finding to locate. Approach from the Grotto Picnic Area, 3.5 miles (5.6m) up Zion Canyon Scenic Drive. Cross the bridge and hike left about 5 minutes (to second or third drainage) then up the drainage 50 yards (46m) past an exposed traverse. Continue via easy 5th class to the first pitch which is a bolted face just right of a right-facing corner. At Pitch 3 avoid a misplaced bolt ladder by climbing a 5.10 short section to its right.

Paraphernalia: Standard Zion free rack.

Descent: Rappel the route.

Cathedral Mountain

Iron Messiah

III, 5.10 R (bottom)

Iron Messiah (top)

The Organ

Organ Grinder

III, 5.9+

The Organ and Angels Landing

The parking pullout for views of the Great White Throne, Organ and Angels Landing is located on the left at 5.5 miles (8.8km) from the visitor center on the Zion Canyon Scenic Drive. However, the pullout is positioned for down-canyon traffic only–1.3 miles (2.1km) downcanyon from the Temple of Sinawava. Three-and-a-half miles (5.6km) from the visitor center is the Grotto Picnic Area (originally Zion's first campground built in 1935) and the Angels Landing trailhead (which leads to the West Rim Trail). It is oil-surfaced for the first mile and gains 1500 feet (457m) in its 2.5 mile (4km) climb to the top of Angels Landing at 5785 feet (1763m) in elevation. The Angels Landing or West Rim Trail is the descent route for all summit climbs up the west walls of the canyon from Angels Landing to the Temple of Sinawava to the north. The West Rim Trail was built in the 1920s. In 1934 the CCC (Civilian Construction Corps) used soil cement on the trail to retard erosion from heavy horse use and frequent afternoon summer thundershowers. The trail climbs 3000 feet (914m) above the floor of Zion Canyon. The first 600 feet (183m) of the Angels Landing trail teeters along a precipitous ledge where the trail zigzags radically as it climbs strenuously up the Navajo Sandstone.

Another formation named by the Methodist minister, Frederick Vining Fisher who visited Zion Canyon in 1916, The Organ is the island of rock which juts to the east from Angels Landing, connecting to the Angel by a narrow ridge.

Descent: Walk a short distance west to the West Rim Trail, hike left to the Angels Landing Trail and take it left to the valley floor or continue down the West Rim Trail to the valley at the Grotto Picnic Area. Descent requires one to one-and-a-half hours.

NOTE: The Angels Landing area is closed in the spring to protect nesting peregrine falcons. Please check at the visitor center for exact dates. The river crossing can be extremely dangerous or impossible during spring runoffs or at high water levels resulting from seasonal thundershowers.

The Organ

ORGAN GRINDER III, 5.9+, 2 pitches

First Ascent: Larry Derby, Mike Weiss, Billy Westbay, March 1975.

Location and Access: The route is located on the left side of the north face of The Organ and climbs about halfway up the landform to a recessed bushy area running east to west across the formation. A prominent overhang is clearly visible (from the parking area across the river) near the top left of the route. Begin by chimneying, jamming and then stemming up the first pitch. Belay from a block on a flake ledge on the left. The second pitch is ascended via a jamcrack.

Paraphernalia: Several large Friends.

Descent: Walk down left and then scramble to the right to the base of the landform.

Photo: Bill Hatcher

Angels Landing

Angels Landing

JOKERS AND THIEVES V, 5.10, A3, 9 pitches

First Ascent: Ken Cook, Galen Kirkwood, 22 March 1978.

Location and Access: The route name is from the Bob Dylan song "All Along the Watchtower." The first ascent team reports: "We are the Jokers and two Thieves stole our jumars at the base of the climb." The route begins in a corner with a bolt at half height and with 5.9 offwidth at the bottom. Join *Northeast Buttress* for the last two pitches.

Paraphernalia: Standard Zion aid rack.

Descent: Rappel the route.

NORTHEAST BUTTRESS IV, 5.11a R, 9 pitches

First Ascent: Randy Aton, Mark Austin, Phil Haney, 1981. First Free Ascent: Conrad Anker, John Middendorf, 21 July 1991.

Location and Access: The northeast buttress is climbed via the arête between the northeast buttress and the north face of Angels Landing, beginning on the east (left) side of the arête. Climb a 5.9 wide crack to gain the ridge between The Organ and Angels Landing, then traverse 300 feet (91m) left to the beginning of the route. Topo on pages 42-43.

Paraphernalia: (1.5) sets of Friends with (1) #3.5 and #4, a #5 or #6 is useful; slings; hexes; stoppers.

Descent: West Rim Trail. See the introduction to The Organ and Angels Landing on page 33.

<$ISWISS-AMERICAN ROUTE VI, 5.10, A4, 11 pitches with bolts placed only at belay stations

First Ascent: John Middendorf, Xaver Bongard, 19-22 October 1991.

Location and Access: Between *Northeast Buttress* and *Lowe Route*. Fourteen holes were drilled on the first ascent (all for belay bolts).

Paraphernalia: Standard Zion aid rack.

Descent: West Rim Trail. See the introduction to The Organ and Angels Landing on page 33.

LOWE ROUTE (North face of Angels Landing) V, 5.10, A2, 13 pitches, 1500 feet (457m)

First Ascent: Jeff Lowe, Cactus Bryan, September 1970.

Location and Access: Begin up the center of three major crack systems, the first prominent system left of *Angel Hair* (a.k.a. *Dunn Route*) when viewed from the parking area. The route may also be identified by the presence of an obvious blind arch located two-thirds of the way up the wall. The climb goes free except for the seventh pitch. Topo on pages 46-47.

Pitch 1-4: Climb chimneys and dihedrals 5.9 then 5.8 to the best bivouac ledge on the route.

Pitch 5: C2, thin nuts to 1½" placements.

Pitch 6: Climb C2 then belay on left diagonal running ramp.

Pitch 7: Traverse on the ramp at 5.7 until it is possible to ascend a thin A2 crack up overhanging steps to a marginal bivouac ledge.

Pitch 8: Above the right edge of the ledge a four-bolt ladder leads to a good crack system beginning wide then thin C2 climbing. Belay beneath a roof.

Pitch 9: C1 climbing for about 15 feet (5m) then 5.10 hands to a belay ledge.

Pitch 10: Begin C1 to 5.10 hands ending with C1 to a double bolt belay.

Pitch 11: Traverse up and left at 5.8 into a large recessed area then right to a second sloping recess which will be a point about 200 feet (61m) below the summit.

Pitches 12-13: The summit is reached by ascending out of the right side of this second recess.

Paraphernalia: Standard Zion free rack; (2) sets of TCUs and Friends to #4 with nuts and slings; (10-15) pitons, mostly knifeblades and Lost Arrows.

Descent: West Rim Trail. See the introduction to The Organ and Angels Landing on page 33.

ANGEL HAIR (aka Dunn Route) V, 5.11, A3, 11 pitches

First Ascent: Jimmy Dunn, Dean Tschappat, two days, 1974.

Location and Access: *Pitch by pitch details are not available at the time of this writing.* The route climbs many difficult chimneys. It is located halfway between *Lowe Route* and *Empty Pages*. It is easily identified by the prominent right-sloping crack system halfway up the wall. No bolts were used on the first ascent. Jimmy Dunn suggests the route will go free at some point in the future. Excellent ledges on the route.

Paraphernalia: Protection from small wires to 6" cracks, with many knifeblades.

Descent: West Rim Trail. See the introduction to The Organ and Angels Landing on page 33.

EMPTY PAGES V, 5.8, A4, 8 pitches

First Ascent: Mark Pey, Dave Jones, 29-31 May 1982.

Location and Access: Right of *Angel Hair* which is joined or crossed at the top of the sixth pitch. Topo on pages 48-49.

Paraphernalia: Standard Zion aid rack with emphasis on smaller sizes.

Descent: West Rim Trail. See the introduction to The Organ and Angels Landing on page 33.

ARCHANGEL VI, 5.8, A3, 16 pitches

First Ascent: Ron Olevsky, solo, 1-8 October 1978.

Location and Access: Between *Empty Pages* and *Prodigal Sun*. The route begins at the same place as *Empty Pages* then traverses right on a ledge to continue up *Prodigal Sun*. At a level near where *Angel Hair* diagonals right, *Archangel* veers left leaving *Prodigal Sun* and joining *Empty Pages* for a short distance before rejoining *Angel Hair* and following it to the summit. (*Angel Hair, Empty Pages* and *Prodigal Sun* all top out at the same place.) There are many bolts and fixed pitons on the route which are not recommended because of the many contrived bolt ladders.

Paraphernalia: Pitons and nuts to 3"; keyhole hangers.

Descent: West Rim Trail. See the introduction to The Organ and Angels Landing on page 33.

PRODIGAL SUN IV+, 5.8, C2, 9 pitches

First Ascent: Ron Olevsky, solo, September 1981.

Location and Access: Just right of *Empty Pages*.

Paraphernalia: Friends (1) each #0.5, #1, #1.5, #2, #2.5, #3.5; Tri-cams #1 through #6; many small nuts to 1¼"; (4) ultra thin wires with sliding heads for use as bolt hangers; ⅜" keyhole hangers; (2) tie-off loops; (1) Chouinard hook; (50) free carabiners; (1) set of Chouinard stoppers and a nut tool. *Prodigal Sun* is a clean aid route and requires no hammer. Topo on pages 50-51.

Descent: West Rim Trail. See the introduction to The Organ and Angels Landing on page 33.

BALL AND CHAIN VI, 5.10, A4, 9 pitches

First Ascent: Glenn Randall, solo, 1978.

Location and Access: A very direct line climbing a major cleft between Angels Landing and Scout's Landing. Begin right of *Prodigal Sun* up a crack system dividing a very dark wall on the left from a light wall on the right.

Paraphernalia: (20) knifeblades; (20) Lost Arrows; (3) angles 2" to 5"; bongs and up to 8" tubes.

Descent: From Scout's Landing, a 1.9 mile (3km) paved trail descends 1000 feet (305m) to the Grotto Picnic Area.

G-MONEY VI, 5.9, A2+, 8 pitches

First Ascent: Barry Ward, Alan Humphrey, 4-7 September 1992.

Location and Access: The route is located 200 feet (61m) right of *Ball and Chain*, left of *Days of No Future*. Begin up a Birdbeak and knifeblade crack.

Paraphernalia: The first ascent party used on ⅜" by 4" bolts. Three sets of Friends up to #6 and TCUs. A selection of hooks, nuts and hexes; (15) Birdbeaks; (18) Lost Arrows; (4) ½" angles; (4) ⅝" angles; (3) ¾" angles; (3) 1" angles; removable hangers.

Descent: See descent for *Ball and Chain*.

DAYS OF NO FUTURE VI, 5.9, A3+, 7 pitches

First Ascent: Barry Ward, John Middendorf, 23-25 May 1991.

Location and Access: The route overhangs most of the distance to the summit at Scout's Landing. Only ten bolts were placed on the first ascent. The route is located up the second major crack system right of *Ball and Chain*.

Paraphernalia: Friends to #7; (15) knifeblades, mostly long; (12) Lost Arrows, mostly long; (4) ½" to ⅝" pitons, (3) ¾", (2-3) 1", 1¼" and 1½"; hooks; stoppers.

Descent: See descent for *Ball and Chain*.

SHEER LUNACY V, 5.9, C2, 11 pitches

First Ascent: Ron Olevsky, solo, August 1992.

Location and Access: The route climbs the prominent right-facing broken dihedral area located right of *Day of No Future* at a point one-third of the way to *Lunar Ecstasy*.

Paraphernalia: Standard Zion aid rack leaning toward the smaller sizes.

Descent: See descent for *Ball and Chain*.

Angels Landing Overview

From left to right:

Northeast Buttress
Swiss-American Route
Lowe Route
Dunn Route
Empty Pages
Archangel
Prodigal Sun
Ball and Chain
G-Money

Moonlight Buttress

Moonlight Buttress is located across the river from the Temple of Sinawava and the park road about 0.5 mile (0.8km) north of Angels Landing. It is a prominent prow of rock with a deep left-facing dihedral forming its left side.

LUNAR ECSTASY V, 5.9, A4, 9 pitches

First Ascent: Linus Platt, Brad Quinn, 2-5 April 1992. Second ascent: Davin Lindy, James Funsten 10-14 April 1992.

Location and Access: Climbs the obvious crack system left of *Moonlight Buttress*, where the buttress meets the main wall. Begin by climbing the first pitch of *Moonlight Buttress* or start to the left in a loose 5.10, A0 corner. Topo on pages 52-53.

Paraphernalia: Standard Zion aid rack with extra Lost Arrows and ½" baby angles.

Descent: West Rim Trail. See the introduction to The Organ and Angels Landing on page 33.

MOONLIGHT BUTTRESS V, 5.12d or 5.9, C1, A0, 10 pitches, ★★★★★

First Ascent: Jeff Lowe, Mike Weiss, October 1971. First Free Ascent: Johnny Woodward, Peter Croft, 24 April 1992. First Female solo: Nancy Feagin. First Night Solo: Calder Stratfond, 5-6 November 1994, 7 P.M. to 5 A.M. Calder, a 17-year-old from Provo, Utah, reported to John Middendorf and me the morning of his ascent, that his headlamp went dead on the eighth pitch and he had to finish the climb in the dark of a moonless night.

Location and Access: The route climbs the prow between light colored rock on the left and green lichen on the right. Begin about 100 feet (30m) below and left of the buttress with a third class scramble up ledges to reach the beginning of roped climbing. Ascend right of the stair-step overhang. Slings are visible from the pullout along the park road. Topo on pages 54-54. Photo on page 77.

Paraphernalia: Standard Zion free rack with extra TCUs.

Descent: West Rim Trail. See the introduction to The Organ and Angels Landing on page 33.

MARCH-FORREST CHIMNEY V, 5.9, A2, 12 pitches

First Ascent: Bill March, Bill Forrest, April-May 1978.

Location and Access: The route ascends the deepest, most prominent chimney system to the right of *Moonlight Buttress*. The route is also recognized by its obvious right-facing dihedral with a stepped roof located at mid-height. Approach after the river crossing by scrambling up to the right-hand side of a large pillar abutting a prominent chimney. From a corner crack, traverse left and begin up a good chimney which is ascended in the traditional back and foot to the top of a block, 5.6. Above is a steep corner crack with an overhang halfway up. This is climbed to gain the top of the pillar, 5.9. An alternative start was climbed by March and Murray Toft and follows the left-hand side of the pillar for two pitches.

Pitch 1: Climb the crack system on the right side of the chimney, pendulum left at 60 feet (18m) into a second crack which brings one to a belay ledge, 5.7.

Pitch 2: Climb the chimney above through a narrow squeeze section to gain the top of the pillar.

Pitch 3: Rappel off a tree on the top of the pillar and scramble into the back of a deep chimney where the route continues to a roof. Back and foot horizontally for 30 feet (9m) to gain a vertical crack which is then followed to a comfortable belay ledge, 5.7.

Pitch 4: Climb a narrowing chimney which becomes an overhanging offwidth jamcrack and gain a tree-shaded alcove, 5.8, A1. Belay on the platform to the right to avoid rockfall.

Pitch 5-7: Climb an excellent chimney in three full runouts of 5.7, over an occasional roof. Belay in a crow's nest deep in the back of the chimney.

Pitch 8: Lead horizontally 40 feet (12m) to the outside of the chimney where a crack is climbed to a good bivouac ledge, "The Haven."

Pitch 9: Ascend a short overhanging wall on the left and aid a corner, then free climb to an overhang and good sling belay.

Pitch 10: Hand traverse 15 feet (5m) right to gain a deep narrow chimney parallel to the great chimney. Belay on a sloping ledge, or there is a good belay at the back of the chimney where good anchors are available.

Pitch 11-12: Climb chimney cracks for two pitches to the top, 5.7.

Paraphernalia: Standard Zion free climbing rack.

Descent: West Rim Trail. See the introduction to The Organ and Angels Landing on page 33.

The Pulpit

The Pulpit is an obvious tower located just across (south) of the north fork of the Virgin River at the Temple of Sinawava parking area.

THE PULPIT II, 5.9+, A2, 2 pitches

First Ascent: Fred Beckey, Pat Callis, Galen Rowell, Eric Bjørnstad, 9 April 1967.

Location and Access: The first pitch climbs a bolt ladder, the second pitch is 5.9+ ending in an offwidth to the summit. There is a top-roped 5.11 free route just left of the original ascent line. Photo on page 91.

Paraphernalia: One set of Friends, a selection of nuts and stoppers.

Descent: Rappel the route.

THE PULPETTE I, 5.9, 1 pitch, 60 feet (18m)

First Ascent: Joede Schoeberlein, Mack Johnson, 5 October 1980.

Location and Access: Immediately south of *The Pulpit*. The climb is on the south side of the tower. Begin up a dihedral to a roof where a face move right to a crack leads to a large ledge with bolts. Unprotected face moves up an arête take one to the summit.

Paraphernalia: A small rack of small to medium wired nuts and (2) larger hexes were used on the first ascent. No pitons, although a drilled pin was used for the rappel anchor.

Descent: One 60-foot (18m) rappel down the route.

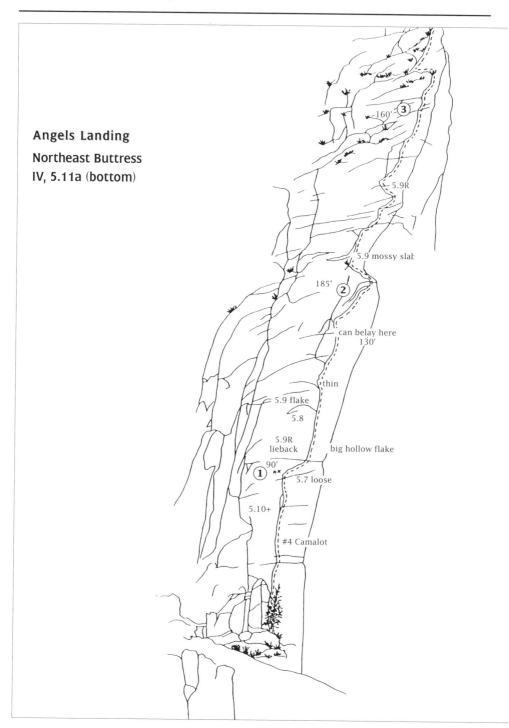

Angels Landing

Northeast Buttress

IV, 5.11a (bottom)

160' ③

5.9R

5.9 mossy slab

185' ②

can belay here
130'

thin

5.9 flake
5.8

5.9R
lieback   big hollow flake

90'
①   xx
5.7 loose

5.10+

#4 Camalot

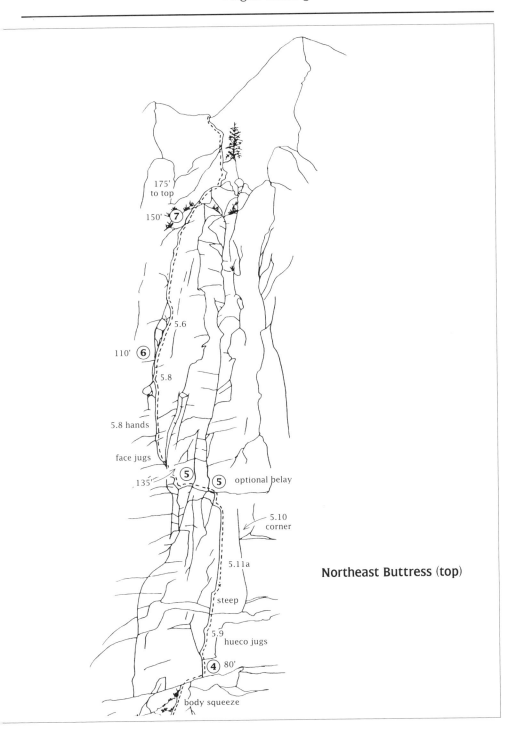

175'
to top

150' ⑦

5.6

110' ⑥

5.8

5.8 hands

face jugs

135' ⑤   ⑤ optional belay

5.10
corner

5.11a

Northeast Buttress (top)

steep

5.9
hueco jugs

④ 80'

body squeeze

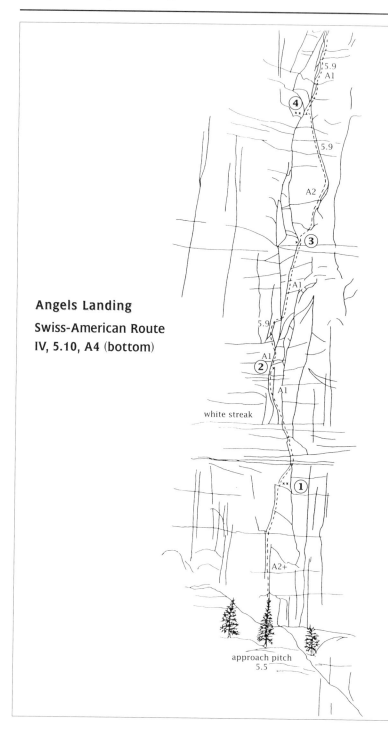

Angels Landing

Swiss-American Route

IV, 5.10, A4 (bottom)

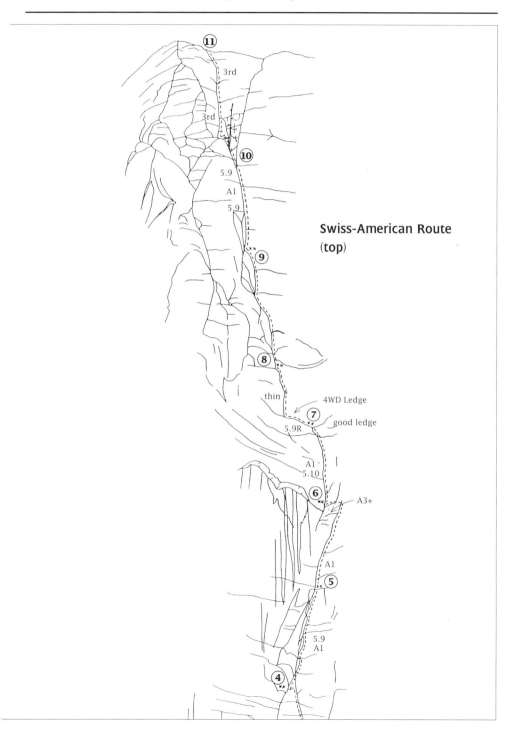

**Swiss-American Route
(top)**

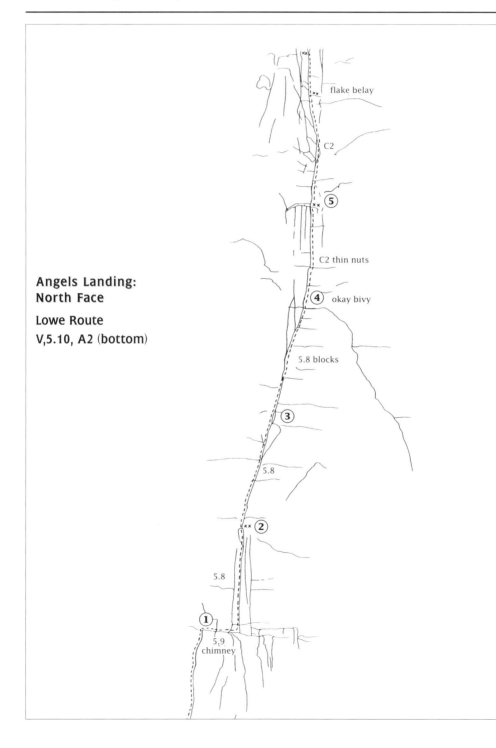

flake belay

C2

⑤

C2 thin nuts

**Angels Landing:
North Face**

Lowe Route

V,5.10, A2 (bottom)

④ okay bivy

5.8 blocks

③

5.8

② ××

5.8

①

5.9
chimney

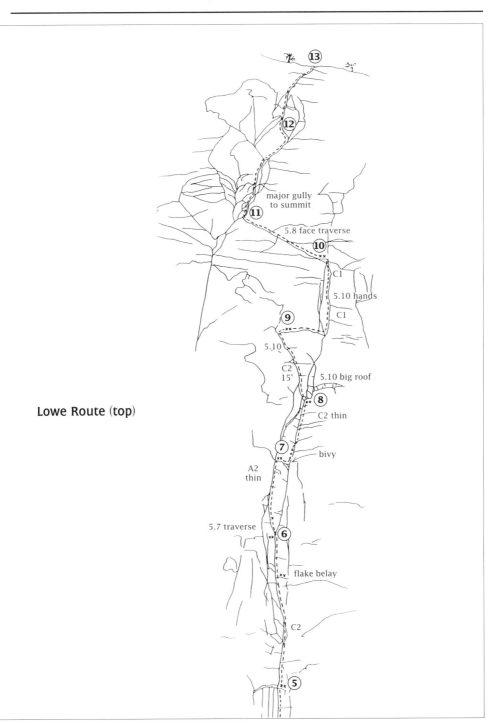

Lowe Route (top)

major gully
to summit

5.8 face traverse

C1

5.10 hands

C1

5.10

C2
15'

5.10 big roof

C2 thin

bivy

A2
thin

5.7 traverse

flake belay

C2

Angels Landing

Empty Pages

VI, 5.8, A4 (bottom)

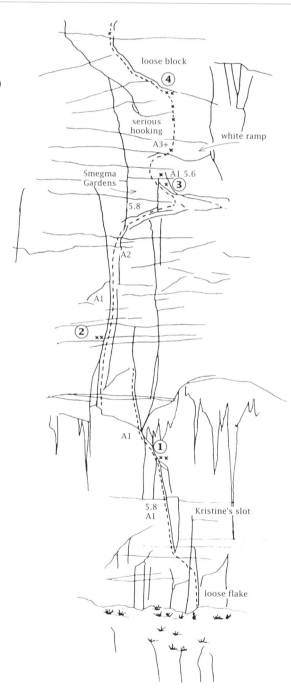

loose block

④

serious
hooking

white ramp

A3+

Smegma
Gardens

A1 5.6

③

5.8

A2

A1

②

A1

①

5.8
A1

Kristine's slot

loose flake

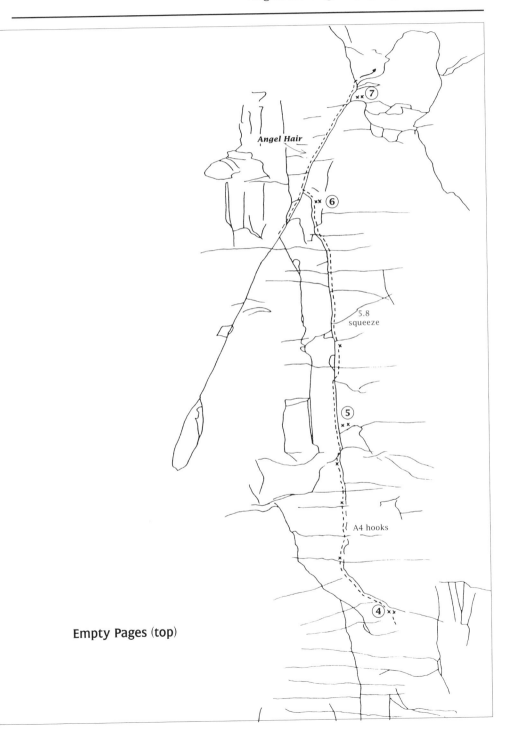

Empty Pages (top)

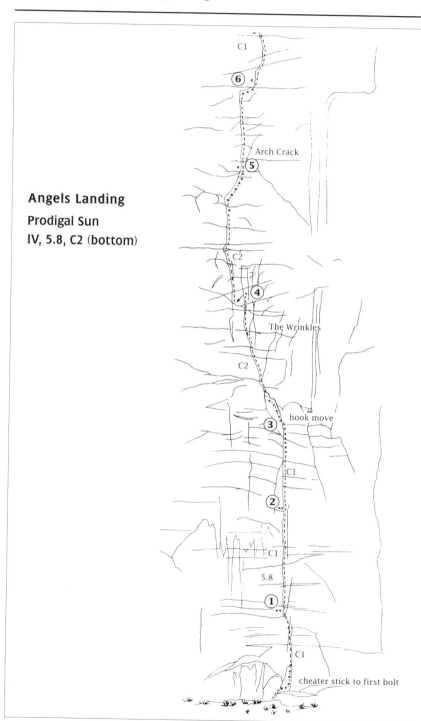

Angels Landing

Prodigal Sun

IV, 5.8, C2 (bottom)

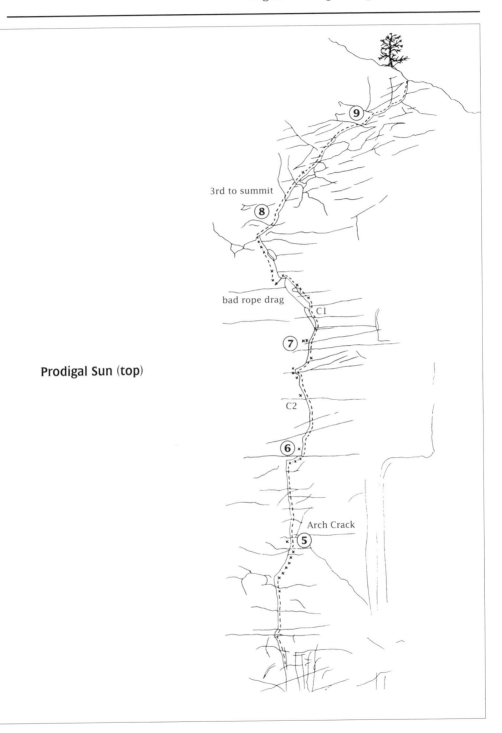

Prodigal Sun (top)

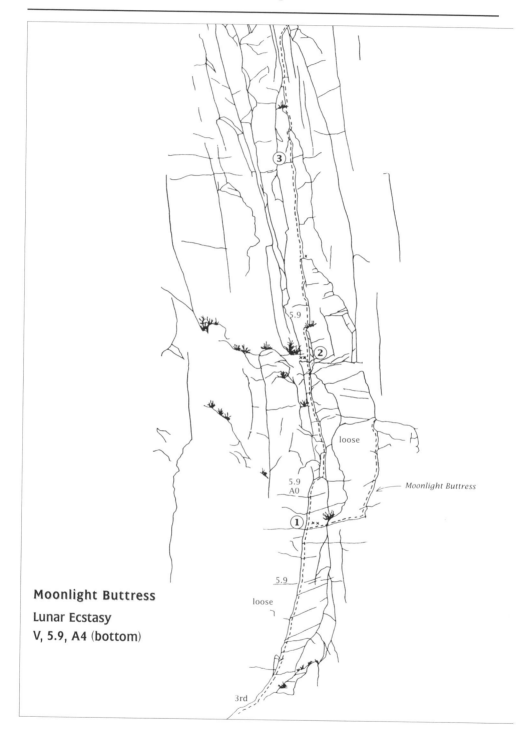

Moonlight Buttress

Lunar Ecstasy

V, 5.9, A4 (bottom)

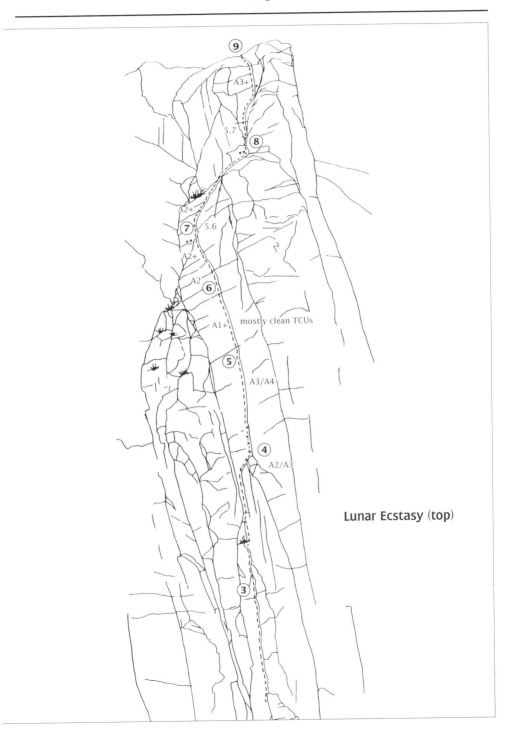

Lunar Ecstasy (top)

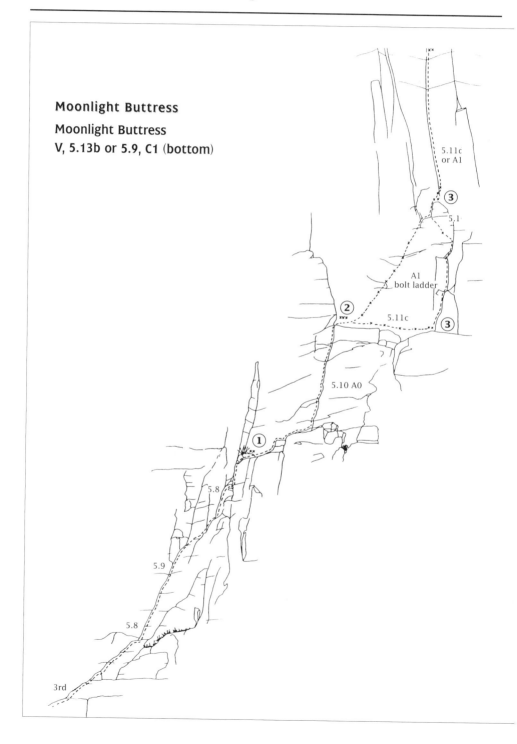

Moonlight Buttress

Moonlight Buttress

V, 5.13b or 5.9, C1 (bottom)

5.11c
or A1

③

5.1

A1
bolt ladder

②

5.11c

③

5.10 A0

①

5.8

5.9

5.8

3rd

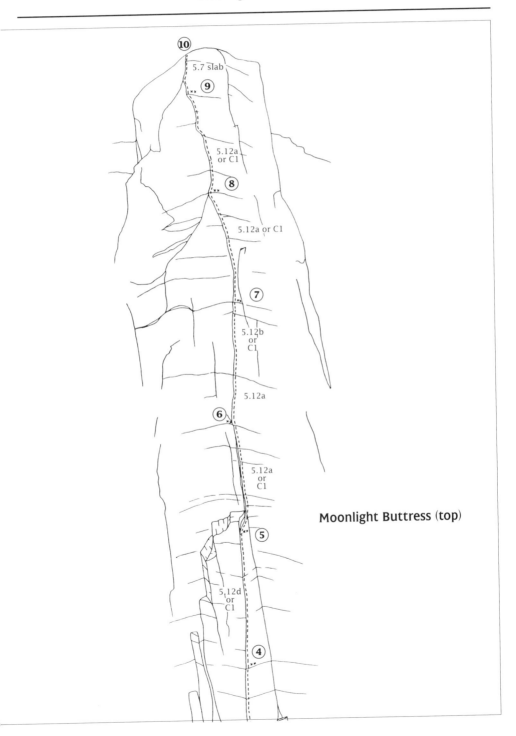

Moonlight Buttress (top)

Cosmic Trauma, *located near* Lunar Ecstasy

Photo: Bill Hatcher

Zion Canyon East

The following two routes are on the walls to the right of the 6.6 mile (10.6km) Zion Canyon Scenic Drive as one drives upcanyon. They begin at the Temple of Sinawava and are listed left to right (north to south) from the Temple back toward the visitor center. They are reached from pullouts on both the left and right sides of Scenic Drive.

Temple of Sinawava Area

The spectacular Temple of Sinawava, coyote-god of the Paiute Indians, is a massive rotunda of 2000 foot (610m) sandstone walls domed high above by a ceiling of sky. It is located at the end of the Zion Canyon Scenic Drive, 6.6 miles (10.6km) from the visitor center. The Temple is also the Gateway to the Narrows, an awesome slot canyon which at one point along its 17 mile (27km) length is 2000 feet (610m) deep and only 20 feet (6m) wide. On the west side of the Temple one of Zion's most spectacular waterfalls drops nearly 1000 feet (305m) from the West Rim after seasonal showers or snowmelt. It is at the Temple that the Navajo sandstone formation reaches its maximum thickness of 2400 feet (732m). Drinking water and restrooms are available at the parking area.

NOTE: Hiking the Narrows can be fatal. It is essential to check flash flood potential at the visitor center.

TOURIST CRACK I, 5.9+, 1 pitch, ★★★★★

First Ascent: Unknown.
Location and Access: In the Temple of Sinawava on the right wall several yards right of the restroom area. Slings are visible from below.
Paraphernalia: Standard Zion free rack.
Descent: Rappel the route.

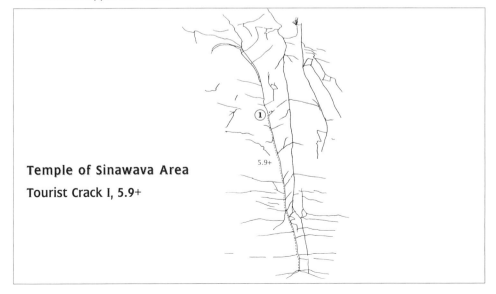

Temple of Sinawava Area

Tourist Crack I, 5.9+

MONKEYFINGER IV, 5.12, 10 pitches, 900 feet (274m), ★★★★★

First Ascent: Ron Olevsky, Rob Schnelker (5.10, A1) 1978. First Free Ascent: Mike O'Donnel, Craig Kenyon, 1989. First Flash Ascent: Johnny Woodward.

Location and Access: The route is located 0.1 mile (0.16km) downcanyon from the Temple of Sinawava parking area at a point directly above a sing reading "No Overnight Parking." It ascends a dark right-facing dihedral with a couple of pods obvious when looking high on the wall. Four sets of rappel slings are visible from below. At the top of the route a large pine tree is silhouetted in the skyline. The crux is at the Black Corner of the fourth pitch. Jeff Lowe says of the route "Monkeyfinger is the Astroman of Zion, a little shorter than its Yosemite brother, but with a more difficult crux....Hand, fist and offwidth cracks, an exciting undercling around a roof, acrobatic stemming on micro-edges in the Black Corner, and a few tricky face moves, all on good sandstone, ensured a great day of climbing. Don't miss it!"

Paraphernalia: Friends through #4; small cams; TCUs; nuts and stoppers up to 3.5".

Descent: Five rappels down the route. An alternate descent is to continue up the northwest ridge to Observation Point, (4th to 5.5), then descend the 5.5 mile (8.8km) East Rim Trail, to the south. This will bring one to Weeping Rock and the East Rim Trailhead located 4.8 miles (7.7km) from the visitor center.

Leaning Wall Area

The Leaning Wall is located 0.6 mile (0.9km) upcanyon from the oneway Organ and Angels Landing viewing pullout. *Spaceshot* is just left from the deep cut right-facing corner. One hundred feet (30m) left is *Vernal Equinox*. Between the two routes are *Moon Patrol* 5.10, A2, and to its right *Cosmic Trauma* 5.10, A3+.

EQUINOX IV, 5.10+, 10 pitches

First Ascent: Ron Olevsky, Mike Strassman, 21–23 March 1984.

Location and Access: Approach by walking to the center and largest of a series of buttresses on the left side of the Leaning Wall, left of the deep cut right-facing corner and left of *Spaceshot*.

Pitch 1: Climb a short 4th class chimney on the left side of this approach butte which leads to a brushy ledge. Hike to the base of a short wall.

Pitch 2: Ascend a 5.8 squeeze chimney past a bolt to the Last Resort, a large ledge.

Pitch 3: From the right edge of the ledge drop down a short step to Servants Quarters and climb a crack that joins a left-facing dihedral higher up, 5.9

Pitch 4: Ascend the right-facing dihedral above, 5.8.

Pitch 5: Continue up a lieback flake to a chimney then a belay ledge, 5.8.

Pitch 6: From the left edge of the belay ledge climb a thin crack at 5.10.

Pitch 7: Climb at 5.8 taking the left of two thin cracks. Belay at a tree at the base of chimney.

Pitch 8: Continue up the chimney to a belay ledge, 5.8.

Pitch 9: Continue up a crack on an arête at 5.9 or move to a 5.10 offwidth chimney.

Pitch 10: The final pitch climbs up and left over slabs at 5.7 then 4th class past trees and enters a gully to the right.

Paraphernalia: Standard Zion free rack.

Descent: Cross the drainage to the east and rappel from a tree past slabs then make four more rappels via excellent ledges.

Photo: Bill Hatcher

Paul Piana leading a pitch on Monkeyfinger

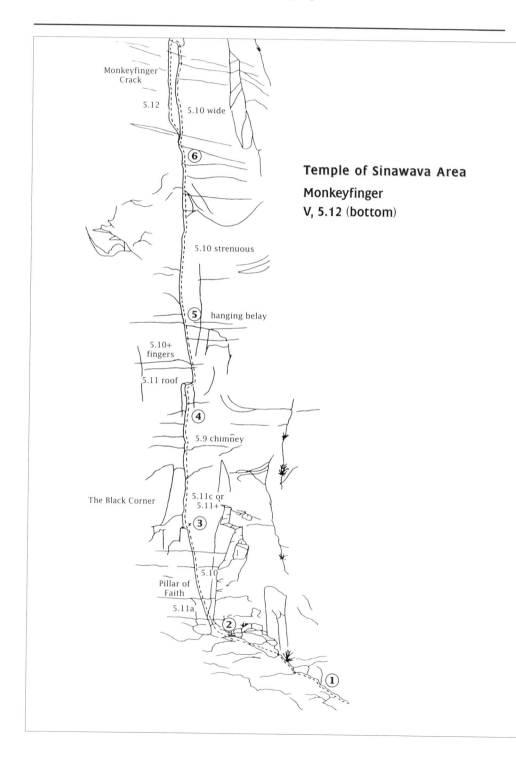

Monkeyfinger
Crack

5.12   5.10 wide

⑥

Temple of Sinawava Area
Monkeyfinger
V, 5.12 (bottom)

5.10 strenuous

⑤ hanging belay

5.10+
fingers

5.11 roof

④

5.9 chimney

The Black Corner   5.11c or
                      5.11+
              × ③

              5.10

Pillar of
Faith

5.11a
              ②

                        ①

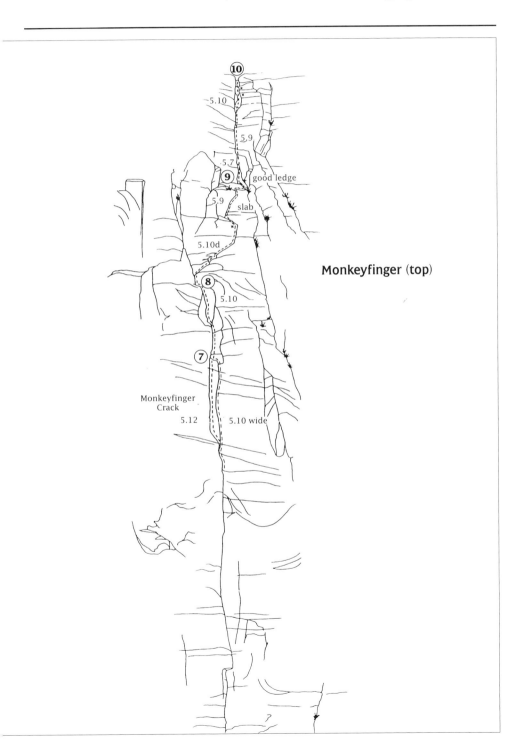

Monkeyfinger (top)

SPACESHOT IV, 5.10, C2, 7 pitches, ★★★★★

First Ascent: Ron Olevsky, Dave Jones, 27-28 November 1978.

Location and Access: *Spaceshot* climbs the first crack system left of the deep cut right-facing corner.

Pitch 1: Begin with a bushwhack then climb the Alpine Start, a 5.9 right-facing dihedral. At the top move left and belay. Climb a 5.6 right-sloping crack system to a good ledge. Wander right and up via 5.4 bushwhacking.

Pitch 2: Ascend a bolt ladder (may be climbed clean) just to the left of Rebozo Pinnacle.

Pitch 3: Continue C2 to a sling belay. From this point on retreat would be difficult.

Pitch 4: Climb C1 or 5.10 to a second sling belay.

Pitch 5: Climb 5.10 or C1 to Earth Orbit Ledge.

Pitch 6: Traverse right on the ledge to a bolt ladder.

Pitch 7: Clean aid to (5.6) free climbing, angle right to timber and the top of the route.

Paraphernalia: (2) sets of Friends with extra #2, #2.5 and #3; double small to medium wires.

Descent: Traverse east past a drainage and rappel from a tree past slabs, then downclimb making four rappels from excellent ledges.

Cereberus Gendarme Area

TOUCHSTONE WALL IV, 5.11– R A0 or 5.9 C2, ★★★★

First Ascent: Ron Olevsky, 1977.

Location and Access: The beginning of the route is marked by a bolt ladder with slings visible just left of a major right-facing corner.

Paraphernalia: Standard Zion free rack with extra carabiners.

Descent: From the summit descend north to a notch on the right side of the Cerberus Gendarme and make several rappels down the gully to the canyon floor.

Cerberus Cragging Area

The five-star Cerberus Cragging area is located along the Cerberus Gendarme and has better than a dozen routes established, located both left and right of the Touchstone Wall route. In Greek mythology Cerberus was a three-headed dog guarding the entrance to Hades.

The routes left to right are: *Cave Route* 5.7, *No Holds Barred* 5.7, *Squeeze Play* 5.10a, *The Fat Hedral* 5.10+, *Fails of Power* 5.11c, *Scarlet Begonias* 5.11a, *Tales of Flails* 5.9, *Electrica* 5.11+ face, *Dire Wolf* 5.12a, *Cherry Crack* 5.10c, *Intruder* 5.11+ fingers, *Flip of a Coin* 5.10d, *Touchstone Wall* IV, 5.11, A0 (or 5.9, C2), *Coconut Corner* 5.10.

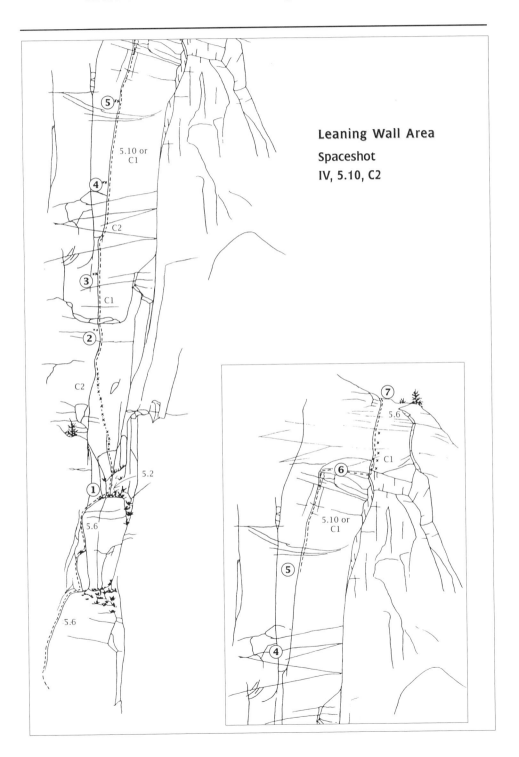

Leaning Wall Area

Spaceshot
IV, 5.10, C2

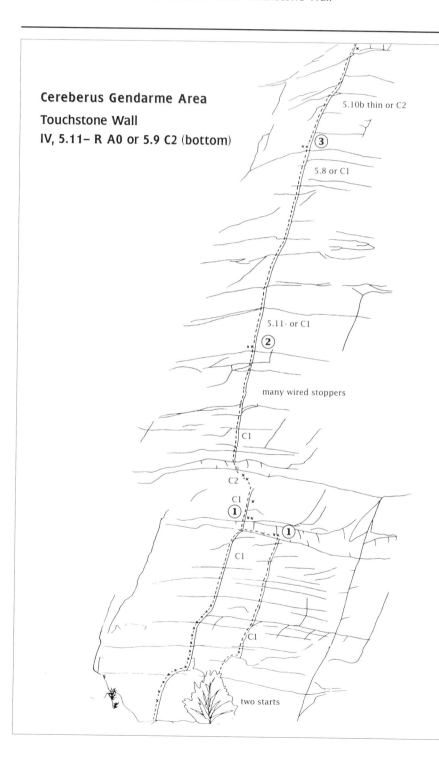

Cereberus Gendarme Area

Touchstone Wall

IV, 5.11– R A0 or 5.9 C2 (bottom)

5.10b thin or C2

③

5.8 or C1

5.11- or C1

②

many wired stoppers

C1

C2

C1

①

①

C1

C1

two starts

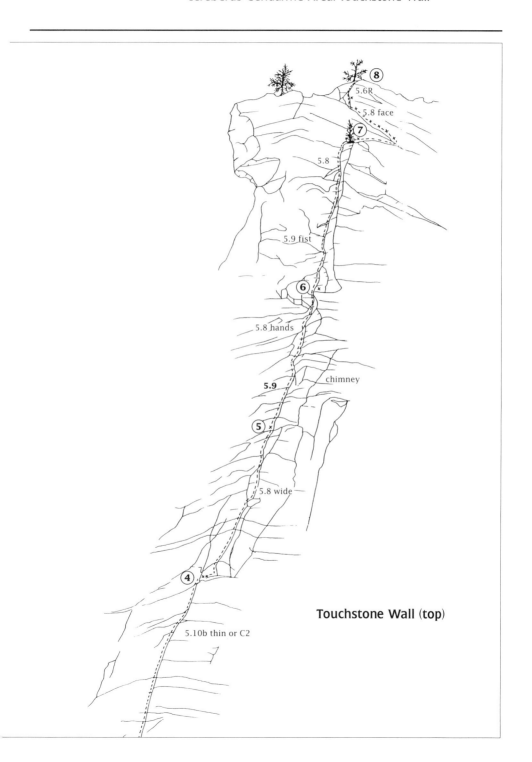

8

5.6R

5.8 face

7

5.8

5.9 fist

6

5.8 hands

chimney

5.9

5

5.8 wide

4

Touchstone Wall (top)

5.10b thin or C2

Red Arch Mountain to Mount Spry

This is the area to the east (right) of the park road, between the Zion Canyon Scenic Drive junction with Zion-Mount Carmel Highway and Red Arch Mountain located left of the Zion Lodge.

NOTE: Routes along these walls include Mountain of the Sun and Mount Spry, both closed during the spring nesting season for the protection of peregrine falcons. Please check at the visitor center for exact dates.

Photo: Ed Cooper

Red Arch Mountain

Red Arch Mountain: North Face

RITES OF PASSAGE IV, 5.11, 9 pitches, ★

First Ascent: Geoff Scherer, Dave Jones, 21-22 April 1994.

Location and Access: The route is left of *Shune's Buttress*. Traverse left from the buttress and begin the climb at 5.10 via a clean right-facing dihedral located just left of a prominent fir tree a few feet up the wall. Approach takes about one hour.

Paraphernalia: (1) set of Friends #0.5 through #4, (1) extra #2, #3 and (2) extra #4; (1) set of Tri-cams; quickdraws for bolts.

Descent: Traverse 200 feet (61m) to the right and rappel *Shune's Buttress*.

SHUNE'S BUTTRESS IV, 5.11c, 8 pitches with a 700-foot (213m) scramble to the top of Red Arch Mountain

First Ascent: Steve Chardon, Dave Jones, 23 September 1980. First Free Ascent: Conrad Anker, Dave Jones, 17 May 1992.

Location and Access: The route climbs the north buttress of the north face of Red Arch Mountain. The 1980 *Shune's Buttress* climb by Chardon and Jones was also the first ascent of Red Arch Mountain. Begin by hiking up the left side to the base of a finger pinnacle. This is a point just to the right of an obvious headwall crack several hundred feet above. A Pitch 1 variation (put up by Bob Yoho and Dave Jones in 1987) begins right of the original line, 5.11-. (There is also a Pitch 2 variation climbed at 5.9 by Wheels in 1992 located to the right of the original 5.10 facecrack.) John Middendorf refers to *Shune's Buttress* as "The Rostrum of Zion," with an incredible 5.11c overhanging thin hands and finger pitch up high."

Paraphernalia: Standard Zion free rack with extra handsize cams and hexes.

Descent: Rappel the route.

Mountain of the Sun

Mountain of the Sun is located opposite the Court of the Patriarchs, 1.7 miles (2.7km) up the Zion Canyon Scenic Drive above the park road. The name comes from its 6723 foot (2049m) summit which reflects the first golden rays of sunrise and the last colors of sunset.

THE TAO OF LIGHT VI, 5.10, A3, 17 pitches plus 500 feet (152m) of 4th class

First Ascent: Paul Turecki, John Middendorf, October 1994.

Location and Access: Begin by working your way up toward the large arch on the right side of the mountain. The route then ascends the arête on the left side of the large corner prominent on the monolith. Good bivouac ledges are located at the top of Pitch 5 and 12.

Paraphernalia: (3) Friends #1 to #3, (2) each #3.5, #4; Camalots (2) #4, (1) #5, (1) #7; (2) each TCUs #.75, #.4; (1) Big Bro or Tri-cam; hexes and Tri-cams; nuts; stoppers; (1) ring angle; (5) Birdbeaks; (3-4) knifeblades; (2-3) Lost Arrows; (3) baby angles ½", ⅜"; (2) each ¾" pitons.

Descent: Rappel the route.

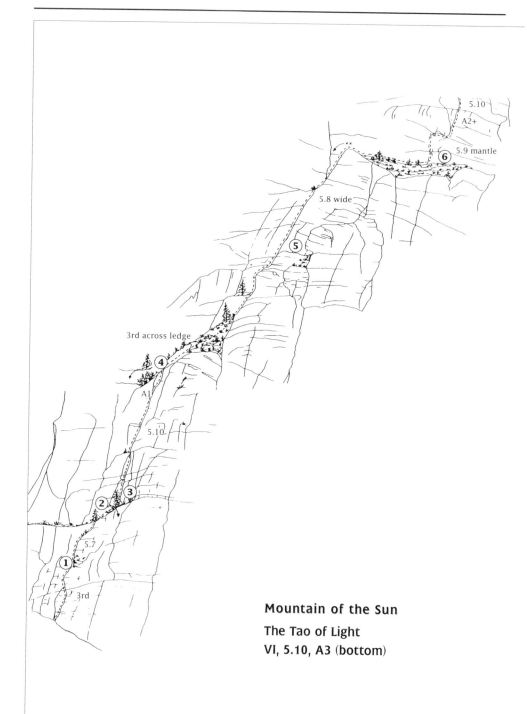

5.10

A2+

5.9 mantle

5.8 wide

3rd across ledge

A1

5.10

5.7

3rd

Mountain of the Sun

The Tao of Light
VI, 5.10, A3 (bottom)

The Tao of Light (top)

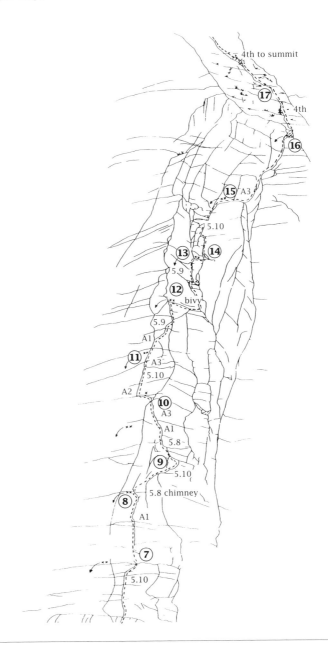

Twin Brothers: Right Twin

Twin Brothers pullout is located 0.3 mile (0.48km) downcanyon from Three Patriarchs pullout.

PEYOTE DREAMS VI, 5.10, A3+, ★★★★★

First Ascent: Eric Rasmussen, Sean Plunkett, November 1994.

Location and Access: The route ascends splitter cracks up the center of the right Twin Brother and is one of the longer routes in the park.

Paraphernalia: Standard Zion aid rack with extra pitons and hooks.

Descent: Scramble and rappel (from trees) down obvious slabs to the south. Once in the prominent drainage, two rappels lead into the canyon where it is a ten-minute walk to the valley floor.

Mount Spry

The peak may be viewed from the Twin Brothers pullout or further downcanyon just before the new road over the 1995 Zion slide area.

SANDBLASTER VI, 5.11, 8 pitches, 800 feet (244m), ★★★

First Ascent: Jeff Lowe, Mark Wilford, September 1987.

Location and Access: The route climbs the west face of the mountain via the right side of the central pillar. The route begins third class left of the *Kraus-Cerf* original Central Pillar climb, joins it for a free ascent over the crux at the top of the sixth pitch then veers left again for an independent finish. Topo on pages 72-73.

Paraphernalia: (3) sets of Friends; Big Bro #4; Tri-cams #0.5, #1.5, #6, #7; (1) set of wired stoppers.

Descent: An intricate descent is made down the canyon behind and left via multiple rappels.

Mount Spry: Northwest Face

MORIA III, 5.8, 5 pitches

First Ascent: Jim Beyer, Bob Sullivan, May 1979.

Location and Access: The route follows a chimney crack system just right of the center of the northwest face. A black roof at half height and an overhanging slot located just right of the beginning of the climb identify the route. The roof is passed on the left side on Pitch 3. At the top of the Pitch 3 it is possible to climb diagonally right via a hard third class gully for 200 feet (61m) and then continue third class and escape onto the south ridge.

Paraphernalia: Protection to 3", with 4", 5" and 6" optional.

Descent: Three long rappels down the southwest ridge then third class to the valley floor.

BLACK CRACK (Bites Back) III, 5.9, 5 pitches

First Ascent: Jim Beyer, Misa Giesey, Fall 1979.

Location and Access: About 200 yards (183m) right of *Moria*. The route starts in a thinly forested and grassy area and is the only clean crack in the region. Begin up 5.8+ hand-and-fist crack and end by third classing 40 feet (12m) to a notch located left of a cone-shaped pinnacle on the upper southwest ridge.

Paraphernalia: Standard Zion free climbing rack.

Descent: Three long rappels down the southwest ridge then third class to the valley floor.

Photo: Jeff Widen

Indian Ruins with The Organ and Angels Landing in the background

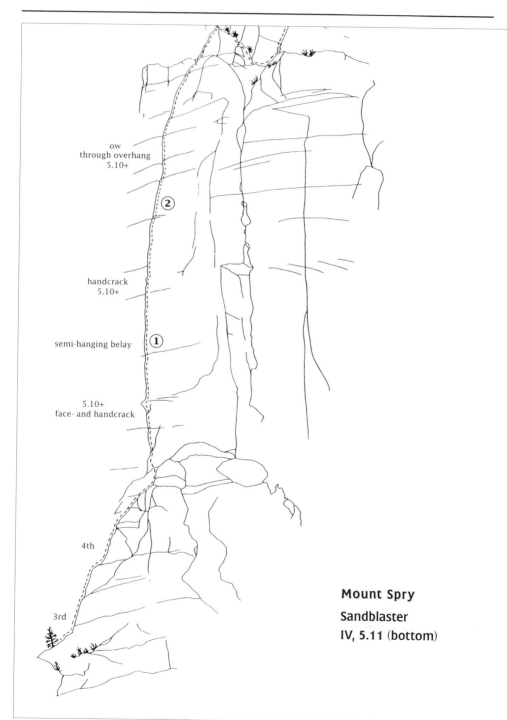

ow
through overhang
5.10+

②

handcrack
5.10+

semi-hanging belay ①

5.10+
face- and handcrack

4th

3rd

Mount Spry

Sandblaster

IV, 5.11 (bottom)

Sandblaster (top)

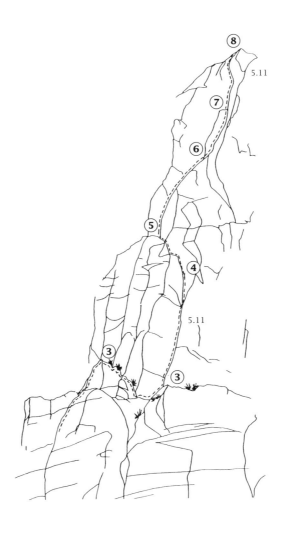

East Temple

East and West Temples were named in a geologic report by Clarence E. Dutton in 1882. Climbs on East Temple are best approached from a parking area at the bridge over Pine Creek. To reach drive about 0.5 mile (0.8km) north of the visitors center to the junction of the Zion Canyon Scenic Drive and the Zion-Mount Carmel Highway and then 0.5 mile (0.8km) east on the Mount Carmel Highway to the parking area at the bridge. This is the bridge located at the bottom of the switchbacks leading to the Mount Carmel Highway tunnels.

NOTE: A number of areas, including East Temple, are closed each year for the protection of nesting peregrine falcons and the lambing or rutting seasons for the Desert Bighorn sheep. Closure for the falcons is usually spring until mid-August and may vary each year as determined by the park biologist. Closures are posted at the visitor center.

LOVELACE V, 5.10, C2+ (1 pitch C2+ with A0 on upper pitches), 1200 feet (366m), ★★★

First Ascent: Dave Jones, Gary Grey, 1983.

Location and Access: *Lovelace* is also known as *Fang Wall*. To approach, park at the bridge located before the first switchback on the Zion-Mount Carmel Highway. Descend to the drainage and hike, then climb, to the left side of the Fang Spire which is obvious from the parking area. *Lovelace* climbs the wall behind The Fang.

Paraphernalia: Standard Zion free rack with extra small wires and larger offwidth protection.

Descent: Rappel the route.

THE FANG V, 5.10, A3+, 6 pitches, 650 feet (198m), ★★★

First Ascent: John Middendorf, Kyle Copeland, 22 May 1988.

Location and Access: Approach as for *Lovelace* from the bridge located before the first switchback on the Zion-Mount Carmel Highway. The spire is obvious as one looks across to East Temple. The route ascends thin cracks on the outer face of the spire. Topo on page 76.

Paraphernalia: Standard Zion aid rack with hooks.

Descent: Begin with one rappel directly south to the ledge at the top of the Pitch 5, then continue rappels straight down to the shoulder below and right of Pitch 2. At this point third class to the right to a ledge and the final rappel.

COWBOY BOB GOES TO ZION V, 5.10+, C2+ (5 moves of aid), 9 pitches, ★★★

First Ascent: Hugh O'Neal, Dave Jones, 6-7 November 1986.

Location and Access: The route ascends the leftmost of the three Towers of Fate that make up the southern side of East Temple. The routes end at the False Rim cliff line which is obvious from the parking area. Begin 100 feet (30m) below the highest point of the scree slope approach and continue up and to the right of a white fingerlike pillar located one-third of the way up the wall. A bold unprotected 5.10+ section is reached near the top of the climb. There are only five moves of aid (on the last pitch). No fixed anchors exist on the route. Topo on pages 78-79.

Paraphernalia: Standard Zion free rack with pieces for offwidth protection.

Descent: Using natural anchors for the descent begin with two rappels down the ridge to the right of the route followed with four rappels down a gully to the top of the scree slope at the base of the climb. This location is the highest talus slope on the south side of East Temple. An alternate descent is to traverse right past the center (*Uncertain Fates*) and right (*Freezer Burn*) of the three Towers of Fate and walk off to the Great Arch Overlook at the upper end of Pine Creek Canyon.

UNCERTAIN FATES V, 5.11+, C1 (5 points of aid), 9 pitches

First Ascent: Stacy Allison, Dave Jones, 9-10 November 1986.

Location and Access: The route climbs just right of center on the middle Tower of Fate. Climb above the talus slope across the upper bushy ledge to a beginning at the left handcracks in the deepest obvious recessed slot at the base of the wall. The final pitch climbs a chimney to easier ground and the False Rim cliff line where the route ends.

Paraphernalia: Standard Zion free rack.

Descent: Hike east, staying high along the ridge of the False Rim to the Great Arch Overlook at the upper end of Pine Creek Canyon.

FREEZER BURN IV, 5.11+, (about 6 points of aid), 7 pitches,
★★★★

First Ascent: Mark Austin, Dave Jones, 1985. First Free Ascent: (*Free or Burn*) Mugs Stump, Lynn Wheeler, February 1991.

Location and Access: The route begins in a sandy alcove right of *Uncertain Fates* between the center and the right Towers of Fate. Begin up a straight-in crack system with a small bush visible low down, even though a more obvious crack line exist just left of this beginning.

Paraphernalia: Standard Zion free rack with (4) #3 cams and (3) #3.5 cams.

Descent: Traverse east to the Great Arch Overlook. See descent for *Uncertain Fates*.

10TH DIVISION IV, 5.10+, C1 (2 points of aid), 9 pitches

First Ascent: Brad Quinn, Dave Jones, 23 October 1988.

Location and Access: Located on the right side of the rightmost Tower of Fate. The route is not visible from the parking area at the bridge because it ascends an eastward facing crack system set back in a recess at the wide upper portion of Pine Creek Canyon. Approach is about 40 minutes from the bridge parking. The route is identified by a tree which overhangs the crack system at the top of the first pitch. Two points of C1 are found on Pitch 6. The route was named in memory of Alexander Jones Jr., Dave Jones' father who served in the 10th Army Division during World War II. Topo on pages 82-83.

Paraphernalia: Friends: (2) #1, #1.5, (2-3) #2, #2.5, (3-5) #3, (2) #4, (2) #6 (Big Dude or tube chock); small to intermediate nuts.

Descent: Forty-minute walk-off east (right) to the Great Arch Overlook.

East Temple

The Fang

V, 5.10, A3+

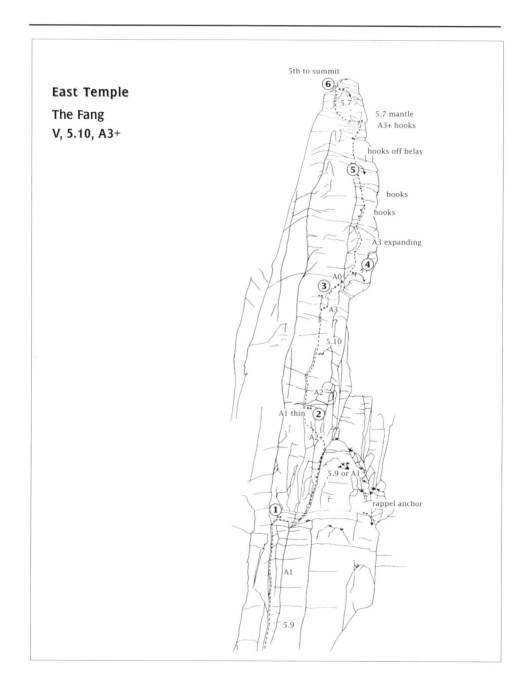

5th to summit

⑥

5.7

5.7 mantle
A3+ hooks

hooks off belay

⑤

hooks

hooks

A3 expanding

④

A0

③

A3

5.10

A2

A1 thin ②

A2+

5.9 or A1

rappel anchor

①

A1

5.9

Eve Tallman soloing Moonlight Buttress

Photo: Bill Hatcher

East Temple

Cowboy Bob Goes to Zion

V, 5.10+, C2+ (bottom)

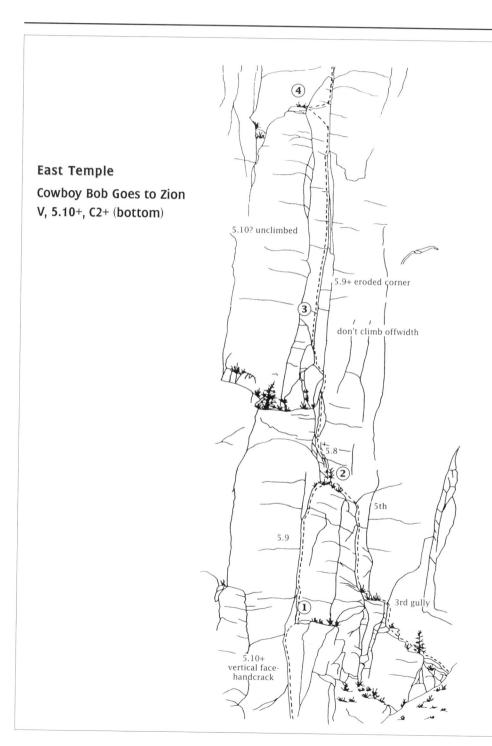

5.10? unclimbed

5.9+ eroded corner

don't climb offwidth

5.8

5th

5.9

3rd gully

5.10+
vertical face-
handcrack

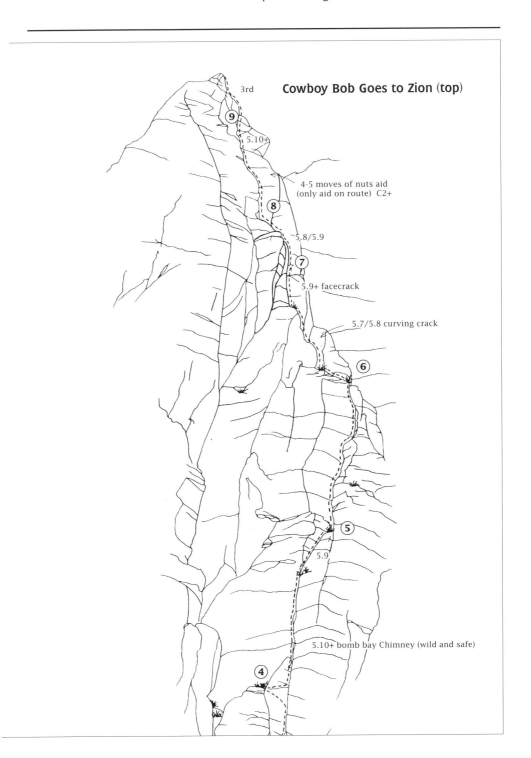

Cowboy Bob Goes to Zion (top)

3rd

5.10+

4-5 moves of nuts aid
(only aid on route) C2+

5.8/5.9

5.9+ facecrack

5.7/5.8 curving crack

5.9

5.10+ bomb bay Chimney (wild and safe)

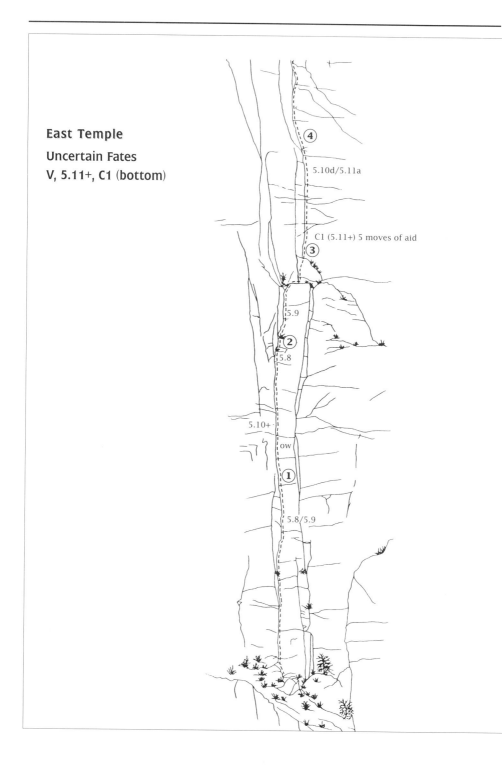

East Temple

Uncertain Fates

V, 5.11+, C1 (bottom)

④

5.10d/5.11a

C1 (5.11+) 5 moves of aid

③

5.9

②

5.8

5.10+

ow

①

5.8/5.9

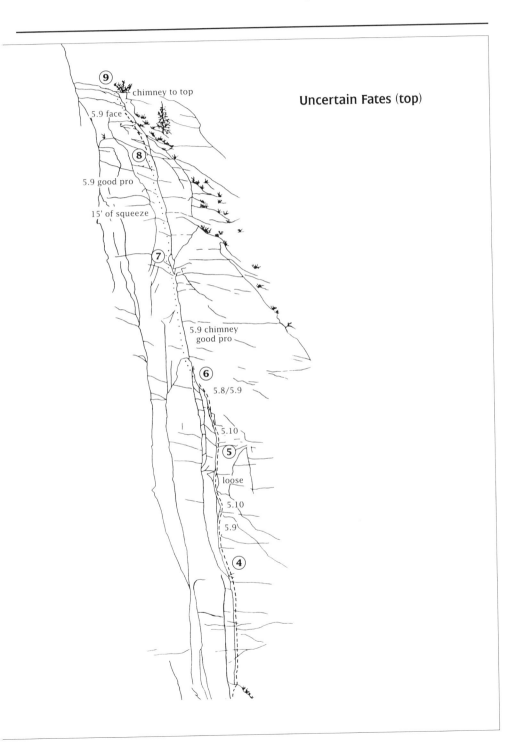

Uncertain Fates (top)

9 chimney to top

5.9 face

8

5.9 good pro

15' of squeeze

7

5.9 chimney
good pro

6

5.8/5.9

5.10

5

loose

5.10

5.9

4

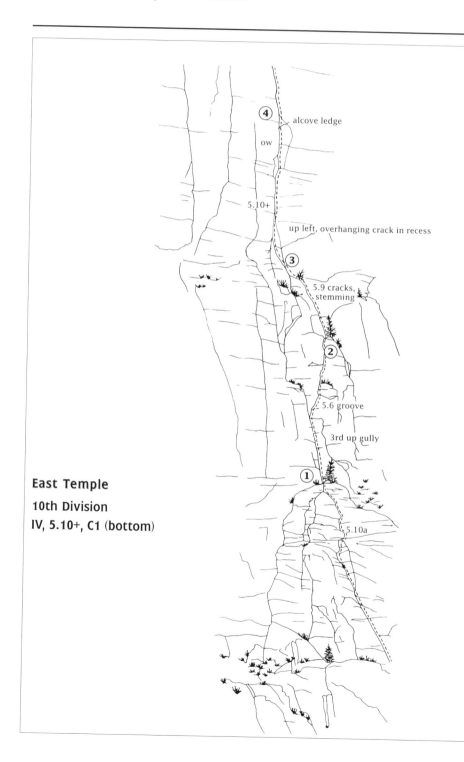

alcove ledge

ow

5.10+

up left, overhanging crack in recess

5.9 cracks, stemming

5.6 groove

3rd up gully

5.10a

East Temple

10th Division

IV, 5.10+, C1 (bottom)

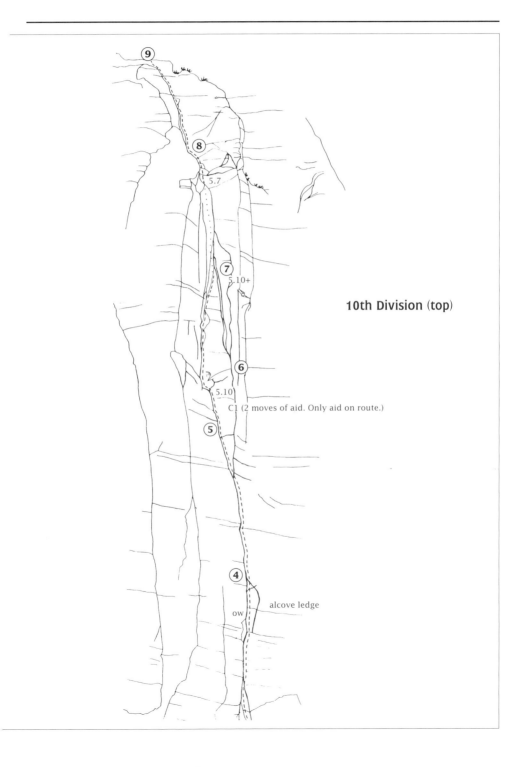

10th Division (top)

9

8

5.7

7

5.10+

6

5.10

C1 (2 moves of aid. Only aid on route.)

5

4

ow   alcove ledge

Tunnel Crags Area

Viewing for the Tunnel Crags free-climbing area is about 2 miles (3.2km) beyond the bridge over Pine Creek at the bottom of the switchbacks leading to the tunnels of the Zion-Mount Carmel Highway. Approach for the climbs is usually from the closest place it is possible to park clear of the busy highway. There are numerous routes established here, mostly one pitch in length.

NOTE: The Tunnel Crag Area is closed in the spring to protect the nesting of peregrine falcons. Please check at the visitor center for exact dates.

NEVER AGAIN III, 5.10, 4 pitches, 3 hanging belays

First Ascent: Gordon Seibel, Kevin Bochne, 24 October 1974.

Location and Access: The first ascent team used no bolts or pitons. The route is located about 50 yards (46m) before the entrance to the west (first) tunnel. It climbs a crack system just left of the popular *Headache* route.

Paraphernalia: Pitch 1: #2 Friends and larger; Pitch 2: (1) set of wire stoppers and Friends to #3; Pitch 3: Wires up to #4 Friends; Pitch 4: Wires to #2.5 Friends. Total of (1) set of wires and (3) sets of Friends.

Descent: Two rappels down the route with 165-foot (50m) ropes, or descend the obvious loose gully immediately to the left of the climb.

THE HEADACHE II, 5.10, 3 pitches

First Ascent: Brian Smith, Dana Geary, 10 August 1975.

Location and Access: Right of *Never Again*, left of the prominent corner viewed from below. Located about 50 yards (46m) before the entrance to the west (first) tunnel. Photo on page 85.

Paraphernalia: Standard Zion free rack.

Descent: Rappel the gully left of the route or rappel the route.

MIGRAINE III, 5.12a, 1 pitch

First Ascent: Paul Turecki, Nancy Pfeiffer, 30 October 1988.

Location and Access: Begin 20 feet (6m) around the corner to the right of *The Headache*. The route climbs thin hands and fingers.

Paraphernalia: Small protection.

Descent: Rappel the route.

NERVOUS TENSION III, 510d, 1 pitch

First Ascent: Paul Turecki, Nancy Pfeiffer, October 30, 1988.

Location and Access: Next crack right of *Migraine* about 100 feet (30m).

Paraphernalia: Small protection.

Descent: Rappel the route.

BORING IV, 5.10, 2 pitches, 180 feet (55m)

First Ascent: Mark Austin.

Location and Access: Slings are visible from below to the right of *Nervous Tension*.

Paraphernalia: Standard Zion free rack with extra protection for finger- to handsize.

Descent: Rappel the route.

WHEELS ON FIRE IV, 5.12a, A0, 180 feet (55m)

First Ascent: Wheels, 1991.

Location and Access: Located right of *Boring* and ending on the same ledge. The route has only been top-roped.

Paraphernalia: Top-roped. No protection used.

Descent: Rappel the route.

Photo: Bill Hatcher

Climber on **The Headache**

South Entrance Bouldering

This is perhaps the most popular bouldering area in the park. It is located on the left (west) side of the park road between the entrance kiosk and the turn into the Watchman Campground.

Virgin River Bouldering

This area is reached by driving 0.5 mile (0.8km) north of the visitor center then crossing the Virgin River bridge and taking the Zion-Mount Carmel Highway a short distance to a large prominent boulder on the right side of the roadway. Cross Pine Creek and hike south ascending up to the obvious Virgin River boulders. Most of the numerous bouldering problems can be top-roped.

The Watchman

Approach via The Watchman Trail which climbs 1.5 mile (2.4km) to a plateau near the base of the impressively fluted monolith. From the south park entrance drive a few hundred yards and enter The Watchman Campground. Turn left at a service road and proceed 0.2 mile (0.3km) to the trailhead. A sign indicates the start of the Watchman Trail. The following routes are listed from left to right on the prominent west face of The Watchman.

NOTE: The Watchman is closed to climbing in the spring for the protection of peregrine falcons during nesting. Please check the visitor center for exact dates.

S & M IV, 5.10+, A0 (one aid move on bolt), 6 pitches

First Ascent: Stacy Allison-Austin, Mark Austin, 1984.

Location and Access: Ascends a clean crack alternating between fingers and offwidth for six pitches with only one aid move. It ascends immediately right of a small tower right of *The Vigil*. When the Watchman is viewed from the north edge of Springdale the route is located just right of the highest point on the skyline.

Paraphernalia: Protection for fingers to offwidth.

Descent: Scramble up either of several choices to the summit ridge or down a gully to the left of the climb, third class with three rappels.

THE VIGIL IV, 5.11, 10 pitches, ★★★

First Ascent: Conrad Anker, Dave Jones, 14-15 May 1992.

Location and Access: To the left of *S & M*. Start in a large, recessed, dirty-looking right-facing dihedral 100 feet (30m) left of a sharper, more solid-looking crack system at the left of a prominent white ramp. An obvious large talus boulder is down and left of the start of the route. To the right is a left-facing corner and further right are two finger pillars. A large tree at the top of Pitch 4 on Violation Ledge is visible from the campground. When The Watchman is viewed from the north end of Springdale, the route ascends up the middle and directly below the first prominent step in the left (north) skyline. Topo on page 87.

Paraphernalia: (2) sets of Friends #.5 through #4 (including half sizes) with extra #3 and #4; (2) #4 Camalots; (2) sets of TCUs; (1) set of RPs and nuts to 1".

Descent: Third to fifth class to the northwest ridge of The Watchman then rappel and scramble right, down a gully.

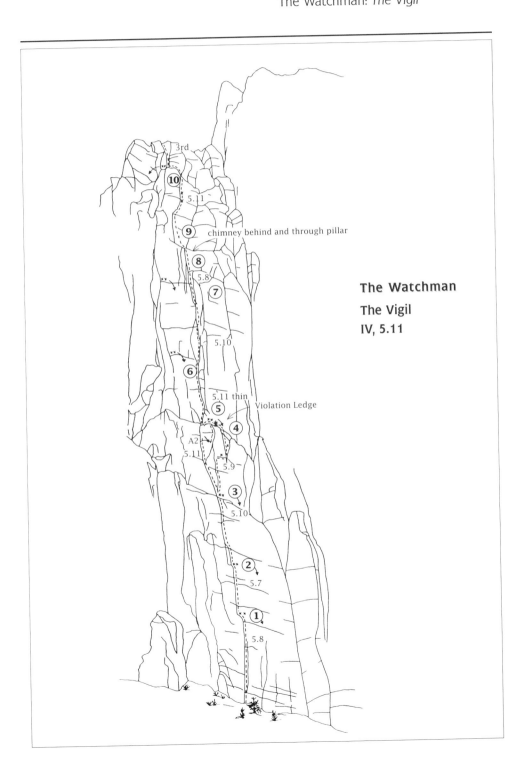

The Watchman

The Vigil

IV, 5.11

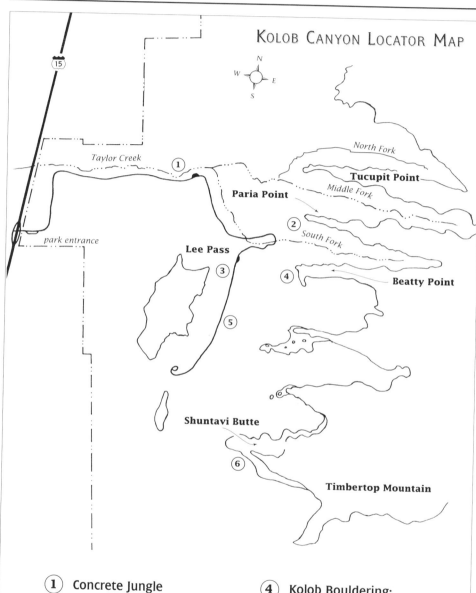

KOLOB CANYON LOCATOR MAP

Taylor Creek

North Fork

Tucupit Point

Middle Fork

Paria Point

South Fork

Lee Pass

Beatty Point

park entrance

Shuntavi Butte

Timbertop Mountain

(1) Concrete Jungle

(2) Paria Point:
Wind, Sand and Stars

(3) Hamburger Bluffs

(4) Kolob Bouldering:
Paria Point, Beatty Point

(5) Kolob Roadside Boulder

(6) Timber Top Mountain:
Ultamahedral

Kolob Canyon

In 1937 the Kolob section (northwest of Zion Canyon) came under protection as Zion National Monument. It was made a part of Zion in 1956. See page 12 for introduction and approach.

Paria Point

WIND, SAND AND STARS V, 5.12c, 11 pitches, 1300 feet (396m), ★★★★★

First Ascent: Jeff Lowe, Catherine Destivelle, May 1991. First Free Ascent: Steve Petro, Lisa Gnade, Jeff Lowe, 15 May 1992.

Location and Access: The climb is located on Paria Point. The route faces south and climbs the major dihedral system just right of the west face beginning via third class slabs up an obvious bowl. Approach to the climb from the nearest overlook parking area is about 45 minutes. The rock is reportedly better than that on Moonlight Buttress. Jeff Lowe comments: "As a free climb, *Wind, Sand and Stars* would be among the very finest long climbs in North America."

Paraphernalia: Friends (2) sets #.5 through #4; Tri-cams #.5 through #1.5; Nuts #2 through #7; (12) quickdraws.

Descent: Five rappels down the west face to the left of the ascent.

Timber Top Mountain

ULTAMAHEDRAL III, 5.11d, A0, 2 pitches

First Ascent: Originally known as *Catharsis.* Dave Jones and party. First Free Ascent: Will Gilmer, Keith Royster, Dave Anderson, 20 May 1989.

Location and Accent: *Ultamahedral* is the free ascent of *Catharsis*. It is the major crack system just right of a huge rockfall scar which leads up to the notch between Timbertop Mountain and Shuntavi Butte.

Kolob Bouldering Areas

Concrete Jungle

Located 1.7 miles (2.7km) from the visitor center. Park at the Interpretive Stop #5 on the left side of the park road. Across Taylor Creek there are numerous boulders composed of the Shinarump Conglomerate, a coarse sand and gravel deposit.

Paria Point and Beatty Point

Numerous problems ranging in difficulty from 5.7 to 5.12.

Hamburger Bluffs

Located 3.8 miles (6.4km) from the visitor center. The location is west of Lee Pass. Problems are on boulders and cliffs up to 50 feet (15m) high and generally in the 5.9 to 5.10 difficulty range. The rock is composed of the Springdale member of Moenave Sandstone. This upper member of the formation is a stream deposited sandstone.

Kolob Roadside Boulder

Four miles (7km) from visitor center. There are numerous problems in the range from 5.4 to 5.11.

Paria Point, Kolob Canyon: **Wind, Sand and Stars**

Photo: Tom Till

Perfection is finally attained, not when there is no longer anything to add, but when there is no longer anything to take away.

Antoine de Saint-Exupéry–Wind, Sand and Stars

One cannot help but be in awe when he contemplates the mysteries of eternity, of life, of the marvelous structure of reality.

Albert Einstein

Photo: Eric Bjørnstad

The Pulpit

Photo: Stewart M. Green

Dennis Jump and Josh Morris on Easter Island, *first ascent*

CAPITOL REEF

The heavenly bodies look so much more remote from the bottom
of a deep canyon than they do from the level. The climb of the walls
helps out the eye, somehow. I lay down on a solitary rock that was
like an island in the bottom of the valley, and looked up...The arc
of sky over the canyon was silvery blue...and presently stars
shivered into it, like crystals dropped into perfectly clear water.

Willa Cather, *The Professor's House*

Capitol Reef National Park, located in south central Utah, was the last territory within the continental U.S. to be explored and mapped. It is an enchanted land, remote, still and majestic. Of the eight national parks on the Colorado Plateau, only Grand Canyon and Capitol Reef boundaries follow a major geographic feature of the land. At Capitol Reef it is the 100 mile (161km) long Waterpocket Fold, considered unique by geologists. Running in a nearly north-south direction, the Waterpocket Fold is the finest, most apparent example of this type of geologic phenomenon on the North American continent. The immense wrinkle (fold) in the earth's crust is a monocline whose origin dates back 65 million years to a time when the drifting continental plate beneath North America collided with the plate that underlies the Pacific Ocean. [A monocline (common on the plateau) links two flat-lying layers of rock at two different levels by a giant step.] It is the same event that resulted in the gradual up-thrust of the Rocky Mountains and the inexorable rise of the Colorado Plateau to over two miles above its previous elevation near sea level. The Waterpocket Fold monocline is a major feature of the earth's surface, consisting of 14 sedimentary strata tilted upward to the west (its steep flanks facing east), creating a 2500 foot (762m) elevation differential between Torrey to the west and Hanksville to the east. Early anglo visitors named the area Capitol Reef for its many domed formations capped with white sandstone, that resemble federal buildings in Washington, D.C. The seemingly endless waterpockets (potholes or 'tanks') within the fold collect moisture with every rainfall. These myriad pits and depressions, when filled after a storm, reflect the bright desert sunlight like a rosette of mirrors facetted across the richly toned sandstone and give the reef of Waterpocket Fold the rest of its name.

In 1880 the geologist Clarence Dutton viewed the Waterpocket Fold while looking east from the Aquarius Plateau and wrote, "It is a sublime panorama. The heart of the inner Plateau Country is spread out before us in a bird's eye view. It is a maze of cliffs and terraces, red and white domes, rock platforms gashed with profound canyons, burning plains barren even of sage–all glowing with bright color and flooded with blazing sunlight. Everything visible tells of ruin and decay. It is the extreme of desolation, the blankest solitude, a superlative desert....The colors are such as no pigments can portray. They are deep, rich, variegated and so luminous are they, that light seems to glow or shine out of the rock rather than to be reflected from it."

History

Archeological finds indicate the park area was visited by the prehistoric Archaic peoples at least 2800 years ago. Around 1200 years ago Fremont Indians farmed, hunted and gathered native wild plant foods in the area of the park. Unlike their contemporaries–the Anasazi Indians who lived and built cliff dwellings east of the Colorado River–the Fremont lived in pit houses to the west. The Fremont were first named in 1931 from evidence of their existence along the Fremont River at present day Capitol Reef National Park. Their culture left behind moki huts (storage bins, which they fabricated from rock and wood), unbaked clay figurines, buffalo-hide shields, black and gray pottery, necklaces, baskets, animal-hide moccasins, digging tools and irrigation ditches, as well as a treasure of petroglyphs. The unique Fremont rock art galleries are predominately composed of desert bighorn sheep and anthropomorphic figures with trapezoidal bodies decorated with necklaces and headdresses. It has been speculated that the Fremont people vacated the territory (as did the Anasazi) approximately 800 years ago in response to a prolonged drought. Next to roam the region were Paiute Indians, who gathered wild foods and hunted game in the area until about the time of the early Mormon settlers in the late 1870s or early 1880s. The Paiute called the great reef of the Waterpocket Fold "the sleeping rainbow."

Capitol Reef was well known for its frequent visits by Butch Cassidy and his wild bunch, riding for their hideout at Robber's Roost. In later years the park area hosted moonshiners, anthropologists, cattlemen, prospectors and tourists. In the 1950s during the uranium boom of the Colorado Plateau, prospectors scoured the region for the mineral. Fortunately for the park lands, little was found and what was mined proved to be economically unfeasible since it was so costly to ship ore to the Grand Junction, Colorado, processing plant over 200 miles (233km) away.

Capitol Reef was first set aside as a 16 acre state park in 1926. It was included then within what was known as The Wayne Wonderland (after Wayne County). In 1937 President Franklin D. Roosevelt proclaimed 37,060 acres a national monument. The area was greatly enlarged in 1958 and 1969 to 254,241 acres, expanding the area nearly seven times. In 1971 the size of the park was fixed at 378 square miles (241,904 acres) and designated a national park. The park ranges in elevation from 3,900 to 8,800 feet (1189 to 2682m) and is approximately 75 miles (121km) long, but generally only 5 to 10 miles (8 to 16km) wide. Old timers have suggested there is as much country standing up as there is lying down. Roy Roylance (author of *The Enchanted Wilderness*) muses, "The park's vertical relief may well exceed that of its horizontal breadth, combining the fantasy of Bryce and the grandeur of Zion...with more variety of color than either and is larger than both combined." He notes, "The Park's vivid colors run in streamers, bands and layers, both vertically and horizontally. There are blues and greens in broad stripes, and purple, orchid and lavender give remarkable softness to the rock walls. Every primary color is visible in any of several different formations, but shades of red and white predominate."

Location and access

Capitol Reef is located 266 miles (428km) south of Salt Lake City or 105 miles (169km) east of Moab. From the town of Green River, located on I-70 (50 miles north and east of Moab), drive 12 miles (19km) west to Utah 24, then 44 miles (71km) south to Hanksville. Capitol Reef's Visitor Center is 37 miles (60km) west of Hanksville on Utah 24.

Utah 24 The original route (and old cattle trail) through the Waterpocket Fold (east-west) followed the Fremont Valley, crossing the Fremont River 72 times. There are still five trails open for cattle drives only. It was the Mormons who improved the route long used by Indians through Capitol Gorge, skirting the river valley 10 miles (16km) south through Capitol Gorge. This Blue Dugway, as it was known, linked Fruita with distant Hanksville. The route begins along the Scenic Drive from the visitor center and served for 80 years as the main highway through the Reef until Utah Highway 24 through the Fremont River valley was completed in 1962.

Fremont River The Fremont River/Dirty Devil was named by Major John Wesley Powell on 27 July 1869. The Powell expedition had come upon an unknown river at the mouth of a narrow canyon. As the party in the lead boat approached they were asked if it was a trout stream. The answer was, "Naw, it's a dirty devil." The name for the Fremont River where Muddy Creek enters it below Hanksville became known as the Dirty Devil. The upper portion in the area of the present day park was named the Fremont River by Powell after he found evidence of Colonel Fremont's earlier cache. Today it is a river with two names.

Visitor Center

The visitor center is located just off Utah 24 at its junction with the park's Scenic Drive. There are books, maps, posters, postcards and film for sale; checklists of plants, birds and mammals; interpretive displays on the area's prehistoric Fremont Indians, pioneer history, plants, birds, animals and geology; and a large relief map giving a bird's-eye overview of the park. Drinking water, restrooms and a slide program are also offered. Rangers at the visitor center offer nature walks, campfire programs and issue the required free backcountry overnight use permits. Visitor center hours are 8 A.M.–7 P.M. June to Labor Day and 8 A.M.–4:30 P.M. thereafter. The center is closed Thanksgiving, Christmas Day and New Year's Day. As in most national parks, pets are not allowed on trails and must be on a leash in picnic and campground areas. Mountain bikes are permissible only on legal vehicular roads.

Communities reached from the visitor center (via Utah 24) and located west are: Torrey 11 miles (17.6km), Bricknell 19 miles (30.5km) and Loa 30 miles (48.2km). East of the visitor center is Hanksville 37 miles (59.5km). From Hanksville it is 44 miles (70.7km) to Hite Marina on Lake Powell, 55 miles (88.4km) to Green River (50 more to Moab) and 266 miles (428km) to Salt Lake City.

The park is open year round. For further information write or call: Capitol Reef National Park, Torrey, Utah 84775, telephone: (801)425-3791.

Geology

Space limitations have precluded a discussion of the extraordinary and very fascinating geology of the park. However, there are a number of excellent books available at the visitor center for those who would like to understand the story behind the rocks upon which they climb.

Flora and fauna

Piñon pine and juniper are the dominate trees in the park. They are usually widely spaced and grow no taller than about 25 feet (8m). Their stunted, knurly and twisted structures form a pygmy forest throughout much of Capitol Reef and the high deserts of the Colorado Plateau, with juniper being the more drought tolerant of the two. Although there are numerous piñon pine trees in Capitol Reef 300 to 500 hundreds years old, two have been dated 800 to 1000 years in age. Wood gathering is not allowed.

Climate

Capitol Reef National Park has an arid climate with an average annual rainfall of a bit more than seven inches (18cm). Temperatures may exceed 100 degrees Fahrenheit (37C) in the summer, with the average in the high 80s to low 90s. It is always important to carry extra water in the desert. Surface water should be treated against giardia, with a one-minute boil the most effective precaution.

Campgrounds

There are three campgrounds within the park. Fruita Campground, elevation 5440 feet (1658m), is located 1 mile (1.6km) down the Scenic Drive from the visitor center and has 71 sites, each with a picnic table and a fire grill (no wood gathering is permitted in the park). Water and flush toilets (during winter months water is turned off, pit toilets are available and there is no camping fee). Loops A and B of the campground are near the Fremont River and have large shade trees and grass. The C loop has younger and thus smaller shade trees. The campground is picturesque with its setting of towering rock walls, the rushing river and pioneer orchards.

In the 1880s, Mormon pioneers settled in present-day Fruita. They grew crops and planted orchards which were irrigated by water from Sulphur Creek and the Fremont River. The site of their community is the location of today's visitor center and the Fruita campground. The park maintains approximately 3000 fruit trees which include pear, apple, apricot, cherry, peach, plum and nectarine. Visitors are welcome to pick and eat fruit free on the premises. From late June through October, visitors may pick and buy fruit for a nominal fee. Fruita was first known as Junction. When the post office was established shortly after the turn of the century, the name was changed because there were too many Junctions in the territory.

The Cedar Mesa primitive campground has five sites and is located in the park's southern district at an elevation of 6000 feet (1829m). The sites have superlative views of Waterpocket Fold, Red Canyon and the Henry Mountains; picnic tables, fire grills and pit toilets, but no water. To reach, drive east 9.2 miles (14.8km) from the visitor center on Utah 24, turn right and drive 22 miles (35km) on the Notom-Bullfrog road.

The Cathedral primitive campground is located in a piñon juniper woodland and serves the northern district of the park at an elevation of 7000 feet (2134m). It has six sites, pit toilets but no water. The campground is located approximately 27 miles (43km) north of Utah 24 on the River Ford Road.

Precautions and regulations

Climbers should check with rangers at the visitor center for current restrictions. Registration is voluntary. Clean climbing techniques are required and no climbing is allowed within 25 feet (8m) of rock art. Due to the considerable archeological value of petroglyphs and pictographs, the rock wall north of Utah 24 between the Fruita Schoolhouse and the east end of the fenced Krueger Orchard is closed to climbing. Hickman Natural Bridge, Chimney Rock, Temple of the Sun and Temple of the Moon areas are also off limits in efforts to protect their sensitive nature.

Afternoon thunder showers are common in July and August. Since sandstone is weak when wet, avoid climbing in damp areas or right after rain.

Rock art sites on federal lands are protected by the Antiquities Act of 1906 (Public Law 59-209) and the Archaeological Resources Protection Act of 1979 (Public Law 960-5). The laws apply to lands managed by the U.S. Forest Service, the National Park Service and the Bureau of Land Management. It's illegal to "remove, damage, or otherwise alter or deface any archaeological resource (including rock paintings and rock carvings) located on public lands or Indian lands...." Penalties include fines up to $20,000 and up to two years in prison for the first offense and fines up to $100,000 and up to five years in prison for the second offense. Our cultural heritage is priceless and must be preserved for all who come after us. Part of the magic of the Colorado Plateau is the mysterious traces of those who came before us.

Paraphernalia

A standard desert climbing rack for free climbs includes two sets of Friends, one set of TCUs, one set of stoppers and quickdraws with 24" slings for multiple pitch climbs.

Order of climbs

With a few isolated exceptions, climbs in Capitol Reef are located along the Scenic Drive which extends south from the Visitor Center for 8 miles (13km). Routes in this chapter begin with the Chimney Rock area 3 miles (4.8km) west from the Visitor Center on Utah 24, then climbs are listed in ascending order as one drives south from the Visitor Center along the Scenic Drive.

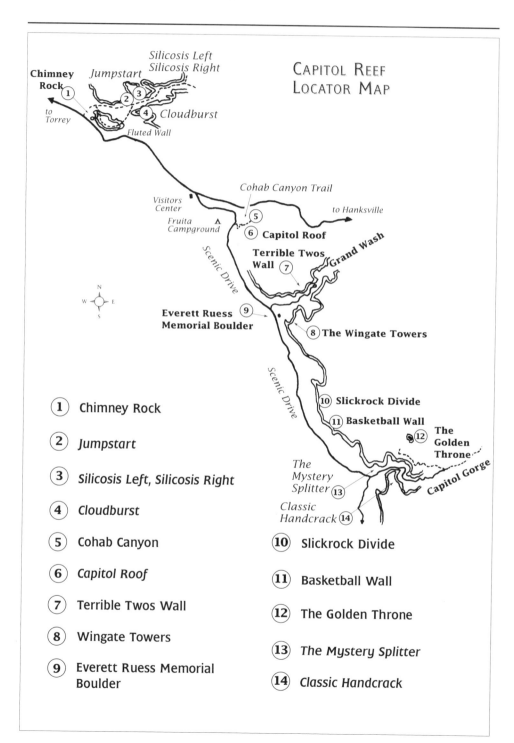

CAPITOL REEF
LOCATOR MAP

Chimney Rock
Jumpstart
Silicosis Left
Silicosis Right
Cloudburst
Fluted Wall
to Torrey

Cohab Canyon Trail
Visitors Center
Fruita Campground
Capitol Roof
to Hanksville

Terrible Twos Wall
Grand Wash
Scenic Drive

Everett Ruess Memorial Boulder
The Wingate Towers

Scenic Drive

Slickrock Divide
Basketball Wall
The Golden Throne

The Mystery Splitter
Classic Handcrack
Capitol Gorge

1. Chimney Rock
2. Jumpstart
3. Silicosis Left, Silicosis Right
4. Cloudburst
5. Cohab Canyon
6. Capitol Roof
7. Terrible Twos Wall
8. Wingate Towers
9. Everett Ruess Memorial Boulder
10. Slickrock Divide
11. Basketball Wall
12. The Golden Throne
13. The Mystery Splitter
14. Classic Handcrack

Chimney Rock Area

Drive to the parking area at the Chimney Rock trailhead. It is located to the right (north) just over 3 miles (4.8km) from the park visitor center driving on Utah 24 northwest toward the town of Torrey. The Moenkopi cliffs along the approach are referred to as the Fluted Wall in old geologic reports. Hike the well marked and maintained 3.5 mile (5.6km) Chimney Rock loop trail climbing 540 feet (165m) to a ridge over looking Chimney Rock, an obvious dark-red fluted Moenkopi spire capped with a block of the Shinarump member of the Chinle formation. The climbs are a short distance beyond the farthest eastern point of the trail where it turns south to return to the parking area.

JUMPSTART I, 5.10, A0, 1 pitch, 150 feet (46m)

First Ascent: Mark Bennett, Seth Shaw, mid-1980s.

Location and Access: Shortly after cresting the rise behind Chimney Rock, the trail descends into a wash that comes in from the left and continues straight ahead to eventually join Chimney Rock Canyon. At the corner of the buttress where the trail enters this wash, there is a nice crack not quite reaching the ground. Reach high and place a nut for protection, with an etrier to get started, then continue free via a handcrack to rappel anchors.

Paraphernalia: Standard desert rack.

Descent: The first ascent party rappelled the route from a two-by-four jammed in a crack. Be careful not to get your foot stuck in this crack as they did both on the ascent and rappel.

CLOUDBURST I, 5.10, 1 pitch

First Ascent: Mark Bennett, Bill Simmons, mid-1980s.

Location and Access: The route is on the right side of the wash opposite Jump Start. Climb the handcrack for one pitch.

Paraphernalia: Standard desert rack.

Descent: The first ascent party rappelled the route from a two-by-four jammed in a crack.

Silicosis

A short distance beyond *Cloudburst* and *Jump Start*, on the left side of the wash, is Silicosis, a tremendous 100 yard (91m) long flake reaching to the rim of the canyon.

SILICOSIS LEFT II, 5.11R, 5 pitches, 400 feet (122m)

First Ascent: Mark Bennett, Bill Simmons, mid-1980s.

Location and Access: Pitch 1 is a short pitch of broken rock, 5.10. Pitch 2 follows a 5.11 offwidth (poorly protected) to a semi-hanging bolt belay where the crack widens to a chimney. From this point, the crack overhangs and appears truly intimidating. Pitch 3 is climbed by a squeeze deep inside a chimney, then ascends an elevator shaft up to a ramp (5.6) leading back out to a stance (and a bolt) at the top of the intimidating section. Pitch 4 leads back over blocks in a small cavern and up a final crack in the left wall to the rim, 5.9. The final crack is climbed with a stem off the opposite wall.

Paraphernalia: Standard desert rack

Descent: Three rappels back down the route. Beware that the ropes are easily jammed on the final rappel.

SILICOSIS RIGHT–FRIENDSHIP CRUISE II, 5.10 R, 3 pitches, 400 feet (122m)

First Ascent: Mark Bennett, Bill Simmons, mid 1980s.

Location and Access: The route ascends the right side of Silicosis, beginning about 100 yards (91m) down wash from the left side of the giant flake. Pitch 1 climbs wide hands to a pod, where a "body-block-belay" is set up, 5.10R. A rack of carabiners was dropped in the pod, unretrievable, and they remain just visible. Pitch 2 continues wide hands, up and then left to a belay on small nuts, 5.10. Pitch 3 climbs straight up to the rim on face holds, 5.10.

Paraphernalia: Standard desert rack.

Descent: The first ascent party hiked off the rimrock. Further details are unknown.

Cohab Canyon

Cohab Canyon is reached from the signed Cohab Canyon trail which begins 1.2 miles (1.9km) from the visitor center, just north of the turn into campground Loops A and B, on the left (east) side of the Scenic Drive. The steep switchbacked trail gains 320 feet (98m) in its first 0.4 mile (0.6km) on its way to the hidden Cohab Canyon. The name is an abbreviation of "cohabitation" and derives from Mormon polygamists taking refuge in the canyon, when pursued by U.S. marshals in the 1880s after federal law made polygamy a felony.

CAPITOL ROOF I, 5.11, 1 pitch, 80 feet (24m)

First Ascent: Mark Bennett, Robyn Rogin, 5 April 1986.

Location and Access: *Capitol Roof* is visible from the Fruita Campground just right of the entrance to Cohab Canyon.

Paraphernalia: Friends (1) #1, #1.5, #2, #3, (2) #2.5, #3.

Descent: Rappel the route.

LOG JAM I, 5.10+, 1 pitch, 150 feet (46m)

First Ascent: Mark Bennett, Seth Shaw, March 1985.

Location and Access: *Log Jam* climbs the first crack system inside Cohab Canyon on the right wall.

Paraphernalia: Friends #2 through #3.5 at the beginning; large pieces to protect a 6" to 2' crack on which the first ascent party used wood two-by-fours for protection.

Descent: Rappel the route with double ropes.

EASTER ISLAND I, 5.10, 1 pitch, 50 feet (15m)

First Ascent: Stewart Green, Ian Spencer-Green, Brett Spencer-Green, Josh Morris, Dennis Jump, Yvonne Botton, August 1993.

Location and Access: The spire sits on a high ridge south of Cohab Canyon. Approach by hiking up the Cohab Canyon Trail from the park campground. Walk east downcanyon to Cassidy Arch-Grand Wash trail. Take the trail south for 1 mile (1.6km). Easter Island becomes visible above the trail as it climbs out of the canyon. The trail eventually passes directly beneath the spire. The route is on the west side of the tower. Begin atop blocks and climb unprotected sandy rock to a ledge, 5.7. Continue up the headwall above past three bolts, 5.10, and pull onto a flat summit, 5.9. Photo page 92.

Paraphernalia: One ¼" angle, quickdraws.

Descent: The summit is too soft for good anchors. Have a ground party fix a rope to a nearby tree and single rope rappel the route.

Scenic Drive

Scenic Drive runs south from the visitor center/campground area. Grand Wash is a spur road branching left (east) from Scenic Drive 3.4 miles (5.4km) from the visitor center. Capitol Gorge is located 4.6 miles (7.4km) further, or 8 miles (12.8km) from the visitor center.

Ninety-nine percent of climbs established in Capitol Reef are located in this area of the park and are established on Wingate sandstone. Boulders in the region rest upon Moenkopi shales and are composed of a Shinarump conglomerate originating from the overlying Chinle formation. See page 15 for a discussion of these rock layers.

SLAPSHOT B1+ lunge

First Ascent: Unknown.
Location and Access: Slapshot climbs an isolated brown boulder which sits on the flats approximately 100 yards (91m) from the left side of Scenic Drive at a point 2.8 miles (4.5km) from the visitor center. The problem is a B1+ lunge over a roof to a bucket, then a scary mantle, 15 feet (5m).

Everett Ruess Memorial Boulders

There are two large boulders immediately to the left of the Scenic Drive, 3.7 miles (6km) from the visitor center, at a point 0.3 mile (0.5km) past the spur road which branches left (east) to Grand Wash. Standout difficulties include *The Lithic Scatter* (a short horrendous, B2 sit-down problem) located just left of a small tree on the large boulder nearest the road and *Dune* (B1) located on the back side of the smaller and farther boulder from Scenic Drive.

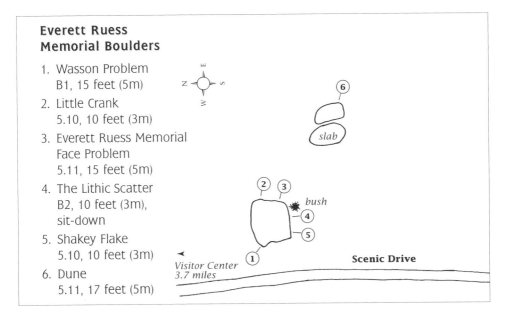

**Everett Ruess
Memorial Boulders**

1. Wasson Problem
   B1, 15 feet (5m)
2. Little Crank
   5.10, 10 feet (3m)
3. Everett Ruess Memorial
   Face Problem
   5.11, 15 feet (5m)
4. The Lithic Scatter
   B2, 10 feet (3m),
   sit-down
5. Shakey Flake
   5.10, 10 feet (3m)
6. Dune
   5.11, 17 feet (5m)

Basketball Wall

Basketball Wall is located high above the Scenic Drive, 5.1 miles (8.2km) from the visitor center. The wall is obvious on the left (east) with its many long, straight-in splitter cracks.

BENCH WARMER I, 5.10a, 1 pitch, ★★★★

First Ascent: Bret Ruckman, Marco Cornacchione, 17 May 1993.

Location and Access: The route is left of *White Boys Can't Jam* and the first crack system right of a deep chimney. The route climbs a handcrack in a right-facing corner.

Paraphernalia: Handsize protection.

Descent: Rappel the route from double anchors visible from below.

WHITE BOYS CAN'T JAM I, 5.10a, 1 pitch, ★★★★★

First Ascent: Marco Cornacchione, Bret Ruckman, 17 May 1993.

Location and Access: The route is located at the first crack system right of *Bench Warmer* and the first system left of *Foul Line*, and ascends an obvious handcrack with rappel anchors visible from below.

Paraphernalia: Hand-size protection.

Descent: Rappel the route from double anchors

Basketball Wall
From left to right:
Bench Warmer
White Boys Can't Jam
Foul Line,
Phi Slamma Jamma

Photo: Eric Bjørnstad

FOUL LINE I, 5.11c, 1 pitch, 100 feet (30m), ★★★★

First Ascent: Marco Cornacchione, Bret Ruckman, 17 May 1993.

Location and Access: Foul Line is the first crack system right of *White Boys Can't Jam*. The route ascends an obvious handcrack with rappel anchors visible from below.

Paraphernalia: Hand-size protection.

Descent: Rappel the route from double anchors.

PHI SLAMMA JAMMA I, 5.11+, 1 pitch, ★★★★★

First Ascent: Bret Ruckman, Marco Cornacchione, 17 May 1993.

Location and Access: The route is located far to the right of *Foul Line* and climbs a splitter crack fingers to hands.

Paraphernalia: Protection small to hand-size.

Descent: Rappel the route from double anchors.

Slickrock Divide

These climbs are located 5.9 miles (9.4km) down the Scenic Drive from the visitor center high on the Wingate walls to the left (east).

CAPITALIST ROOF I, 5.12a, 1 pitch, 50 feet (15m), ★★★★★

First Ascent: Marco Cornacchione, Bret Ruckman, 19 May 1993.

Location and Access: From the Slickrock Divide parking area, hike directly up the talus to the rimrock, then right (south) along the wall for 100 yards (183m) to the base of the climb. The crux of the climb is near the top where the route angles to the vertical after a rightward traverse below a prominent overhang.

Paraphernalia: Friends in order of placement: #2, #2.5, #3, #3.5.

Descent: Rappel straight down on a single rope. Slings visible from below.

MAN ALIVE I, 5.11, 1 pitch, 140 feet (43m), ★★★★★

First Ascent: Bret Ruckman, Marco Cornacchione, 19 May 1993.

Location and Access: The route is located 75 yards (69m) right (downhill) of *Capitalist Roof* and climbs a splitter crack beginning with 5.11 thin stemming. This is a point just left of an obvious overhang with a tree below it.

Paraphernalia: Protection in order of placement #2, #2.5, #3 Friends.

Descent: Rappel the route with double ropes. Slings are visible from below.

Left to right: Capitalist Roof, Man Alive

Photo: Eric Bjørnstad

Photo: Eric Bjørnstad

Washed Up

Grand Wash

At mile 3.4 (5.4km) on the Scenic Drive from the visitor center, a dirt spur branches left into Grand Wash.

Radioactivity Boulders

The large chocolate-brown wafers visible behind the low ridge on the left (north) are the Radioactivity Boulders. The bouldering area is located 0.2 miles (0.3km) down the Grand Wash spur from Scenic Drive. Standout problems in this area include *Wild Isotopes*, a 5.10 aréte, and *U-235*, a scary 5.11 problem. Further details are unknown.

WASHED UP I, 5.11d, 1 pitch, 130 feet (40m)

First Ascent: Karen Budding, Steve Hong, April 1983.

Location and Access: The route is located 0.4 mile (0.6km) down Grand Wash from Scenic Drive. If approaching from the *Terrible Twos'* route, walk along the cliff base approximately 0.25 mile (0.4km) left (west). Begin up a handcrack in a shallow right-facing corner a little left of the prominent right-facing dihedral/chimney system, part of a narrow, indistinct pillar.

Paraphernalia: Many #2, #2.5, #3 Friends.

Descent: Rappel the route.

Necco Wafer

The route begins at point 0.6 mile (0.9km) down Grand Wash from the Scenic Drive, just visible 100 yards (91m) on the right (south) of the road, atop a small knoll. Necco Wafer is a blade-like boulder sitting on edge. It is the location of many "killer" problems. Further information unknown.

LIVERPOOL KISS I, 5.12a, 1 pitch, 80 feet (24m), ★★★★

First Ascent: Bret Ruckman, Marco Cornacchione, 19 May 1993.

Location and Access: The route is located 0.6 mile (0.9km) down Grand Wash from the Scenic Drive on the right wall, above and left of Necco Wafer. The route climbs a fantastic splitter crack on the wall just left of a shallow left-facing dihedral. Begin up badly undercut rock and pass to a stance, 5.12. Just below the rappel ledge it is possible to climb from the left side of a stance at 5.12 or the right side at 5.11a.

Paraphernalia: Friends in order of placement #.75, #1 to the first rest; #1.5, #2, #.75 to the stance below the top. If climbing the left side via 5.12, protect with a #2, #1.5. If climbing the right side via 5.11a, protect with a #1.5.

Descent: Rappel the route.

Terrible Twos Wall

The climbs are located on the left wall 0.65 mile (1.04km) down Grand Wash from the Scenic Drive. The two obvious straight-in splitter cracks are *Terrible Twos* and *Unknown Thin Crack*. Left of *Terrible Twos* is *Soapstone Dihedral*.

SOAPSTONE DIHEDRAL I, 5.11c, 1 pitch, 40 feet (12m)

First Ascent: Doug White, Lloyd Johnson.

Location and Access: *Soapstone Dihedral* is located 20 feet (6m) left of *Terrible Twos* and is obvious from the road.

Paraphernalia: Unknown.

Descent: Rappel the route.

TERRIBLE TWOS I, 5.11+, 1 pitch, 80 feet (24m), ★★★

First Ascent: Bret Ruckman, Marco Cornacchione, 15 May 1993.

Location and Access: The route is located between *Soapstone Dihedral* on the left and *Unknown Thin Crack* on the right. This is a point just left of a prominent juniper tree. The route climbs a south-facing lightning-bolt crack, easily identified from the road.

Paraphernalia: (1) #2 Friends; (2-3) #2.5, (1) #3 TCUs.

Descent: Rappel the route.

UNKNOWN THIN CRACK I, 5.12a, 60 feet (18m), ★★★★

First Ascent: Ron Olevsky and unknown party.

Location and Access: The route climbs an obvious splitter crack and is just right of *Terrible Twos* and right of a prominent juniper tree.

Paraphernalia: Fingercrack protection.

Descent: Rappel the route from double anchors.

CAPITOL REEF NATIONAL PARK   107

Grand Wash • Terrible Twos Wall: *Soapstone Dihedral, Terrible Twos,*
Unknown Thin Crack, Left Practice Crack, Right Practice Crack

Photo: Eric Bjørnstad

Grand Wash Area
Left to right: Soapstone Dihedral, Terrible Twos, Unknown Thin Crack, Left Practice Crack, Right Practice Crack

LEFT PRACTICE CRACK I, 5.10, 1 pitch, 40 feet (12m)

First Ascent: John Wasson, Sharon Wasson.

Location and Access: The *Left Practice Crack* is located 40 feet (12m) right of *Unknown Thin Crack* and climbs a splitter hands crack with a small pod halfway up. The route ends atop a fingertip like pinnacle at obvious rappel anchors.

Paraphernalia: Hand-size protection.

Descent: Rappel the route.

RIGHT PRACTICE CRACK I, 5.11c, 1 pitch, 40 feet (12m), ★★★

First Ascent: John Wason, Sharon Wason.

Location and Access: The route ascends the next crack system right of *Left Practice Crack*. Climb a fingers to offwidth crack to obvious anchors.

Paraphernalia: Finger to large protection.

Descent: Rappel the route.

Wingate Towers

The climbs in this area are located 0.7 mile (1.1km) down Grand Wash from the Scenic Drive immediately right (south) of the road. The three routes (one toprope) share the same rappel anchors.

PUSSY BOLT I, 5.8 R, 1 pitch, 60 feet (18m), ★★

First Ascent: Unknown.

Location and Access: *Pussy Bolt* climbs an obvious right-leaning flake with a bolt halfway up.

Paraphernalia: Unknown.

Descent: Rappel the route from a double-bolt anchor shared with *Sharon's Crack*.

THE WINGATE ARETE I, 5.12a, TR, 1 pitch, 60 feet (18m), ★★★★

First Ascent: John Wason.

Location and Access: This is a classic toprope which climbs directly up the arête of the Wingate landform.

SHARON'S CRACK I, 5.10a, 1 pitch, 60 feet (18m)

First Ascent: Sharon Wason.

Location and Access: The route climbs right of *Pussy Bolt* and *The Wingate Arête*. Ascend a left-leaning hand-and-finger crack.

Paraphernalia: Finger to handsize protection.

Descent: Shared rappel anchors with *Pussy Bolt*.

BOULDER OVERHANG I, 5.10d X, 1 pitch, 35 feet (11m)

First Ascent: Unknown.

Location and Access: The route climbs a splitter overhanging hand-and-fist crack in a boulder on the left (north) side of the road 1 mile (1.6km) into Grand Wash from Scenic Drive. The route is rated X or toprope.

NOT FREE (YET) I, 5.12+, A1, 1 pitch, 50 feet (15m)

First Ascent: Eve Tallman, et al.
Location and Access: The climb is on the right side of the road 0.1 mile (0.16km) beyond *Boulder Overhang* or 1.1 miles (1.7km) down Grand Wash from the Scenic Drive. Climb a right-leaning splitter fingercrack to a double-bolt rappel anchor.
Paraphernalia: Unknown.
Descent: Rappel the route.

Photo: Eric Bjørnstad

Wingate Towers
From left to right: Pussy Bolt, The Wingate Arête, Sharon's Crack

SANDY DIHEDRAL I, 5.10b, 1 pitch, 80 feet (24m)

First Ascent: Unknown.

Location and Access: *Sandy Dihedral* is located on the left side of the road 0.1 mile (0.16km) beyond *Not Free (Yet)* or 1.2 miles (1.9km) down Grand Wash from the Scenic Drive. The route is located just right of two obvious right-facing dihedrals and climbs to broken rock visible from below.

Paraphernalia: Finger-size protection.

Descent: Rappel from anchors visible from below.

Photo: Eric Bjørnstad

Sandy Dihedral

Photo: Eric Bjørnstad

The Mystery Splitter

Capitol Gorge

Capitol Gorge is located 8 miles (12.8km) from the visitor center on Scenic Drive.

THE MYSTERY SPLITTER I, 5.13, 1 pitch, 60 feet (18m), ★★★★★

First Ascent: Unknown.

Location and Access: *The Mystery Splitter* is located 8.1 miles (13km) from the visitor center or 0.1 mile (0.16km) via dirt road past the picnic veranda and gate at the end of the paved Scenic Drive (near the entrance into Capitol Gorge). The climb is on the wall left of the road, on the left side of a shallow right-facing dihedral. The route (with rappel slings visible) begins up a right-leaning 1¼" crack system behind a large pointed boulder. Climb unrelenting 1¼" fingers with no rests and nothing for the feet for 60 feet (18m) to triple rappel anchors.

Paraphernalia: Many #1.5 Friends.

Descent: Rappel the route from triple anchors.

Capitol Gorge Boulders

The Capitol Gorge Boulders are located on the left 8.2 miles (13km) from the visitor center, or 0.2 mile (0.32km) down the dirt road at the end of the paved Scenic Drive. Standout problems include *Desert Archaic* (B1), an excellent overhanging arête and *Right Side of the Triangle* (B1+). See locator map on page 98 for approach.

CLASSIC HANDCRACK I, 5.10a, 1 pitch, 120 feet (37m), ★★★★★

First Ascent: Unknown.

Location and Access: The route is on the right (south) side of the Grand Wash road 8.4 miles (13.5km) from the visitor center or 0.4 mile (0.6km) from the end of the paved section of the Scenic drive. It climbs its namesake, a classic handcrack.

Paraphernalia: Many #1.5 through #3 Friends.

Descent: Double-rope rappel via the route from two anchors.

Capitol Gorge Boulders

1. Broken Jug B2, 12 feet (4m)
2. Desert Archaic B1, 12 feet (4m)
3. Chert Corner 5.11, 12 feet (4m)
4. Sandslab B1, 12 feet (4m)
5. Slab Seam 5.10, 15 feet (5m)
6. Right Side of the Triangle B1+, 17 feet (5.2m)

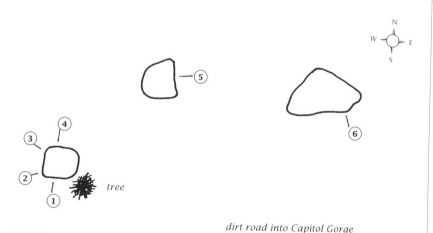

tree

dirt road into Capitol Gorge

The Golden Throne

The Golden Throne is a prominent landmark located in the Waterpocket Fold. To reach from the visitor center, take the Scenic Drive to the Capitol Gorge parking area, then follow signs to the Golden Throne viewpoint. The 2 mile (3.2km) hike to the base of the landform is strenuous with steep grades and uneven terrain, gaining about 1100 feet (335m) in elevation.

SOUTHWEST ROUTE II, 5.8, 3 pitches, 320 feet (97m)

First Ascent: George Hurley, Jean Hurley, Dave Rearick, 25 April 1974.
Location and Access: Approach from the Golden Throne viewing area.
Pitch 1: The route begins in a chimney at the southwest corner of the rock.
Pitch 2: The first pitch chimney widens to a broad gully.
Pitch 3: Traverse south to an easier line for the summit lead.
Paraphernalia: Standard desert rack.
Descent: Rappel the route.

*Beyond the low-slung ridge that separates this part of the valley
from the upper, the valley head turns pink in alpenglow, beginning
and changing and deepening to a spectacular lavender-salmon,
finally glowing like a hot coal. The color lasts only a moment or
two, then dims and dies to gray. And finally the sky congeals
to navy blue behind a barque-shaped moon.*

Ann Zwinger Run, River, Run

*Unlike the graceful outlines of mountains and valleys in humid
climates, the landscape is bold and rugged; curves are replaced
by angles. In further contrast the protecting cover of vegetation
is largely lacking; the dominant grays and greens of humid regions
give way to whites, reds, and browns—the colors of the rocks themselves.*

Herbert E. Gregor,
The San Juan Country,
A Geologic and Geographic Reconnaissance of Southeastern Utah, 1938

The Three Gossips

Photo: Chris Begue

ARCHES NATIONAL PARK

The wind blows, unrelenting, and flights of little gray birds whirl up and away like handfuls of confetti tossed in the air....In the evening the wind stops. A low gray ceiling of clouds hangs over the desert from horizon to horizon, silent and still. One small opening remains in the west. The sun peers through as it goes down. For a few minutes the voodoo monuments burn with a golden light, then fade to rose and blue and violet as the sun winks out and drops.

Edward Abbey–*Desert Solitaire*

The finest workers in stone are not copper or steel tools, but the gentle touches of air and water working at their leisure with a liberal allowance of time.

Henry David Thoreau

Of the eight national parks within the vast desert lands of the Colorado Plateau, Arches is the most recent to be elevated to park status (together with Capitol Reef, also established in 1971). Arches is also the northernmost park and the most frequently visited by climbers. Although over 2000 arches with 3- to 306-foot spans have been documented, the spectacular hoodoos, towers and fins are for many an equal attraction. Added to the magnificent landforms of the park is the spectacular backdrop of the nearly 13,000 foot (4,000m) La Sal mountains.

The park land ranges in elevation from 3960 (1207m) to 5653 feet (1723m). Twenty-five percent is steppe covered by shrub and forty five percent by a "pygmy forest" composed of juniper and piñon. The rest of the region is barren rock.

Location and access

Located only five miles north of Moab, Utah, and half-an-hour south of the transcontinental Interstate 70, Arches is reached by auto four hours from Salt Lake City and seven or eight hours from Denver or Phoenix.

The main park road extends 18 miles (29km) from the entrance kiosk/visitor center to Devils Garden with a 2.5 mile (4km) spur to the Windows section of the park, and another 2.5 miles (4km) spur to Delicate Arch viewpoint. All climbs are within a few minutes' approach from these paved roads, with the exception of *Dark Angel* which involves a 2.5 mile (4km) hike through some of the most beautiful terrain found anywhere in canyon country.

History

The first human residents were likely Paleo-Indians hunting big game which roamed the territory 9,800 to 12,000 years ago. Next, the so-called Archaic people were hunting and foraging nuts, seeds and berries in the region from about 2,000 to 9,000 years ago. After they left the territory, it was 20 centuries before the area was again inhabited. About 1,300 years ago the Anasazi (coming from the south) and the Fremont (coming from the north) planted crops and gathered native foods in and near the province of present day Arches. Although it is thought that the two cultures spoke different languages, they are known to have engaged in trading activities. Both tribes left the area about 900 years ago. Their exodus is thought to be the result of an extensive drought, the adversities of dealing with marauding Utes, as well as a depletion of resources from over-use of the land.

The first white men to enter the region were probably fortune seekers looking for silver or gold. Spanish trappers and traders entered the territory in the early nineteenth century. In the winter of 1830–31, a trail connecting Santa Fe to Los Angeles was opened. The Old Spanish Trail, as it became known, was an important trade route in the years to follow. It forded the Colorado River at the southern border of Arches, near the present site of the river bridge north of Moab.

In 1898 John Wesley Wolfe and his son Fred homesteaded in Arches at the junction of Salt Wash and Winter Camp Wash just west of Delicate Arch. John Wolfe had sustained a leg injury in the Civil War, and after returning to his home in Ohio he traveled west, it is believed, in search of more favorable climate for his ailing leg. In 1910 the Wolfes abandoned their frontier site and returned to the midwest.

In 1923 the prospector Alexander Ringhoffer suggested to supervisors at the Denver and Rio Grand Western Railroad that the Klondike Bluffs, located a few miles south of the rail crossing, be developed as a tourist attraction. Following a tour by railroad officials, Stephen Mather, first director of the National Park Service, viewed the area and in 1929 upon his recommendations, President Herbert Hoover proclaimed a seven square-mile area Arches National Monument.

Throughout the years additions were made to the land area of the monument, including 53 square miles in 1938 by Franklin D. Roosevelt. The elevation to National Park status came in 1971 when about 115 square miles (73,379 acres) were set aside to protect the densest collection of natural stone arches on earth.

Visitor Center

A stop at the visitor center is highly recommended. The center is open daily except Thanksgiving, Christmas and New Year's. Winter hours are 8 A.M. to 4:30 P.M.; extended hours in summer. At the visitor center weather forecast, road conditions, closures, ranger-led hikes, nature walks, evening programs and a variety of other information is given. Every half-hour a 15-minute slide program is given (a must see introduction to the park). Also at the center is a geology museum and history exhibit. Canyonlands Natural History Association offers a good selection of books, maps, postcards, posters, slides, audio tapes, film and water bottles for sale. Water is available year 'round at the visitor center and in season at Devils Garden (at the end of the park road).

Also highly recommended is the ranger-led hike through the Fiery Furnace. This dramatic hike is 2½ to 3 hours long and covers 2 miles (3.2km) of moderately difficult terrain. Hikes are twice daily (morning and afternoon) and are limited to 25 persons, with advanced registration at the visitor center. To experience the hauntingly beautiful Fiery Furnace is sure to highlight one's visit to this unique region of the desert. To enter the Furnace without a ranger, it is necessary to obtain a permit and view a short slide show at the visitor center (violation subject to a $50 fine). It is not recommended one attempt to explore the labyrinthine maze of Fiery Furnace fins independently. There is little chance that one will experience much of this complicated place without a guide.

Geology

The major landforms of the park are composed of Entrada Sandstone underlain by Navajo Sandstone. Entrada is divided into three layers: The base (and oldest) is the Dewey Bridge Member, the middle layer is the Slickrock, and the topmost (youngest) member is the Moab Tongue. The Dewey Bridge Bridge Member has few climbs on it and is made up of relativly soft reddish-brown mudstones and siltstones. It appears as a wrinkled, undulating layer and is the pedestal upon which many routes rest (The Three Penguins are an excellent example). The middle member of Entrada, the Slickrock, is much lighter in color than the Dewey Bridge. Most arches in the park are formed at the bedding seam between the Dewey Bridge and Slickrock Members. It is on the Slickrock that nearly all climbs have been established. The layer is not as dense as the popular Wingate south of Arches but it is not far different. The upper Moab Tongue is shallow and outsrops atop Delicate Arch and in the northwestern perimeters of the park in the Klondike Bluffs.

Flora and Fauna

Plant and animal adaptation to the arid land of Arches (8.5 inches, 22cm, average rain per year and desiccating winds) is a commanding study. The parkland supports a surprisingly rich assemblage of flora and fauna: 357 species of vascular platns, 128 types of birds, 38 different mammals, 20 kinds of reptiles, 14 fish species, and 8 types of amphibians.

Cryptobiotic soil Two thousand square miles of the earth are lost to desertification each year. On the Colorado Plateau the vulnerable ecosystem of the desert is being dramatically impacted. Cryptobiotic soil crust is the critically fragile skin of the desert upon which the health of this unique ecosystem depends. It is the product of a symbiotic relationship between moss, lichen, fungus and algae. It traps nutrients, fixes nitrogen and is crucial to the development of vascular plants. Without the aid of cryptobiotic soil the majority of indigenous flowers and shrubs on the desert would not exist. The subsurface fibrous network of crypto soil plays a major role in controlling wind and water erosion, but once damaged by tire or foot, it is estimated that recovery takes 50 to 250 years. In addition, tire- or footprints aesthetically degrade the land. Such prints remain visible for decades. Not only is the black crusty cryptobiotic soil to be avoided, but its fledgling form of reddish or light brown crust, known as cyanobacteria soil (nearly invisible in early stages) must also be preserved for the critical health of the desert.

If we are to preserve this beautiful land, it is most important that we walk only on slickrock (rock devoid of soil or vegetation), in drainages or on an established trail. If this is not possible, it is important to keep impact at a minimum by not walking abreast but following single file in companions' footsteps. Direct cross-country travel is unconscionable. I implore all who visit this unique land to act responsibly, not only out of our own love of the land, but for the generations yet to be thrilled by this magical place.

Campgrounds

A 52-site campground is maintained at Devils Garden on a first-come, first-served basis, plus two walk-in group sites limited to tenting and available by reservation for 11 or more persons. Campground registration is made at the park entrance kiosk. Facilities at the campground include flush toilets and running water until the first frost. From November through mid-March a reduced fee is charged, the water is turned off and only chemical toilets are available. Campfire programs are held nightly in the spring, summer and fall at the amphitheater located within the campground.

The park superintendent's address is Arches National Park, Post Office Box 907, Moab, Utah 84532, telephone (801)259-8161, voice or (801)259-5279, TTY.

Climate

The average annual temperature at Arches is about 54°F. Clear skies night and day are common most of the year, creating a large margin of temperature change. Temperature fluctuates dramatically, with changes of 50°F or more possible within a few hours. Highs during the summer months may reach 110°F in the shade, and rocks exposed directly to the sun can be a scorching 150°F or more.

The number of frost-free days is about 177 between the last frost in the spring and the first frost of autumn. Some winters are cold enough for the Colorado River, which borders the park for 11 miles (17.7km) at its southern edge, to freeze over.

The mean yearly precipitation for the park is approximately 8.5 inches.(22cm). October is the wettest month, receiving about an inch (2.5cm) of moisture. June is the driest month, with approximately 0.5 inch. The driest months–May, June and July–collectively receive only about 1.6 inches (4cm) of precipitation.

Most precipitation in the park is in the form of summer thunderstorms which are often of cloudburst magnitude. They are generally accompanied by lightning, thunder and violent winds. Such storms advance with great velocity across the open landscape, appearing then disappearing with the same swiftness. During and immediately after thunderstorms, dry arroyos can fill with alarming speed as runoff over the slickrock gathers in volume to dramatic proportions.

The mean annual snowfall at Arches is about 10.65 (27cm) inches. In winter months, it sometimes accumulates to depths of several feet in drifts and at higher park elevations.

Both spring and autumn are windy, but it is in the spring that the winds can be especially intense–irritating and relentless, occasionally sandblasting the barren park lands with gale force. Although these are the seasons when nearly all climbing is done in the region, one must expect to lose a day now and then to traditional turbulence.

Precautions and regulations

Although at present a climbing permit or prior registration is not required, it is important to become familiar with the park's current climbing regulations, including the closures of critical resource areas for nesting raptors or natural, cultural or scenic resources protection. Areas are subject to periodic change in status, so check with the Visitor Center. Backcountry permits are required for all overnight backcountry stays. (Nearly all climbs in the park are within five minutes' hike from the main road and thus backcountry camping is not favored.) Wood gathering and fires in the backcountry are prohibited; camp stoves must be carried. It is of course, important to carry water throughout the desert. One gallon (4 liters) is the recommended minimum per person per day for hikers. Strenuous climbing will certainly require more.

The use of white chalk has been banned in Arches and Canyonlands National Parks to "preserve the scenic integrity which is the Parks' primary purpose and to provide a 'pure climb' without having the route marked by the chalk of earlier climbers" (from the Superintendent's Directive 11 December 1986). All climbers are encouraged to abide by a clean climbing ethic and to use dull-colored webbing at belay and rappel stations. The Park Service, and the public in general, view the use of chalk and fixed anchors as a visual impact. Climbers must take the first step in resolving this issue before it is resolved for them by the closure of entire areas to rock climbing. Bicycles are considered the same as vehicles and are allowed only on designated roads. Dogs must be kept on a leash at all times and are not allowed in the backcountry or on any hiking trail. The use of battery-powered drills and portable radios is prohibited. Disturbing archaeological sites and rock art is a serious violation of the law. Climbing near these areas is strongly discouraged.

The Park Service recommends that no new bolts or other hardware be left in a fixed location unless an existing bolt or hardware is deemed unsafe.

Paraphernalia

A standard desert climbing rack for free climbs includes two sets of Friends, one set of TCUs, one set of stoppers and quickdraws with 24" slings for multiple pitch climbs.

Order of climbs

Climbs begin at the parkland's southern border located across the Colorado River from The River Road (Highway 128) just north of Moab. Following the southern border, climbs are arranged from Headquarters Hill above the Visitor Center in ascending order out to the Windows Spur Road 9 miles (14.5km) from the park entrance, then east along the 2.4 mile (3.9km) Windows Spur. Beyond the Windows area, climbs are documented from the Devils Garden area at the end of the 18-mile-long (29km) park road, then in the Klondike Bluffs at the remote northwestern corner of the park.

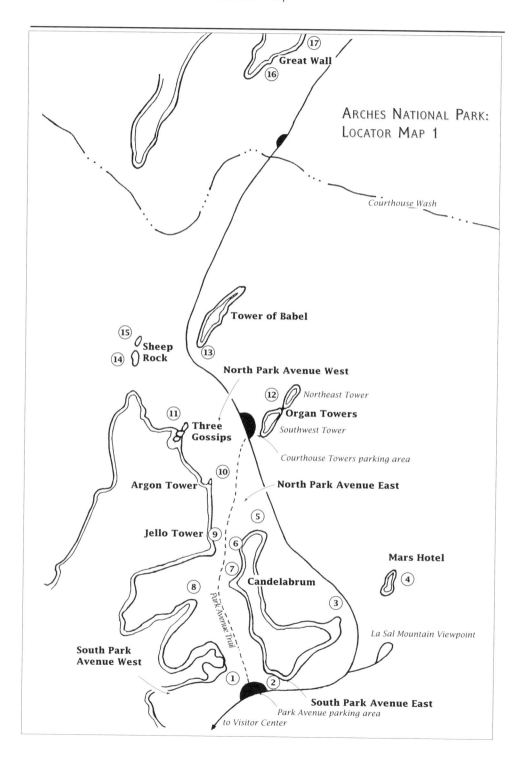

ARCHES NATIONAL PARK:
LOCATOR MAP 1

Courthouse Wash

Great Wall

Tower of Babel

Sheep
Rock

North Park Avenue West

Northeast Tower

Organ Towers

Southwest Tower

Courthouse Towers parking area

Three
Gossips

North Park Avenue East

Argon Tower

Jello Tower

Mars Hotel

Candelabrum

La Sal Mountain Viewpoint

South Park
Avenue West

Park Avenue Trail

South Park Avenue East

Park Avenue parking area

to Visitor Center

(1) South Park Avenue West:
Tilting at Windmills
Cinnamon Rose
Another Zinger
Red Zinger

(2) South Park Avenue East:
Robber's Roost
The Hideout
The Carrot Cannibal

(3) La Sal Mountain View Area:
Sand Tear

(4) Mars Hotel:
If I Only Had a Brain
Lost in Space

(5) North Park Avenue East:
Sand Bag
Weapons of Love

(6) *Heart of the Desert*

(7) Candelabrum:
Hall of Flame
A Company of Candles
Play with Fire

(8) North Park Avenue West:
I Need Friends
Sand of a Beach
Black Celebration
Many Miles Away
Skin Deep

(9) Jello Tower

(10) Courthouse Towers
Argon Tower:
North Face
Pratt-Robinson Route
West Face
North Northeast Arête

(11) The Three Gossips:
West Face
Lyon-Trautner Route
The Crystalline Entity
Be There or Be Talked About
Variation
Knockfirst Sandwitch
Speak No Evil

(12) The Organ: Southwest Tower
Thelma and Louise

(13) Tower of Babel:
Zenyatta Entrada

(14) Sheep Rock: *Virgin Wool*

(15) The Lamb:
Sheepish Grin
Sheep in Wolf's Clothing

(16) The Great Wall: *Chinese Eyes*

(17) Mr. Sombrero
Great Wall Crack
Great Wall Crack Too
Beyond Great Wall Crack Too

Southern Edge Area

The Southern Edge region of the park is accessed via the River Road (Scenic Byway 128), 1 mile (1.6km) north of Moab. First ascent parties crossed the Colorado River by rubber raft.

Goose Island

FUN RAMP III, 5.9, A2 (2 points of aid), 6 pitches, 350 feet (107m)

First Ascent: Layton Kor, Kyle Copeland, October 1988.

Location and Access: Ascends the obvious right-to-left running diagonal fracture system in view across the river (north) between Mile Marker 1 and 2 on the River Road. This region is known as Goose Island by Moab locals.

Paraphernalia: One set of Friends.

Descent: Walk east along rim to a low-angle slab with one bolt. One 90 foot (27m) rappel to ground.

Barney Rumble Tower

RAVEN'S DELIGHT II, 5.9+, 2 pitches, 140 feet (43m)

First Ascent: Bego Gerhart, Jeff Widen, Tony Valdes, Dawn Burke support.

Location and Access: Obvious small tower across from Mile Marker 4 on the River Road. The shelf the tower sits upon is gained via a series of right facing ramps. *Raven's Delight* follows the line of weakness on the east side of the tower.

Paraphernalia: Friends (1) #1.5, (2) #2, #2.5, (3) #3, #4; stoppers.

Descent: One double-rope rappel to the north.

Headquarters Hill Area

Headquarters Hill is the steep, switchbacked grade located between the park entrance kiosk (and visitor center) and the Moab Fault viewing area 1.2 miles (1.9km) beyond.

The Three Penguins

The Three Penguins is the prominent monolith left of the switchbacks on Headquarters Hill. Parking is available on a gravel pullout located directly below the rock on the opposite side of the park road.

RIGHT CHIMNEY I, 5.10c, 2 pitches, 120 feet (37m), ★★★★★

First Ascent: Molly Higgins and Michael Kennedy, November 1976. Second ascent: Tony Valdes and Sonja Paspal, June 1987.

Location and Access: Approach as for *Center Chimney*. Pitch 1 climbs a right-facing corner fingers to fists/offwidth, 80 feet (24m). Pitch 2 climbs steep hand to offwidth crack, then face climb onto the summit.

Paraphernalia: Two sets of Friends with extra #3.5, #4; (1) Camalot #1.

Descent: Rappel route.

CENTER CHIMNEY I, 5.9, 2 pitches, 120 feet (37m)

First Ascent: Larry Bruce, Molly Higgins, Michael Kennedy, November 1976.

Location and Access: Approach the base of The Three Penguins by climbing The Pedestal (upon which the formation sits). It is a moderate pitch which begins at the park road and climbs the soft mudstone of the Dewey Bridge member of Entrada sandstone. Ascend a south-facing crack system below and in line with the left edge of The Penguins when viewed from the east. Or climb the crack system directly below *Center Chimney* (center of the three crack systems on the east face of The Penguins). This is a shorter but more difficult approach. Belay on the ledge beneath *Center Chimney*. Pitch 2 climbs a difficult squeeze chimney which exits on the summit. An alternate route to the base of The Three Penguins avoids The Pedestal by traversing from the east side to the base of the climb from the rimrock behind the formation.

Paraphernalia: One set of Friends, plus (4) #2.5, (2) #3, #4.

Descent: Rappel from summit anchors on *Right Chimney*.

ANOREXIA I, 5.10a, 1 pitch, 120 feet (37m)

First Ascent: Alan Nelson, Alan Bartlett, 14 April 1989.

Location and Access: The route ascends the left chimney on the east face of the tower, left of *Center Chimney*. See *Center Chimney* for the approach. The climb begins with 5.9 fist up overhanging rock. Continue up an 8" squeeze chimney (the crux) and up to the top of the left Penguin.

Paraphernalia: TCUs #2, #4, #5; Big Bro #4; stoppers.

Descent: Traverse up and over the center Penguin, and on to rappel anchors above *Right Chimney*.

Moab Fault Area

These climbs are opposite the Moab Fault Plaque at the top of Headquarters Hill.

STRONGER THAN DIRT I, 5.12, 1 pitch, 70 feet (21m)

First Ascent: Charlie Fowler, Chris Coplerud, November 1986.

Location and Access: This and the following routes on Headquarters Hill are in view from U.S. Highway 191 as one nears the turnoff to Arches National Park. To reach, drive up the switchbacks from the visitor center to the Moab Fault viewing area pullout near the top of Headquarters Hill, 1.2 miles (1.9km) from the visitor center. *Stronger than Dirt* is located on the lower wall directly opposite the lower end of the Moab Fault viewing area. It is the only right-facing dihedral in the area on the lower wall.

Paraphernalia: Friends (2) #0.5 to #2.5 with extra #0.75, #1, #3, #4; Tri-cams #0.5, #1, #7.

Descent: Rappel the route from a fixed anchor or walk down upper ramp.

CREATURES OF THE DESERT I, 5.11−, 1 pitch, 100 feet (30m)

First Ascent: Kyle Copeland, Alan Bartlett, Eric Johnson, March 1989.

Location and Access: Ascends an obvious left-facing dihedral located on the lower wall 150 yards (137m) right of *Stronger than Dirt*. The route summits the upper ramp, just left of the beginning of *Libbus Maximus* on the upper wall.

Paraphernalia: Friends (2) #1.5, (1) #2, (2) #2.5, #3, #3.5. (3) #4; Tri-cams #3 through #7 or Big Bros. Hexes useful.

Descent: Rappel from drilled angles or walk down the upper ramp.

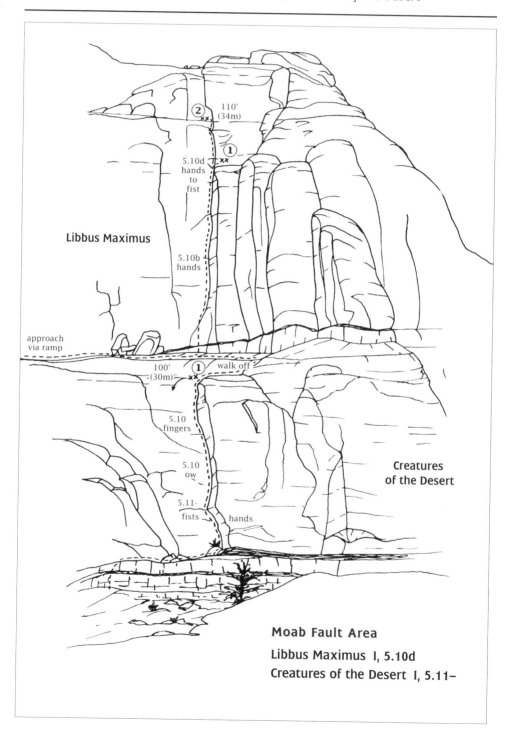

Libbus Maximus

2 xx 110'
(30m)

1 xx

5.10d
hands
to
fist

5.10b
hands

approach
via ramp

100'
(30m) 1 xx walk off

5.10
fingers

5.10
ow

5.11-
fists hands

Creatures
of the Desert

Moab Fault Area

Libbus Maximus I, 5.10d

Creatures of the Desert I, 5.11–

LIBBUS MAXIMUS I, 5.10d, 2 pitches, 110 feet (34m)

First Ascent: Pitch 1 Tony Valdes, Sonja Paspal, Bob Milton, 14 September 1986; Pitch 2 Tony Valdes, Jeff Widen, November 1986.

Location and Access: Park as for the previous routes. *Libbus Maximus* is located on the prominent shelf above *Stronger than Dirt*. The route ascends the angular dihedral, the third such dihedral in from the right side of the shelf. Approach the shelf from the extreme left (west) end.

Pitch 1: Begin left of the dihedral and climb up to a right-ascending ramp about 6 feet (2m) above the bench. Continue up the ramp 25 feet (8m) to where it meets the dihedral. Ascend the corner, first with 5.10b hands, then 5.10c hands and fist to a fixed anchor 70 feet (21m) up the wall.

Pitch 2: Climb 40 feet (12m), 5.10d fist to rappel anchors.

Paraphernalia: Friends: (3) #2.5, #3, (1) #3.5, (4) #4.

Descent: Rappel the route.

ALAN'S CRACK HOUSE I, 5.9, 1 pitch, 100 feet (30m)

First Ascent: Kyle Copeland, Eric Johnson, Alan Bartlett, March 1989.

Location and Access: Ascends the first crack system left of the east edge (far right end) of the lower wall. This is 300 yards (274m) right of *Creatures of the Desert*. Approach from the left of the route, scrambling fourth class to a rotten bedding seam, then begin the route with 5.9 stemming. Continue up a four-inch crack system. Near the top of the climb, branch left, climbing hands into 5.6 wide hands, up to triple fixed anchors.

Paraphernalia: Many #3.5 to #4 Friends; #4 Camalot.

Descent: Rappel 100 feet (30m) from bolts.

HAMBURGER HELL I, 5.11+, 1 pitch

First Ascent: Kyle Copeland, Alison Sheets; 5.10, A2. First free ascent: Katy Cassidy, Earl Wiggins.

Location and Access: Located on the shelf above *Stronger than Dirt*. It ascends a straight-in offwidth crack.

Paraphernalia: Standard desert rack.

Descent: Rappel the route.

The 100-Yard Wall Area

Drive 1.7 miles (2.7km) from the park visitor center to a small pullout (difficult to see) on the left side of the roadway. An indication that you have gone too far is a sign regulating outward bound traffic to 20 mph with a serpentine arrow. Turn around and drive back a few hundred yards toward the visitor center. The small pullout will now be easier to see on the right side of the road. Approximately 80 yards (73m) northwest, a 100-yard long (91m) bench can be seen halfway up the rimrock wall. The 100-Yard Wall is the Slickrock Entrada wall above the bench.

THE NUTCRACKER I, 5.8, 1 pitch, 65 feet (20m)

First Ascent: Steve Swanke, Tom Wesson, 1982.

Location and Access: The route climbs the right side of an 80-foot (24m) pillar attached to the extreme lower right end of the 100-yard (91m) long bench. To start, hike up a prominent boulderfield to the right of the route. The climb begins with 5.8 stemming, leads to 5.8 hands and finishes with a 5.4, then a 5.2 chimney. One may diagonal right near the top of the route for a more difficult finish.

Paraphernalia: One set Friends.

Descent: Walk off talus to the right of the climb via a prominent slide of giant boulders. This also serves as the approach to *Fledgling* and *Doil* and descent from all the routes in the 100-Yard Wall area.

DOIL I, 5.8, 1 pitch, 65 feet (20m)

First Ascent: The first ascent party is unknown.

Location and Access: The route begins atop the bench directly above *The Nutcracker*. It ascends a crack system behind an 80-foot (24m) pillar that resembles a drumstick, for 65 feet (20m). To start, hike up a prominent boulderfield to the right of the route. The climb begins up loose blocks to a chimney inside the pillar. Continue up a hand-and-fist crack, then up tight stemming to rappel slings.

Paraphernalia: One set of Friends with extra large pieces.

Descent: Rappel the route from slings around a chockstone, then walk off the talus to the right of the climb.

FLEDGLING I, 5.4, 1 pitch, 90 feet (27m)

First Ascent: Terre Lashier, Steve Swanke, 1 January 1987.

Location and Access: The *Fledgling* is located two formations left of *Doil*. It is the center of three broad leaning towers on the 100-yard (91m) bench.

Paraphernalia: One set of Friends.

Descent: Downclimb the route and walk off talus to the right of the climb.

Zippy Zebra Wall

Drive 1.7 miles (2.7km) from the visitor center and park behind a sign regulating outward bound speed to 20 mph with a serpentine arrow indicating curves ahead. Zippy Zebra Wall is the prominent south-facing wall left (north) of the park road. This is a point just before a post with a number 2 on it, which is a designated stop for the audio cassette tour sold at the park visitor center.

ZIPPY ZEBRA I, 5.10a, 1 pitch, 120 feet (37m)

First Ascent: Jeff Widen, belayed by Dawn Burke, August 1985.

Location and Access: The route ascends the prominent left-facing dihedral on the south-facing wall directly above the sign regulating outward bound speed to 20 mph. Begin up a 5.10a lieback which ascends to a small shelf which provides a good resting point. Continue up a 5.9 handcrack in the dihedral.

Paraphernalia: Friends (2) #1, #1.5, #2, #3 and #4; medium to large stoppers.

Descent: Walk left 100 feet (30m) and rappel from a juniper tree (visible from below) using two ropes, or walk 50 feet (15m) to the right and rappel from a boulder. There are also rappel anchors on the shelf a few feet left of the route.

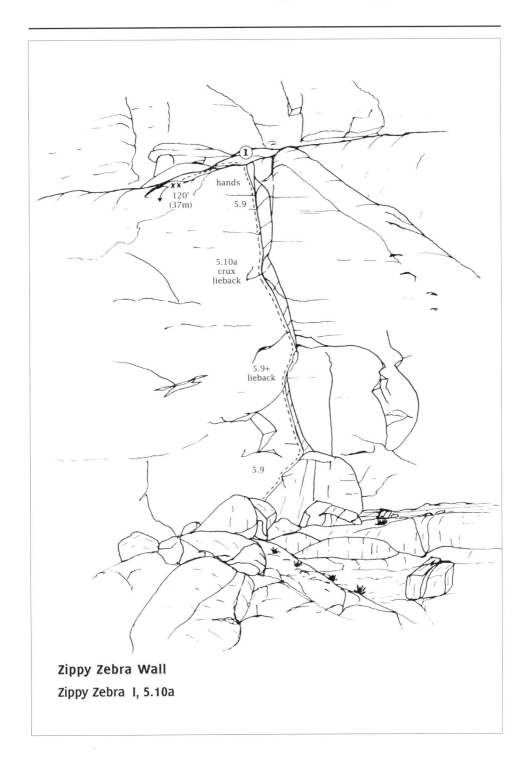

Zippy Zebra Wall

Zippy Zebra I, 5.10a

Photo: Eric Bjørnstad

Charlie Fowler on The Dumpster

PORTABLE TRASH UNIT I, 5.9, 1 pitch, 70 feet (21m)

First Ascent: Doug Cochran, Jeff Widen, August 1985.

Location and Access: Park at a post with the number 2 on it. This is a designated stop for the audio cassette tour sold at the park visitor center. *Portable Trash Unit* is located 300 feet (91m) north on the south-facing Zippy Zebra Wall. The climb is up a rounded right-facing dihedral, the first one when walking right (east) from *Zippy Zebra*. Begin with a 5.6 climb to a rounding shelf, then continue up a 5.9 fingercrack on a steep wall.

Paraphernalia: Friends (2) #1 through #3; medium stoppers.

Descent: Third class to the left of the route.

THE DUMPSTER I, 5.10+, 1 pitch, 85 feet (26m)

First Ascent: Charlie Fowler, belayed by Eric Bjørnstad, 13 October 1986.

Location and Access: Climbs the prominent right-facing dihedral two cracks right of the previous route, *Portable Trash Unit*. The two routes are separated by only a few feet. *The Dumpster* may also be recognized as the first dihedral left of the end of the south facing wall.

Paraphernalia: Friends: (2) #1 through #3, (1) #3.5.

Descent: Third class to the left of the route.

OFF THE COUCH I, 5.11b, 1 pitch, 125 feet (38m)

First Ascent: Katy Cassidy, Earl Wiggins, 8 February 1988.

Location and Access: *Off the Couch* is a right-facing flake off the ledge above and left of *The Dumpster*. The route angles up and left, just left of a straight thin crack. Approach from ramps left of the route.

Paraphernalia: Standard desert rack.

Descent: Rappel the route, then walk off the approach ramp. Slings are visible from below.

THE WHOLE THING I, 5.11+, 1 pitch, 110 feet (34m)

First Ascent: Katy Cassidy, Pete Gallagher, Earl Wiggins.

Location and Access: The route is located above *The Dumpster*. Approach from ramps left of the route and ascend the straight thin crack just right of *Off the Couch*.

Paraphernalia: Standard desert rack.

Descent: Rappel the route, then walk off the approach ramp. Slings are visible from below.

EARTH, WIND AND TIRE I, 5.10, 1 pitch, 60 feet (18m), ★

First Ascent: Bret Ruckman, Gary Olsen.

Location and Access: The route is located left of *Wind, Sand and Cars*, around the corner from *The Dumpster*. Park at a pullout on the right side of the road across from the route. Approach by scrambling in from the far right of the lower rock. The climb faces east and ascends the higher Slickrock member of Entrada sandstone.

Paraphernalia: Standard desert rack.

Descent: Rappel the route.

WIND, SAND AND CARS I, 5.11+, 1 pitch, ★

First Ascent: Bret Ruckman, solo.

Location and Access: The route is located between *Earth, Wind and Tire* and *Blood, Sweat and Gears*. Approach as for *Earth, Wind and Tire*. Climb an overhanging crack up a right-leaning and right-facing corner to a two-bolt rappel station.

Paraphernalia: Standard desert rack.

Descent: Rappel the route from a double-bolt anchor.

BLOOD, SWEAT AND GEARS I, 5.10+, 1 pitch, ★

First Ascent: Gary Olsen, Bret Ruckman.

Location and Access: The route is located up the crack system right of *Wind, Sand and Cars*. Approach the same as for *Earth, Wind and Tire*.

Paraphernalia: Standard desert rack.

Descent: Rappel the route.

South Park Avenue West

The South Park Avenue West walls overlook the Park Avenue parking lot which is located about 2.2 miles (3.5km) from the visitor center.

TILTING AT WINDMILLS II, 5.8, A3, 3 pitches, ★★★

First Ascent: Tom Bepler, Kyle Copeland, 3 December 1988.

Location and Access: The route is 95% clean aid with only the start of Pitch 1 and Pitch 2 requiring pitons (about 5 points total). It is the only route in the area that climbs to the top of the rimrock. Begins immediately left of *Cinnamon Rose*. Pitch 1 begins A3 up to A1 and finishes A2 at the rappel point for *Cinnamon Rose* and *Another Zinger*. Pitch 2 climbs A0 up 5 bolts angling left to a A1 (1" piton) crack system which climbs up an obvious right-facing dihedral to a belay stance 160 feet (49m) up the route. Pitch 3 continues via 5.8, then 5.6 climbing to the top, 80 feet (24m).

Paraphernalia: Friends (2) #1, #1.5, #2, (4) #2.5, #3, #3.5, (3) #4; many TCUs and small Tri-cams; pitons (2) ¾", (1) 1".

Descent: Walk west 100 feet (30m) and make two 165 foot (50m) rappels to the ground from bolts west of the summit.

CINNAMON ROSE I, 5.9, 1 pitch, 75 feet (23m)

First Ascent: Charlie Fowler, solo, 12 October 1986.

Location and Access: *Cinnamon Rose* is just right of the prominent buttress left at the beginning of Park Avenue West. The climb ascends the crack system on a pillar formation attached to the rimrock wall. Climb 5.9 fingers, then 5.9 hands and fingers to a point 60 feet (18m) up the pillar. At this point, *Cinnamon Rose* joins *Another Zinger* for the last few feet to rappel slings visible from below.

Paraphernalia: Friends (2) #1 through #3.

Descent: One-rope rappel from slings around a chockstone.

ANOTHER ZINGER I, 5.9, 1 pitch, 75 feet (23m)

First Ascent: Unknown.

Location and Access: Located just to the right of *Cinnamon Rose*, *Another Zinger* is a prominent offwidth crack. The route climbs 5.9 offwidth to a shelf about 60 feet (18m) up the wall, then ascends another 15 feet (5m) up a 5.7 chimney to rappel slings, joining *Cinnamon Rose* for the last few feet of the climb. Rappel slings are visible from below.

Paraphernalia: Hex #6, #7, #11; a selection of stoppers; sling for chockstone on the crux.

Descent: One-rope rappel from slings around a chockstone.

RED ZINGER I, 5.9+, 1 pitch, 110 feet (34m)

First Ascent: Unknown.

Location and Access: Located a few yards right of *Another Zinger*, the climb ascends the left side of a broken looking pillar leaning against the rimrock wall. Begin in a crack system formed by the pillar, then climb to rappel anchors on the wall via finger-and-hand cracks.

Paraphernalia: Standard desert rack.

Descent: One double-rope rappel down the route.

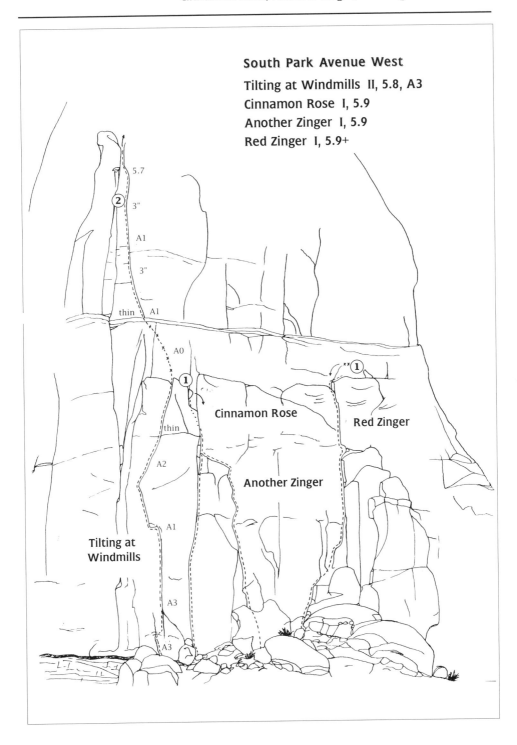

South Park Avenue West

Tilting at Windmills II, 5.8, A3

Cinnamon Rose I, 5.9

Another Zinger I, 5.9

Red Zinger I, 5.9+

South Park Avenue East

ROBBER'S ROOST I, 5.10+, 1 pitch, 80 feet (24m)

First Ascent: Carl Horton, solo 1985.

Location and Access: This climb is the most prominent left-facing dihedral nearest the east end of the parking lot. Begin with fingers and exit the route via an offwidth crack system.

Paraphernalia: Standard desert rack.

Descent: One double-rope rappel down the route. Rappel anchors are visible from below.

THE HIDEOUT I, 5.9, 1 pitch, 50 feet (15m)

First Ascent: Charlie Fowler, solo, 29 December 1986.

Location and Access: The prominent right-facing dihedral located three cracklines to the right of *Robber's Roost*.

Paraphernalia: One set of Friends.

Descent: Rappel *Robber's Roost*.

THE CARROT CANNIBAL I, 5.12a, 1 pitch, 80 feet (24m), ★★★★

First Ascent: Kyle Copeland, Sonja Paspal, June 1989.

Location and Access: An obvious right-facing dihedral with a prominent roof halfway up, located above and left of *Robber's Roost*. Slings are visible on the right wall a few feet above the roof. It may be reached by walking 200 yards (183m) to the right of *Robber's Roost* to the end of the wall. Climb 5.8 through the Dewey Bridge sandstone layer and a 5.9 short finger to offwidth flake then walk back across the bench through a notch.

Paraphernalia: Friends (1) #1, many #1.5, several #2, (1) #3, #4.

Descent: Rappel the route 80 (24m) feet from double fixed anchors.

La Sal Mountain Viewpoint Area

Drive from the visitor center about 2.6 miles (4.1km) to the La Sal Mountain Viewpoint and park. Walk down the park road north 0.1 mile (0.16km). *Sand Tears* is located on the left wall and Mars Hotel is the landform obvious just right of the roadway.

SAND TEARS I, 5.11, 1 pitch, 50 feet (15m)

First Ascent: Charlie Fowler, belayed by Eric Bjørnstad, 18 October 1986.

Location and Access: The first crack from the left side of the wall above the highway. The wall is north-facing and most easily approached from the right side. The route begins with a 5.11 move over the undercut Dewey Bridge sandstone then continues up 5.10+ fist and finally loose offwidth rock to a good ledge and rappel anchors.

Paraphernalia: Friends (1) #1 through #3, (2) #3.5 through #4.

Descent: One-rope rappel down the route from a fixed piton.

Mars Hotel

Mars Hotel is located east of the park road from *Sand Tears*. It is the first butte on the right side of the park road north of the La Sal Mountain Viewpoint.

LOST IN SPACE II, 5.10, A0, 4 pitches, 165 feet (50m)

First Ascent: Mike Baker, Leslie Henderson, October 1992.

Location and Access: Climb the east face beginning up a 5.8 chimney in a line with the left summit of the landform. Belay on the prominent bedding seam from a point left of the chimney. Pitch 2 climbs 5.9 hands, then up a 5.8 chimney to a belay in the back of the chimney. Pitch 3 traverses out of the chimney, then makes an exposed step across to the beginning of a crack system. Angle right, then continue up A0 and 5.9 offwidth to the base of the summit block from which it is a scramble to the top.

Paraphernalia: A selection of Camalots; TCUs through #3.

Descent: Downclimb from the summit to bolts, then rappel the east side of the tower. Rappel slings are visible from the ground.

IF I ONLY HAD A BRAIN II, 5.9, A2, 4 pitches, 165 feet (50m)

First Ascent: Kyle Copeland, Eric Johnson, March 1989.

Location and Access: Begin 100 yards (91m) right of *Lost in Space* at the low point of the saddle between the two summits of the landform. Begin at the left side of the saddle and climb approximately 40 feet (12m) up a crack system (5.9, A0) to a prominent bedding seam. Pitch 2 moves right on the bedding seam, then climbs A1 (protected by a #1.5 Friend), then A2 to reach the prominent saddle which is about 50 feet (15m) above the bedding seam. Pitch 3 ascends the ridge approximately 100 feet (30m) to a belay. The last pitch continues to the base of the summit block. Climb 5.9 offwidth with one point of A0 to a shoulder where it is possible to friction 5.6 left to the far side of the base of the summit block from which it is a scramble further left and up to the top.

Paraphernalia: One set of Friends with (2-3) #1.5; TCUs; small to medium wires.

Descent: Same as for *Lost In Space*.

North Park Avenue East

This section describes routes and formations that lie on the east side of Park Avenue. From the visitor center drive about 3.5 mile (5.6km) to the Courthouse Towers parking area.

SAND BAG I, 5.10b, 1 pitch, 80 feet (24m)

First Ascent: Kyle Copeland, Sue Kemp, 29 August 1986.

Location and Access: Hike to the left walls of lower Park Avenue. *Sand Bag* is the first crack left of the northwest corner of the north end of Park Avenue. The route begins in a left-facing dihedral and works up hands and fingers to a sloping shelf.

Paraphernalia: Friends (1) #1.5, #2, #2.5, (2) #3, #3.5, #4; (1) #7 Tri-cam.

Descent: On the first ascent the summit rock was found to be too soft for rappel anchors. Unless future parties have innovated an anchor, it is necessary to lower the climber down the route with a rope wrapped around a bollard at the top of the pitch. Rappel slings are visible from below the climb.

WEAPONS OF LOVE I, 5.10d, 3 pitches, 140 feet (43m)

First Ascent: Tony Valdes, Kirk Miller, 1987.

Location and Access: The route climbs *Sand Bag*, traverses left 250 feet (76m), then ascends to rappel anchors.

Paraphernalia: For Pitch 3: Friends (8) or more #0.5 through #1.5, (4) #2, (2) #3, (1) #4.

Descent: Two double-rope rappels; the first rappels *Weapons of Love* pitch, the second to the ground.

HEART OF THE DESERT I, 5.10c, 1 pitch, 80 feet (24m), ★★★★★

First Ascent: Jeff Widen, belayed by Dawn Burke, August 1985.

Location and Access: *Heart of the Desert* is the first dihedral visible on the lower rock on the left (east) side of Park Avenue. (It is obscured from view from some areas of Courthouse Towers parking area by a small Dewey Bridge sandstone tower in the foreground.) The climb is a prominent left-facing dihedral which begins atop the lowest bench at the far end of a long crackless wall located about 200 feet (61m) before the north end of the left wall of Park Avenue. The route ascends a 5.10c handcrack to a rappel from fixed anchors.

Paraphernalia: Friends (1) #2, (2) #2.5, (4) #3, (2) #3.5, (1) #4.

Descent: One double-rope rappel back down the route.

Photo: Chris Begue

Heart of the Desert   Photo: Chris Begue

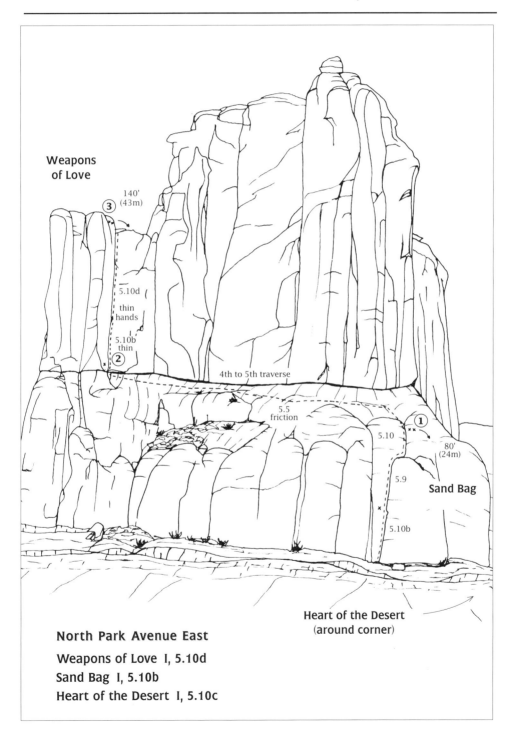

Weapons
of Love

140'
(43m)
3

5.10d

thin
hands

5.10b
thin
2

4th to 5th traverse

5.5
friction

5.10

1

80'
(24m)

5.9

Sand Bag

5.10b

Heart of the Desert
(around corner)

North Park Avenue East

Weapons of Love I, 5.10d
Sand Bag I, 5.10b
Heart of the Desert I, 5.10c

The Candelabrum

The Candelabrum is located up Park Avenue from the Courthouse Towers parking area about 100 yards (91m) beyond the *Heart of the Desert* dihedral on the same (left) side. The formation is a stout tower that is the farthest west projection of the east walls of Park Avenue.

SOUTHEAST CRACK II, 5.11, A1, 3 pitches

First Ascent: Katy Cassidy, Earl Wiggins.
Location and Access: The route ascends a crack on the southeast side of the landform.
Paraphernalia: Unknown.
Descent: Rappel from anchors 20 feet (6m) below the top.

HALL OF FLAME II, 5.11d, 3 pitches, 85 feet (26m)

First Ascent: Kyle Copeland, Alison Sheets, 5.11, A2, 2 November 1987. First free ascent: French climbers Stevie Haston, Gouault Lawrence, Spring 1994.
Location and Access: The route begins atop a broad bench of Dewey Bridge sandstone, at the far left side of the west face. Fixed anchors and rappel slings are visible from below.
Paraphernalia: Small Tri-cams; Friends (3) #1, (1) #2.5, (2) #3, (1) #3.5, (1) #4.
Descent: Rappel the *Play with Fire* route.

A COMPANY OF CANDLES (rating unknown)

First Ascent: Unknown.
Location and Access: The route ascends the first crack system to the left of *Hall of Flame*. Rappel slings are visible about 40 feet (12m) up.

PLAY WITH FIRE III, 5.9, A2, 3 pitches, 240 feet (73m)

First Ascent: Charlie Fowler, Chris Coplerud, November 1986.
Location and Access: As the Candelabrum is viewed from the Courthouse Towers parking area, *Play with Fire* ascends the farthest right (west) crack system of the tower.
Paraphernalia: Friends (3) #1 through #4; Tri-cams (3) #7; small assortment of medium nuts and some assorted small angle pitons.
Descent: Downclimb on aid from the summit, then rappel the face below.

North Park Avenue West

This section describes routes and formations that lie on the west side of Park Avenue. From the visitor center drive about 2.2 miles (3.5km) to the Park Avenue parking lot. An alternate approach is to hike up Park Avenue from the Courthouse Towers parking area, located 3.5 miles (5.6km) from the visitor center.

I NEED FRIENDS I, 5.9, 1 pitch, 80 feet (24m)

First Ascent: Unknown.
Location and Access: One-fourth mile (0.4km) north of Park Avenue parking area. The route is located left into the first opening when approaching from Park Avenue parking area. Scramble up to the base of the climb. The route ascends a 90-degree corner beginning with fist and ending with fingers.
Paraphernalia: Standard desert rack.
Descent: Hike northwest 200 yards (183m) and downclimb 5.2 rock.

Photo: Michele Goldstein

Park Avenue

SAND OF A BEACH I, 5.10a, 1 pitch, 50 feet (15m)

First Ascent: Chris Begue, Scott Carson, March 1987.

Location and Access: The route is located on the prow of rock at the entrance to the second canyon on the west as one walks north from the Park Avenue parking area. The landform first becomes visible to the left (west) about 150 yards (137m) down the Park Avenue trail. From the Courthouse Towers parking area the prow is located directly across (west) from The Candelabrum.

Sand of a Beach begins on the southeast side of the prow, at the bedding seam between the lower Dewey Bridge member and the upper Slickrock member of Entrada sandstone. Climb up a sloping block to a short chimney stemming section. An alternate approach is to traverse to the climb from the west end of the shelf formed by the bedding seam. The route begins with fingers and ends with hands.

Paraphernalia: Friends (1) #1.5 to #3.5, plus (2) #2.

Descent: One simultaneous rappel down opposite sides of the rock.

BLACK CELEBRATION I, 5.10c, 1 pitch, 50 feet (15m), ★★★

First Ascent: Chris Begue, Scott Carson, March 1987.

Location and Access: Located on the northwest side of the prow (opposite *Sand of a Beach*), beginning at the bedding seam between the Dewey Bridge member and the upper slickrock. To reach, traverse right from *Sand of a Beach*, around the prow to the other side of the landform via a narrow ledge system. An alternate approach is to traverse to the climb from the west end of the shelf formed by the bedding seam. The route ascends a prominent crack two lines north of *Sand of a Beach*, but on the opposite side of the formation.

Paraphernalia: Friends (3) #0.5, (1) #2, #2.5, #3; hexes #4, #5, #6.

Descent: Same as for *Sand of a Beach*.

MANY MILES AWAY I, 5.11c, 1 pitch, 50 feet (15m)

First Ascent: Chris Begue, Scott Carson, April 1987. First free ascent: Kent Wheeler, Chris Begue, Bret Ruckman, 6 May 1988.

Location and Access: Located one crack system north of *Sand of a Beach*, on the opposite side of the formation. It is easily identified by the fracture line between *Black Celebration* and *Sand of a Beach*, but on the northwest side of the landform. The route begins in a right-facing corner, proceeding with thin fingers, to perfect hands, then finally hard offwidth near the top.

Paraphernalia: Friends and TCUs #1 through #4; wired stoppers.

Descent: Rappel the route.

SKIN DEEP I, 5.11c, 1 pitch, 50 feet (15m)

First Ascent: Chris Begue, March 1988. First free ascent Bret Ruckman, Gary Olsen, 8 May 1988.

Location and Access: Located 10 feet (3m) right of *Many Miles Away*.

Paraphernalia: Fingersize to handsize pieces.

Descent: Rappel *Many Miles Away*.

Jello Tower

Jello Tower is located directly opposite *Heart of the Desert*, across the Park Avenue wash. It is most easily approached from the Courthouse Towers parking area.

SOFT PARADE I, 5.10+, A4, 2 pitches, 130 feet (40m)

First Ascent: Charlie Fowler, Sue Wint, November 1986.

Location and Access: The route ascends a right-facing corner on the right side of the small tower which is viewed as the farthest point projecting from the west walls of Park Avenue. Pitch 1 is enjoyable 5.10 thin hands leading to 5.10+ fist, climbing for 80 feet (24m) to a shelf. The hard aid of Pitch 2 can be avoided with a rappel.

Paraphernalia: One set of Friends protects Pitch 1. Pitch 2 climbed with aid is not recommended.

Descent: Rappel down the northwest face.

Courthouse Towers

The Courthouse Towers are a loose cluster of towers located on both sides of the park road, north, west and east of the main Park Avenue. Approach these formations from the Courthouse Towers parking area, about 3.5 miles (5.6km) from the visitor center. Each have multiple routes which may be researched at the visitor center or through Moab Adventures Outfitters at the Moab Rock Shop.

The Three Gossips

The Three Gossips are located on the southwest side of the park road and are quite visible from the Courthouse Towers parking area. See photo on page 114.

WEST FACE II, 5.11, 3 pitches, 255 feet (78m), ★★★★

First Ascent: Allen Steck, Steve Roper, October 1970. First free ascent: Glenn Randall, Jeff Achey, 1982, during the third overall ascent of the tower.

Location and Access: The route is on the west face, the opposite side of the tower from the park road, and ascends to the northern summit via the rightmost crack system. A hidden four-foot-wide (1.2m) chimney splits the summit block.

Paraphernalia: Standard desert rack; many small wires.

Descent: Two double-rope rappels down the route.

LYON-TRAUTNER ROUTE II, 5.11, 3 pitches, 300 feet (91m)

First Free Ascent: Charles Lyon, Todd Trautner, 1981. (This was the first free and second overall ascent of The Three Gossips.)

Location and Access: Ascends the crack system left of the original ascent line and joins the few feet of summit rock at the notch between the northern and middle summits of the landform.

Paraphernalia: Standard desert rack plus many small wires, TCUs.

Descent: Two double-rope rappels down the *West Face* route.

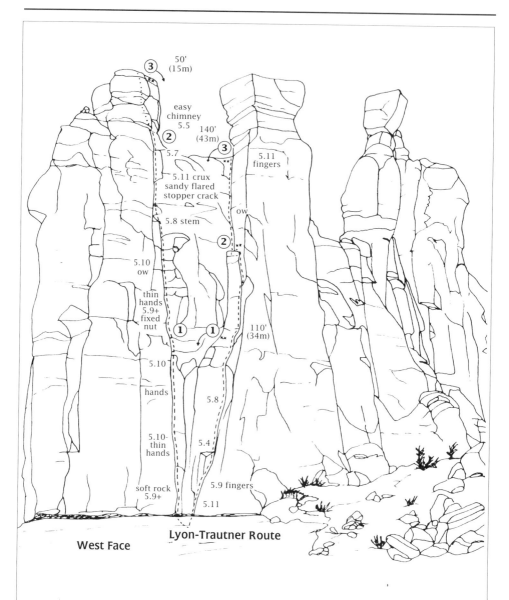

West Face

Lyon-Trautner Route

The Three Gossips West Face

West Face II, 5.11

Lyon-Trautner Route II, 5.11

THE CRYSTALLINE ENTITY III, 5.9, A3, 4 pitches
First Ascent: David Evans, Tom Sherman, Margy Floyd, with Jim Angione and John Furlong on lower pitches, Easter 1994.
Location and Access: The route ascends the crack system left of *West Face*.
Paraphernalia: Standard desert rack; Friends (3) to #5; pitons to 1".
Descent: Rappel *West Face*.

BE THERE OR BE TALKED ABOUT (South Tower via West Face) II, 5.11, A1, 4 pitches, 280 feet (85m)
First Ascent: Pete Gallagher, Bego Gerhart, 1988.
Location and Access: West face of the South Gossip. The summit cap is ascended via a five-bolt ladder.
Paraphernalia: Camalots #1.5 to #4.
Descent: Rappel the route.

VARIATION 5.11d
First Ascent: Bret Ruckman, Marco Cornacchione, 3 October 1989.
Location and Access: The variation begins up the crack barely right of the second pitch fist crack.
Paraphernalia: Small Friends #0.4 through #2.5; TCUs.

KNOCKFIRST SANDWITCH III, 5.7, A3, 3 pitches, 350 feet (107m)
First Ascent: James Funsten, solo, 4, 15, 16 April 1993.
Location and Access: Climbs the east face of the south summit, facing the road and following a steep crack to an obvious corner. Funsten suggests "second pitch has scary rock that looks solid from the ground and that one should knock first and find where one shouldn't place a piton or nut."
Paraphernalia: Camalot #4; Tri-cam (2) sets #0.4 through #4; Rocks (1-2) sets; short, thin knifeblade; bugaboos (2-3); RURP (1); Birdbeak (1).
Descent: Rappel the route.

SPEAK NO EVIL III, 5.10, C2, 4 pitches, 350 feet (107m)
First Ascent: Duane Raleigh, Lisa Raleigh.
Location and Access: The route climbs the east face of The Three Gossips (side facing the park road), via obvious thin crack system located opposite *Lyon-Trautner*.
Paraphernalia: Camming devices 0.5 to 5 inches and 2 sets of Lowe Balls.
Descent: Rappel the *Lyon-Trautner Route*.

VARIATION A1, 1 pitch, 150 feet (46m)
First Ascent: Jeff Widen, John Plvan, Fall 1994.
Location and Access: The variation climbs the crack system 30 feet (9m) left of *Speak No Evil*, joining at the top of Pitch 1.
Paraphernalia: Friends (3) sets, (4) #3; TCUs (2) sets.

Argon Tower

Argon Tower is the slender free-standing pinnacle at the far left end of Park Avenue when viewed from the Park Avenue viewpoint, 2.2 miles (3.5km) from the visitor center.

NORTH FACE III, 5.11c, 3 pitches, 260 feet (79m)

First Ascent: Layton Kor, Bob Bradley, Charlie Kemp, 17 January 1964. First free ascent (III, 5.11-) Paul Turecki. (This was the second ascent of the North Face and the first free ascent of Argon Tower.)

Location and Access: To approach the climb, park at the Courthouse Towers parking lot, a mile (1.6km) further up the road from the Park Avenue viewpoint. Argon Tower will be the free-standing tower on the lower right (west) end of Park Avenue wash. The route climbs the prominent crack system on the slender north side of the tower.

Paraphernalia: Three sets of Friends up to #3; a selection of medium stoppers. No pitons.

Descent: Rappel the *West Face*.

PRATT-ROBINSON III, 5.9, A3, 4 pitches, 260 feet (79m)

First Ascent: Chuck Pratt, Doug Robinson, 15 April 1969.

Location and Access: The route ascends the crack system left of *North Face*.

Paraphernalia: Standard desert rack.

Descent: Rappel the *West Face*.

WEST FACE III, 5.11+, A1, 4 pitches, 260 feet (79m)

First Ascent: Steve Cheyney, John Pease, Spring 1972. Subsequent ascents are responsible for much of the free climbing.

Location and Access: The route climbs a right-facing crack on the right side of the West Face. Begin A1 and climb to 5.11+ fist into a 5.10b squeeze.

Variation: During the fourth ascent of the tower, George Hurley and Bill Forrest climbed the crack system to the right of the route for the first pitch.

Paraphernalia: Three sets of Friends #1 through #3.5, (5) #4; Tri-cam #7; a small selection of medium wires; pitons ¾", 1", (3) ⅜".

Descent: Three double-rope rappels down *West Face*.

NORTH-NORTHEAST ARETE III, 5.11-, 4 pitches, 260 feet (79m)

First Ascent: Todd Gordon, Dave Evans, 5.9 A2, Spring 1984. First free ascent (5.11-) Tim Coats, Bret Ruckman, October 12, 1987.

Location and Access: The route ascends a crack system left of *Pratt-Robinson*. Climb past a 5.10b squeeze to double fixed anchors, then continue over a small roof to the summit.

Paraphernalia: Standard desert rack.

Descent: Rappel *West Face*.

The Organ: Southwest Tower

It is the nearest landform to the Courthouse Towers parking area, on the right side of the road, about 3.5 miles (5.6km) from the visitor center. In addition to *Thelma and Louise*, there are several routes established on The Organ which require considerable amounts of aid. Since aid climbing in the park is discouraged, details of the routes are not included in this guide.

Photo: Bill Duncan

Argon Tower

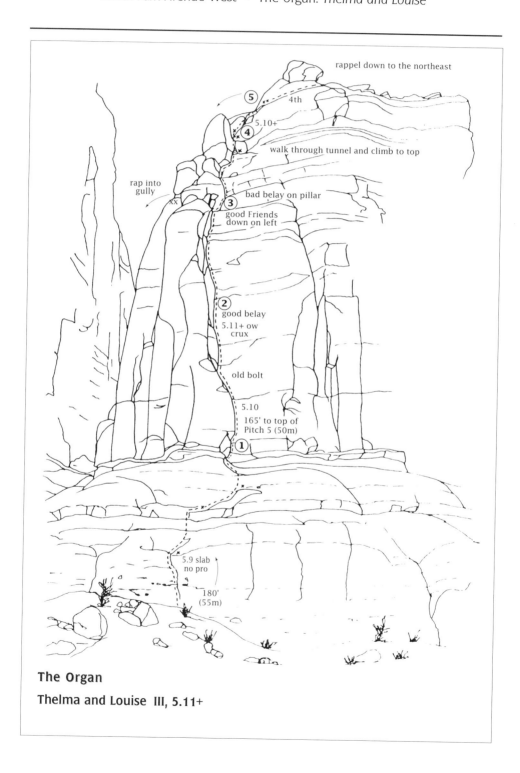

rappel down to the northeast

⑤ 4th

5.10+

④

Ⓐ walk through tunnel and climb to top

rap into gully

xx

③ bad belay on pillar

good Friends down on left

② good belay

5.11+ ow crux

old bolt

5.10

165' to top of Pitch 5 (50m)

①

5.9 slab no pro

180' (55m)

The Organ

Thelma and Louise III, 5.11+

THELMA AND LOUISE III, 5.11+, 5 pitches, 500 feet (152m)

First ascent and first free ascent: French climbers Stevie Haston, Gouault Lawrence, Spring 1994.

Location and Access: The Organ when viewed from the west end of the parking area is divided into two towers. *Thelma and Louise* is located on the far left side of the right (southwest) tower, and is not visible from the parking area. It shares Pitches 1 and 7 (the first and last) with *Death By Hands*, which climbs with aid, a continuous crack system just left of *Thelma and Louise*. The first pitch climbs slickrock with poor protection.

Paraphernalia: Friends (2) #1, #1.5, #2, (1) #2.5, (2) #3, #3.5, #4; a selection of wires and RPs. No pitons.

Descent: Rappel *Death By Hands* which ascends the continuous crack system on the far left side of the right (southwest) tower when viewed from Courthouse Towers parking area. Four rappels are necessary using double ropes–two rappels lead into the gully between the two towers and two rappels lead to the ground on the southeast side of the tower (opposite side from the parking lot). Using only one rappel from the gully creates a tremendous rope drag upon retrieval.

Tower of Babel

ZENYATTA ENTRADA IV, 5.4, A2, 6 pitches, 550 feet (167m)

First Ascent: Charlie Fowler solo, with Eric Bjørnstad on the lower pitches and Lin Ottinger to the summit via prusiks, 14-17 October 1986.

Location and Access: The route ascends the obvious system of cracks on the southwest buttress directly above the park road. Each lead involves overhanging rock with fair belay stances fixed with drilled angles. The climb is 5.4, C2 with A2 on Pitch 3.

Paraphernalia: Friends (2) sets #1 through #3, (1) #3.5, #4; Tri-cams (2) sets #0.5 to #2; small to medium stoppers; (3) Lost Arrows; (3) baby angles; (3) standard angles; large (sawed-off) angles helpful; hooks for piton scars..

Descent: Ropes should be fixed from the second belay onward to facilitate a descent.

Sheep Rock

VIRGIN WOOL III, 5.9, A2, 4 pitches, 440 feet (134m)

First Ascent: Jim Bodenhamer, Sandy Fleming, 30 November 1986.

Location and Access: The route begins on the east side of the tower, facing the park road, and begins where Sheep Rock and The Lamb meet.

Paraphernalia: Several sets of TCUs and Lowe Balls.

Descent: Rappel 70 feet (21m) from drilled angles to the top of Pitch 3. Rappel 150 feet (46m) from drilled angles to top of Pitch 2. Rappel 150 feet (46m) from drilled angles to the ground.

Photo: Cameron M. Burns

Ann Robertson rappelling off Owl Rock

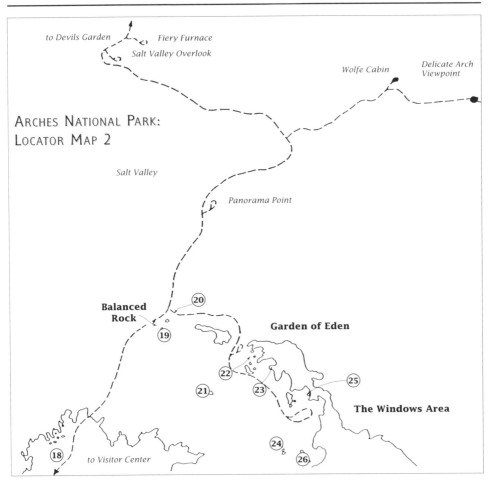

ARCHES NATIONAL PARK:
LOCATOR MAP 2

Garden of Eden Area

⑱ The Lovers, The Phallus,
The Testes: *Left Nut*

⑲ *Bubo*

⑳ Off-Balanced Rock:
*Northeast Chimney, Camino
Route*

㉑ Squaw Pinnacle: *Variation*

㉒ Owl Rock: *Owl Rock One, Ala
Sinistra, Rasta Magnola*

㉓ Bullwinkle Tower:
West Chimney, East Chimney

㉔ The Remnant

㉕ The Windows Area:
The Wishbone

㉖ Tonka Tower

The Lamb

The Lamb is the landform adjacent to and north of Sheep Rock at the west edge of the Courthouse Towers region of the park.

SHEEPISH GRIN I, 5.10, 1 pitch, 90 feet (27m)

First Ascent: Charlie Fowler, solo, October 1986.

Location and Access: The route follows a crack system on the southwestern (backside) of The Lamb. Begin at the closest point between The Lamb and the western rear of Sheep Rock. Easy fifth-class moves to the 5.8 thin fingers which becomes 5.9+ hand and fist. Continue up the chimney to 5.10 offwidth ending on a belay shelf. Easy fifth-class climbing 15 feet (4.6m) to the summit.

Paraphernalia: Friends (2) sets #1 through #4; Tri-cams (2) #7.

Descent: First ascent party lowered off the other side of the rock from a rope previously fixed at the start of the route.

SHEEP IN WOLF'S CLOTHING I, 5.10, 1 pitch, 90 feet (27m)

First Ascent: Charlie Fowler, solo, December 1986.

Location and Access: The route is on the northeast face, facing the park road.

Paraphernalia: Standard desert rack.

Descent: Rappel the route which may need anchors.

The Great Wall

The Great Wall is a long escarpment of Entrada sandstone paralleled by the park road on its west side as it runs for 4 miles (6.4km) north from the Courthouse Wash.

CHINESE EYES I, 5.9+, 1 pitch, 70 feet (21m), ★★★★★

First Ascent: Charlie Fowler, Dan Grandusky, November 1986.

Location and Access: Located 4.6 miles (7.4km) from the visitor center. Park at the pullout on the left side of the roadway, just after crossing Courthouse Wash Bridge. The route ascends the central crack system on the broken slabs leaning against The Great Wall, northwest of the parking area. The route is obvious; there are no other broken areas along The Great Wall for 100 yards (91m) in either direction.

Paraphernalia: Friends (2) sets #1 through #3.5; Tri-cam (1) #7.

Descent: Rappel the route from fixed anchors.

MR. SOMBRERO I, 5.11c, 1 pitch, 75 feet (23m), ★★★★★

First Ascent: Mark Lemmons, Rob Slater, Jim Bodenhamer, December 1987.

Location and Access: An obvious left-facing dihedral 300 feet (91m) northeast of *Chinese Eyes*. It is located 0.04 mile (0.6km) from the Courthouse Wash Bridge. Best parking is at the location for *Chinese Eyes* just north of the Courthouse Wash Bridge. Slings are visible from below.

Paraphernalia: Standard desert rack.

Descent: One 75-foot (23m) rappel from two drilled angles.

GREAT WALL CRACK I, 5.11, 1 pitch, 140 feet (43m)

First Ascent: Jimmy Dunn, Mike Lockhart, 1979.

Location and Access: The route is located at the right edge of a long, crackless, east-facing portion of The Great Wall, 0.05 mile (0.8km) beyond Courthouse Wash bridge. Park on the west (left) side of the road (when coming from the visitor center). The route is visible 1000 feet (305m) to the southwest, just right of a prow of rock in The Great Wall which extends toward the park road.

The route faces northeast. Scramble atop a white ledge dividing the soft Dewey Bridge member of the Entrada from the Slickrock member. Stand on a boulder at the entrance to a shallow cave and climb a 5.9+ fingercrack to a 5.10b roof which is turned on the left. There is an optional belay stance between the 5.9+ fingercrack and the roof. Continue via 5.11 offwidth which thins to 5.10c hands and lieback. The pitch finishes with 5.9 fists.

Paraphernalia: Friends (2) sets; stoppers #7 through #9.

Descent: One double-rope rappel from an alcove at the top of the climb.

GREAT WALL CRACK TOO I, 5.11, 1 pitch, 140 feet (43m)

First Ascent: Scott Gilbert, Jim Newberry, 1977.

Location and Access: Located about 1.07 miles (2.7km) beyond Courthouse Wash Bridge or 0.8 miles (1.2km) beyond *Great Wall Crack*. The route faces south southeast. When viewed from the Petrified Dunes parking area, the route is about ten o'clock to the left of the park road on a prominent, protruding, south-facing dihedral. The route follows a left-facing dihedral on a portion of rock that is only two-thirds as high as the walls framing it from behind. Begin with a 5.10a start and continue up 5.9+ fingers. There is an optional belay or continue via hands at 5.11, then lieback and hands ending at the top via fist.

Paraphernalia: Standard desert rack.

Descent: A rappel anchor is on the right side of a chimney "V" hidden from below. Make one rappel on a doubled rope back down the route.

BEYOND GREAT WALL CRACK TOO (rating unknown), 1 pitch, 70 feet (21m)

First Ascent: Scott Gilbert, Glenn Randall, circa 1970s.

Location and Access: Located about 300 feet (91m) to the right of *Great Wall Crack Too* on the same protrusion of rock. It faces northeast. The route begins on the right side of a slab formation leaning against the wall. Traverse left once the top of the slab is gained and continue up a vertical crack to rappel slings, visible from the ground.

Paraphernalia: Standard desert rack.

Descent: Rappel the route.

The Lovers, The Phallus, The Testes

From the Courthouse Wash Bridge, just beyond the Courthouse Towers parking area, drive 2.8 miles (4.5km) north and park on the west (left) side of the road. Miss Rosa Coldfield, The Phallus and The Testes are clearly in view about 600 feet (183m) to the west.

The Lovers

This tower is the first landform south of The Phallus.

MISS ROSA COLDFIELD II, 5.8 R, A2, 1 pitch, 140 feet (49m)

First Ascent: Dave Gloudemans, solo, 16 October 1995.

Location and Access: The route climbs the south face of the tower. Begin 5.8 and climb to a pillar. Stem behind the pillar and sling it. Continue 5.6R then A2 on overhanging crack in white rock to summit anchors. Slings are visible from below.

Paraphernalia: Firends #1.5, #2.5, #3, (2) #3.5, #4; Metolius TCUS #2; rocks (3) #2, #5, (2) #7, #8; pitons Lost Arrows #5, #8; angles (1) ¾", 1"; bugaboos (4); knifeblades (2); 15-foot sling for pillar halfway up.

Descent: Rappel the route from the bottom two of three summit anchors.

The Phallus

The Phallus is the obvious tower immediately west of the park road.

THE PHALLUS II, 5.7, A2+, 1 pitch, 90 feet (27m)

First Ascent: Peter Geyser, solo.

Location and Access: Route is on the southeast face. Begin on the south side and traverse right to the southeast side of the landform.

Paraphernalia: Fiends #2 through #3½; Tri-cams #2½, #3; Rocks #6 through #8; (6) long Bugaboos; (2) ¾", 1", 1½", ½" and ⅝" angles..

Descent: One double-rope rappel. Slings are visible from the ground.

The Testes

Two-tower formation immediately north (right) of The Phallus.

LEFT NUT II, 5.9, A1+, 1 pitch, 150 feet (46m)

First Ascent: Cameron Burns, Ann Robertson, 20 March 1993.

Location and Access: The route climbs the higher tower via the west face (opposite the park road). Begin in the crack system dividing the two towers (Left Nut from Right Nut). There is a fixed piton on the route located just above the height of the lower (Right Nut) tower. Slings are visible on the Right Nut but details of the route are unknown.

Paraphernalia: Friends (2) sets; (3) baby angles; medium nuts; slings for rappel.

Descent: One double-rope rappel from slings around summit knob.

Balanced Rock Area

From the visitor center drive about 9 miles (14.5km) and park at the Balanced Rock view area. **NOTE:** The rock is a critical resource area for nesting birds and is closed to climbing from

1 January through 30 June.

Balanced Rock and Bubo

BUBO I, 5.7, 3 short pitches, 140 feet (43m)

First Ascent: Unknown.

Location and Access: From the parking area, a short trail circles Balanced Rock. At its farthest southeast point the trail passes beneath the north face of Bubo. The route follows the deep chimney system on the north face, facing Balanced Rock.

Bubo virginianus is the genus name for the great horned owl, also known as the night owl or hoot owl. Its mournful "hoo, hoo-hoo-hoo" is a commonly heard nocturnal call in the park.

Paraphernalia: Standard desert rack.

Descent: One double-rope rappel down the route.

Off-Balanced Rock

The landform directly north of Balanced Rock. The routes are best viewed from a gravel pullout located immediately after turning onto the spur road to The Windows section of the park, a few yards beyond the Balanced Rock parking area.

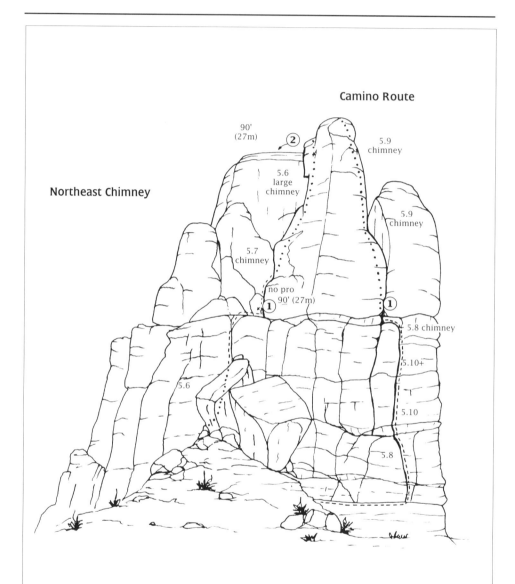

Off-Balanced Rock

Northeast Chimney I, 5.7
Camino Route I, 5.10+

NORTHEAST CHIMNEY I, 5.7, 2 pitches, 90 feet (27m)

First Ascent: Unknown.

Location and Access: The route follows the crack chimney system on the left of a stout pillar-like structure in the center of the north wall.

Paraphernalia: Pitch 1 Friends (3) #2.5; Pitch 2 is difficult to protect.

Descent: One double-rope rappel down the route from long slings around a chockstone.

CAMINO ROUTE I, 5.10+, 2 pitches, 90 feet (27m)

First Ascent: Italian climbers Marco Ferrari, Patrizia Spadon, 28 March 1987.

Location and Access: The route ascends the chimney system right of the stout pillar-like structure on the north face of the landform. "Camino" is Italian for chimney.

Paraphernalia: Friends (1) #1 to #4, (3) #2.5.

Descent: One double-rope rappel from long slings around a chockstone. The rappel is made down *Northeast Chimney*.

Garden of Eden

The Garden of Eden area of the park is located about 10 miles (16km) from the visitor center, or 1 mile (1.6km) from the intersection of The Windows road and the main park road.

Squaw Pinnacle

Squaw Pinnacle is a prominent spire about 2000 feet (610m) south of and across the park road from Owl Rock. It is easily distinguished as the nearest tower when viewing to the east (toward The Windows) from the first pullout south of Balanced Rock.

SQUAW PINNACLE I, 5.10–, A3, 2 pitch, 100 feet (30m)

First Ascent: Keen Butterworth, Dave Gloudemans, 24 November 1991.

Location and Access: The route faces north.

Paraphernalia: Friends (1) #1.5 through #2.5, (2) #3-4; a selection of stoppers and RPs; small selection of KBs, LAs, baby angles.

Descent: Rappel the route.

VARIATION 5.9+

First Ascent: Mike Bryan, Frosty Weller, November 1991. (This was the second ascent of the tower.)

Location and Access: This 5.9+ variation begins 30 feet (9m) right of the original ascent line and requires no pro. It is an easy bypass to the 5.10- original beginning.

Owl Rock

From the Garden of Eden parking area, Owl Rock is 100 feet (30m) southeast. When driving south (toward the visitor center) from the Fiery Furnace, Owl Rock is visible for several miles as the sole tower on the southern horizon between Elephant Butte on the left and Ham Rock on the right. Owl Rock is also known as Eagle Rock, deriving its name from the bird-shaped rock that was once perched atop the tower. Although the formation toppled in March of 1941, the rock retains the name.

OWL ROCK ONE I, 5.8, 1 pitch, 100 feet (30m), ★★★★★

First Ascent: Ron Olevsky, solo, February 1978.
Location and Access: Arches' most popular climb. A rappel chain is visible from the parking area.
Paraphernalia: One set of Friends.
Descent: One rappel via the route from a rappel chain visible from below.

VARIATION 5.12a TR

First Ascent: Jimmy Dunn, Bob Palais, Betsi McKittrick, 1991.
Location and Access: The variation begins left and meets *Owl Rock One* near the crux high on the climb.

ALA SINISTRA I, 5.11, 1 pitch, 100 feet (30m)

First Ascent: Italians Marco Ferrari, Patrizia Spadon, 28 March 1987.
Location and Access: The route is located on the west face of the tower, about 20 feet (6m) right of *Owl Rock One*. The Italian name means "left wing."
Paraphernalia: Friends (3) #2.5.
Descent: One double-rope rappel down *Owl Rock One*.

RASTA MAGNOLA I, 5.11, 1 pitch, 100 feet (30m)

First Ascent: Jimmy Dunn, Bob Palais (5.9, A2), September 1991. First free ascent (I, 5.11) Jimmy Dunn, Craig Luebben, 7 November 1994.
Location and Access: Ascends the tower on the opposite side (east) of *Owl Rock One*, following the left of the two obvious crack systems.
Paraphernalia: Two sets of Friends.
Descent: Rappel *Owl Rock One*.

Bullwinkle Tower

First tower south of Owl Rock. The formation is recognized by a chimney splitting its upper half. It may also be located by driving from The Windows parking area back toward the main park road. Just before the turn to the Garden of Eden, there is a sign which reads: "Garden of Eden Viewpoint" with an arrow indicating the upcoming pullout. The arrow points directly to Bullwinkle Tower.

WEST CHIMNEY I, 5.7+, 1 pitch, 60 feet (18m)

First Ascent: Sara Holloway, Keen Butterworth, April 1992.
Location and Access: Traverse to the base of the climb from the left of the obvious chimney, 5.4.
Paraphernalia: Standard desert rack.
Descent: Rappel west off slings around the summit blocks.

EAST CHIMNEY I, 5.9, 1 pitch, 60 feet (18m)

First Ascent: Randall Weekley, Jonathan Auerbach, May 1992.
Location and Access: Approach by traversing right from *West Chimney* around the base to *East Chimney*, 5.2.
Paraphernalia: Standard desert rack.
Descent: Rappel west off slings around summit blocks.

Photo: Randall Weekley

Bullwinkle Tower

The Remnant

The best view of this pinnacle is from the first pullout south of Balanced Rock. It is the southernmost isolated tower when looking east toward The Windows section of the park.

THE REMNANT I, 5.9+, 1 pitch, 80 feet (24m)

First Ascent: Frosty Weller, Mike Bryan, October 1990.

Location and Access: Climb the north face to a short corner with a 4" to 6" crack to a belay on a ledge. Solo up the last 15 feet (5m) to the summit.

Paraphernalia: Friends (1) set; a few wired nuts.

Descent: One single-rope rappel from belay ledge on the west end of the formation. A sling around a block was used by the first ascent party.

The Windows

From the visitor center drive 9.1 miles (14.6km) to The Windows spur road which branches to the right (east). From the intersection drive 2.4 miles (3.9km) further to The Windows parking and viewing area. Restrooms without water, are available.

THE WISHBONE I, 5.8, A2+, 1 pitch, 80 feet (24m)

First Ascent: Keen Butterworth, solo, 24 November 1994 (Thanksgiving Day).

Location and Access: This spire is located just north of the trail to North Window, 100 yards (91m) northeast of the parking lot. As one hikes to North Window it is the closest tower to the parking area. The route climbs an obvious crack system on the north face of the landform.

Paraphernalia: Two sets of Friends, many nuts and a small selection of knifeblades and Lost Arrows (minimal nailing).

Descent: One rappel down the route from double anchors.

Tonka Tower

Tonka Tower is located in the furthest tower group right and south of Turret Arch. As viewed from The Windows parking area, the tower is second from the left of the landforms.

TONKA TOWER II, 5.8, A0, 2 pitches, 150 feet (46m)

First Ascent: Earl Wiggins, Katy Cassidy, Chris Begue, Bill Schmausser, George Hurley, Fall 1988.

Location and Access: The route is at the left edge of the west face. Slings are visible from below.

Paraphernalia: Friends (1) set; a selection of Tri-cams; hexes; stoppers.

Descent: One 150-foot rappel (46m) down the east face to the ground.

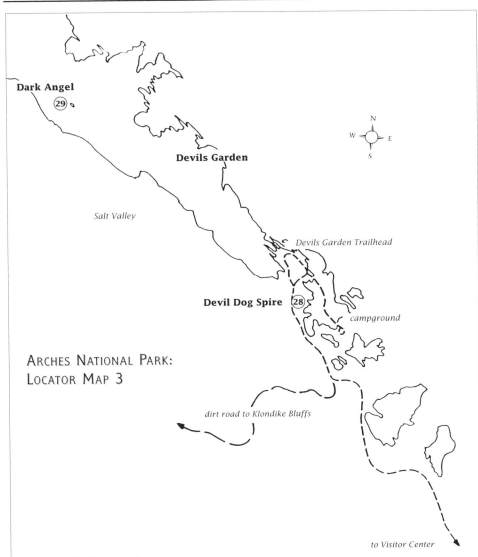

Dark Angel
(29)

Devils Garden

Salt Valley

N
W ✦ E
S

Devils Garden Trailhead

Devil Dog Spire (28)

campground

ARCHES NATIONAL PARK:
LOCATOR MAP 3

dirt road to Klondike Bluffs

to Visitor Center

Devils Garden Area

(28) **Devil Dog Spire:**
Industrial Disease

(29) **Dark Angel:** *West Face*

Devils Garden

Drive 18 miles (29km) from the visitor center to Devils Garden at the end of the park road. Restrooms and water are available in season only.

Devil Dog Spire

Devil Dog Spire is located near the main park road in the south Devils Garden area. As one approaches Devils Garden and can see the beginning of the oneway loop, the spire will be visible just to the right (east) of the road. **NOTE:** The rock is a critical resource area for nesting birds and is closed to climbing from 1 January through 30 June.

INDUSTRIAL DISEASE I, 5.11, 3 pitches, 170 feet (52m)

First Ascent: Scott Reynold, Max Kendall, October 1986.

Location and Access: Park on the right side of the road at the first paved pullout (picnic area) on the oneway loop road at Devils Garden. Cars parked at non-designated areas will likely be towed away. Devil Dog Spire is the nearest landform to the right of the park road at the point where the Devils Garden loop is first seen. *Industrial Disease* climbs the prominent crack system (facing the park road) splitting the two-tower formation of Devil Dog Spire. There is a drilled angle piton and a bolt fixed on Pitch 1. Pitch 2 climbs the short summit block by first pulling over a roof, then Pitch 3 continues via jams to the top.

Paraphernalia: One set of Friends and large hexes.

Descent: Two double-rope rappels down the north face.

Dark Angel

Dark Angel is the prominent spire visible for miles as one travels on the park road north from Balanced Rock. From the Devils Garden trailhead take the path to Double O Arch (2 miles, 3.2km). The spire is visible 0.5 mile further north from the arch.

WEST FACE I, 5.10 (or 5.9 A0), 2 pitches, 125 feet (38m)

First Ascent: Dave Rearick, Bob Kamps, 29 November 1962. First free ascent: Tim Toula, Kathy Zaiser (free-climbing the bolt ladder on the west, northwest side) 16 November 1986.

Location and Access: Begins on the south face, diagonals left and finishes on the west corner of the tower.

Pitch 1: Begin in a 40-foot (12m) 5.7 chimney on the left side of a detached flake on the southwest face. Above the chimney climb 15 feet (5m) of steep 5.9 finger and hands, then diagonal left to a belay on the west corner of the tower. The right side of the detached flake at the start of the pitch was climbed (5.8) by Harvey T. Carter, Steve Miller and David Hiser in the spring of 1965 during the second ascent of the spire.

Pitch 2: Make an awkward 5.7 move over a block directly above the belay. Continue 5.10 or 5.9 A0 past fixed anchors. The summit is gained after a loose 5.4 runout.

Paraphernalia: One set of Friends; medium stoppers.

Descent: One double-rope rappel from anchors on the summit.

(3) scramble to summit
20'

(2) 30'
(9m)

(1) 120'
(37m)

5.11 fingers

Devil Dog Spire

Industrial Disease I, 5.11

Klondike Bluffs

This region is located in the remote northwestern corner of the park. It is a mesa-like area that has been eroded away to form a series of buttes and towers. To approach, drive about 17 miles (27.4km) from the visitor center to a point near Skyline Arch. A dirt road branches to the southwest (left) and, if dry, is passable with 2-wheel drive vehicles. After several miles a sign marks the Tower Arch trailhead into the Klondike Bluffs.

The Marching Men
The Marching Men are a series of towers that are aligned in a north-south direction.

NORTH MARCHER I, 5.10+, 2 pitches, 140 feet (43m)
First Ascent: Leonard Coyne, Dennis Jackson, Stewart Green, November 1979. Second ascent: Todd Gordon, Diane Stang, 1984.

Location and Access: *North Marcher* can be seen by looking south from the middle section of the Tower Arch Trail. From this point *North Marcher* is the second tower north. The route is from the southwest.

The Marching Men   Photo: Charlie Fowler

Pitch 1: Make an easy traverse onto a ledge at the southwest side of the tower.
Pitch 2: Ascend a 5.4 chimney to a 5.9 handcrack which climbs to a 5.10+ offwidth overhand. Continue with poor protection to a 5.9 squeeze near the top.
Paraphernalia: Standard desert rack.
Descent: One double-rope rappel from drilled angles.

CUDDLEBUNNY TOWER I, 5.11, 1 pitch, 140 feet (43m)

First Ascent: Charlie Fowler, Rob Slater, Geoff Tabin, 30 December 1986.
Location and Access: The tower is located three formations south of *North Marcher*. Begin at the crack in the middle of the southwest face. Climb 5.11 fingers, then hands, then a 5.10 offwidth near the summit.
Paraphernalia: Three sets of Friends.
Descent: Rappel off the other side.

Perhaps this is the loveliest hour of the day, though it's hard to choose. Much depends on the season. In mid-summer the sweetest hour begins at sundown, after the awful heat of the afternoon. But now, in April, we'll take the opposite, that hour beginning with the sunrise.

Edward Abbey–*Desert Solitaire*

Photo: Jim Bodenhamer

Rob Slater on the first pitch of Islet-in-the Sky

CANYONLANDS NATIONAL PARK

The shadows of foliage, the drift of clouds, the fall of rain upon leaves, the sound of running waters - all the gentler qualities of nature that minor poets love to juggle with - are missing on the desert. It is stern, harsh, and at first repellent. But what tongue shall tell the majesty of it, the eternal strength of it, the poetry of its wide-spread chaos, the sublimity of its lonely desolation. And who shall paint the splendor of its light; and from the rising up of the sun to the going down of the moon over the iron mountains, the glory of its wondrous coloring! It is a gaunt land of splintered peaks, torn valleys, and hot skies.

John C. Van Dyke, 1901

Edward Abbey succinctly describes the area of Canyonlands National Park as "the least inhabited, least inhibited, least developed, least improved, least civilized,...most arid, most hostile, most lonesome, most grim, bleak, barren, desolate, and savage quarter of the state of Utah–the best part by far."

Situated in southeastern Utah, the park is trisected by the Green and Colorado Rivers, which form a great "Y," the west side created by the canyons of the Green River, the east side by the canyons of the Colorado. The land in between is a high level mesa. At its southern tip is the Island-in-the-Sky, a 12 mile (19.3km) long remnant of a large mesa.

The area comprising the park is unique in that the vast region was not first a national monument or protected by a wilderness designation as were many other national parks; it was simply public domain and vulnerable to exploitation. Its relatively pristine condition at the time it was entered into the national park system is due largely to its isolation. President Johnson signed the proclamation creating Canyonlands National Park on 12 September 1964. It was enlarged in 1971 and now at 527 square miles (848 square kilometers), is Utah's largest national park. Elevation ranges from 3,700 feet (1,128m) at the southwest boundary near the head of Lake Powell, to more than 7,000 feet (2,134m) above Salt Creek, at its southeast border.

Location and access

Island-in-the-Sky The Island-in-the-Sky is a large 6000 foot (1829m) high and relatively flat mesa, the apex of land separating the canyons of the Green and Colorado Rivers lying 2000 feet (610m) below. It is reached via State Highway 313 located 9 miles (14.5km) north of Moab on U.S. 191. Seventeen miles (27km) from its junction with U.S. 191, the road branches 4 miles (6.5km) southeast to Dead Horse Point State Park, a dramatic view of a Colorado River section known as the upper Grand Canyon. A short distance straight ahead from the Dead Horse Point turnoff the road leads to the Island-in-the-Sky visitor center where permits, upgraded road conditions, maps, books, film, posters, and other visitor amenities are available (but no free water). The center also has a small display of the regions geology, flora, and fauna.

At the entrance to Island-in-the-Sky is The Neck, a narrow strip of land blocked by early Indians and ranchers so they could used the steep-walled island mesa as a natural corral. At the southern tip of Island-in-the-Sky is Grand View Point, located at the apex of the mesa, 6080 feet (1853m) above sea level. From the overlook at Grand View Point the towers of Monument Basin can be seen directly below the rim. Grand View Point is described in a park brochure as having "overwhelming vistas of almost incomprehensible dimensions." The views span canyon upon canyon to a horizon nearly 100 miles (160km) distant. Dotted throughout the vista are the island mountains - the Abajos south, the La Sals east and the Henrys southwest. A few miles just north of the Island the panorama includes the 180 mile (290km) Book Cliffs and the vast majority of the twenty-eight thousand square mile area of the Canyonlands Province of the Colorado Plateau.

White Rim of the Island-in-the-Sky Twelve hundred feet (366m) below the commanding Island-in-the-Sky, the White Rim member of the upper Cutler Formation circumvents the mesa through some of the most spectacular scenery in all of the Colorado Plateau. This broad bench encircles the east, south, and west perimeters 1,000 feet (305m) above the river, forming a middle world in the park that is only accessible by vehicle via the rough Shafer Road, descending 1200 feet (366m) in about 4 miles (6.4km) from the Island, the Potash Road which joins the White Rim Road near the bottom of the Shafer Road, or from Mineral Bottom via the Horsethief Trail near the northwest boundary of the park. The White Rim Road loop covers a distance of 99.8 miles (160.5km). It generally requires two days of slow four-wheel driving. Reservations are required for any camping along the way.

The Needles The Needles district of the park is located south and east of the confluence of the Green and Colorado Rivers. It is reached from U.S. 191 via State Highway 211, 40 miles (64km) south of Moab (14 miles–22.5km–north of Monticello, then 38 miles–61km–west down Indian Creek). This district includes a dense array of buttes, arches, sheer walled canyons with numerous petroglyphs and pictographs, and many ancient Indian ruins. Part of the region encompasses Chesler Park, a 960 acre grassy meadow offering a stunning contrast to surrounding barren rock. The Needles district is one of the best developed in the park. Entrance to numerous hiking trails, and four-wheel-drive roads in a variety of canyons is over Elephant Hill, located 3 miles (5km) from Squaw Flat Campground. This difficult entrance to the interior of the district passes over a 40 percent grade and should be attempted only by veteran four-wheel-drivers.

The Maze The Maze district of the park is the distant land west of the Green River, south and east of the confluence of the Green and the Colorado. The early Indian name for the region, toom-pin wu-near' tu-weap , translates to "Land of Standing Rocks." This district is considered one of the most remote and inaccessible regions in the continental United States. Difficult to reach, it receives comparatively few visitors. Included in this primitive area are the mesas, buttes, and towers of the Doll House, the Fins, Ernies Country, and a 30 square mile (48km) "maze" of chaotically jumbled canyons.

The Maze, isolated from the other districts of the park by the Green and Colorado Rivers, and the jumbled nature of the terrain, makes its approach long and roundabout. The Hans Flat Ranger Station is the principal entrance into this region. It is reached from Utah 24, located 36 miles (58km) south of Green River and 21 miles (34km) north of Hanksville. This is a point just south of the west turn to Goblin Valley State Park. The approach to Hans Flat crosses 46 miles of open San Rafael Desert. At the Hans Flat Ranger Station three roads branch to remote regions of the district. A dirt track spurs northeast to Cleopatra's Chair and Panorama Point (four-wheel-drive). Another four-wheel-drive track branches north along The Spur rounding the head of Millard Canyon and on to Horseshoe Canyon. Branching south from the Ranger Station a dirt track goes to the head of the Flint Trail (difficult four-wheel-drive) where it descends sharply over the rim of the Orange Cliffs. Three miles (5km) beyond, the road meets the Hite approach road (40 miles, 64km, north of the marina). A branch of this road leads out past Ernie's Country to the Land of Standing Rocks (toward the Doll House) where The Wall, Lizard Rock, the Plug, and Standing Rock preside near the heart of the Maze canyon system. A north turn at the foot of the Flint Trail leads to Elaterite Butte, 80 miles (129km) from the nearest pavement (170 miles, 274km, from park headquarters in Moab). Beyond Elaterite Butte the trail passes Ekker Butte and continues many miles beyond to the looming Buttes of the Cross.

Approach from Hite Marina is made by an unmarked north turn from Utah 95 on the only road (four-wheel-drive) between the bridges over the Colorado and Dirty Devil Rivers. This road passes the Middle Finger and Sewing Machine Needle and continues via a circuitous route through terrain cut by spectacular canyons, buttes and towers. It ends at a 4-way junction where two Maze district four-wheel-drive roads converge.

Glen Canyon National Recreation Area Since Glen Canyon National Recreation Area border Canyonlands National Park on the west and south, it is included in this chapter. John Wesley Powell writes during his 1869 maiden voyage down the Colorado "This lands is...a curious ensemble of wonderful features–carved walls, royal arches, glens, alcoves, gulches, mounds and monuments. We decided to call it Glen Canyon." This unit of the National park Service is the largest park area in Utah and Arizona and is one of the largest in the continental U.S. It comprises 1875 square miles (1,200,00 acres) of rugged and remote terrain. From north to south its boundaries extend over 150 air miles (241km). It includes nearly all of the Colorado River from Canyonlands National Park in the north to near the Grand Canyon border in the south. Included in the recreation area are regions reaching far up the arms of the San Juan and Escalante rivers. It borders Canyonlands at the northwest perimeter of the park and includes spectacular sections of the Orange Cliffs (Robbers Roost) and the Green River. Formal boundaries were established by an act of Congress in 1972, through a large part of the region was established by executive order in 1958 during the construction of Glen Canyon Dam.

The Glen Canyon National Recreation Area differs from National Parks, because it is open to multiple use, including mining and grazing, with recreation being its primary use. Central to the area is Lake Powell, one of the world's largest man-made reservoirs, extending for nearly 200 miles (322km) north from Glen Canyon Dam to the lower reaches of Cataract Canyon. Because the lake is contained in the rugged finger tributaries of the Colorado River, the topography of the lake's shoreline is ten time longer that the lake itself. Although the lake is enormous–it is 186 miles (288km) long with 96 major side canyons and 1,960 miles of shoreline, longer than Washington, Oregon and California combined–it comprises only 13% of the park's 1875 Square miles. Before the remote vastness of Glen Canyon became inundated by the static reservoir of Lake Powell (water began flooding the canyon in 1963) the canyon was known as one of the most beautiful regions on the planet. It was named by the Powell expeditions of 1869 for its many lovely oases of vegetation and wildlife and the serene and gentle river. With the flooding, the national treasure of thousands of Anasazi ruins and writings were lost. Today the lake is a playground for millions, where heavily used beach areas are occasionally closed. Boaters and campers should bring and use porta-potties. There are five marinas giving easy access to the region's vast remoteness. It was originally predicted by the planners of Lake Powell that annual visitation would approach half a million by the year 2000, Its location is within a day's drive of Albuquerque, Phoenix, Los Angeles, San Diego, Las Vegas, Salt Lake City and Denver. In 1995, annual visitation exceeded 3 million and is climbing season by season.

For the most part, the lake is a reservoir entombing the undisputed jewel of the Colorado Plateau so that hydroelectric power may be generated to support modern communities as far away as California, Colorado and Nevada. But the land beyond the lake, the remote rugged land of Glen Canyon National Recreation Area is only arbitrarily separated from Canyonlands National Park and Capitol Reef National Park. All the splendor of the parkland and more is to be found there.

History

The earliest people to enter this area were prehistoric Indians who hunted game and gathered berries, seeds, nuts, and other native foods thousands of years ago. About 1300 years before present time Ancestral Puebloans (Anasazi) migrated from the area around Mesa Verde. At first only a few families lived in Canyonlands, but by the 1200s up to 1000 people lived here is stone pueblos. The Anasazi planted corn, beans, squash and foraged for food. They are believed to have been responsible for the rock art in the region. The two forms of rock art in existence, petroglyphs and pictographs are frequently confused. An easy way to differentiate between them is to remember that petroglyphs are "pecked" into the rock with a hammerstone and pictographs are painted on the rock with organic or mineral pigments. As in other area of the Colorado Plateau the ancient Puebloans abandoned this region about 700 years ago for reasons thought to be a combination of extensive drought and lack of resources. They are believed to have moved south to the Rio Grand.

The earliest penetration of what is now southeastern Utah by white men was the Dominquez-Escalante expedition of 1776. They crossed the Colorado River Gorge at an area that became known as the Crossing of the Fathers, now Padre Bay of Lake Powell; however, for the most part their explorations skirted the heart of canyon country. There is evidence that trappers and prospectors entered the area of the present parkland in the early 1800s, but few physical indications of their passing remain.

In 1859 an expedition of the U.S. Army Corps of Topographical Engineers, led by Captain John N. Macomb, left Santa Fe, and followed the Dominquez-Escalante route into southwestern Colorado. The survey team then branched west, entering Utah east of the Abajo Mountains. The focus of the expedition was to explore and map the confluence of the two great rivers, the Green and the Grand (now the Colorado), and to take notice of any mineral value in the terrain they crossed. The expedition succeeded as the first to map southeastern Utah, outline the geologic structure of the region, and describe in detail a segment of the Old Spanish Trail– an important trade route used for many years between Santa Fe and Monterey, California. Also they made the first discovery of dinosaur fossils in North America. Their accomplishments contributed significantly to scientific understanding of the Colorado Plateau.

Dr. John S. Newberry, the expedition diarist, was the first to describe the area of present day Canyonlands National Park. Dr. Newberry writes, "In the southwest was a long line of spires of white stone [the Needles], standing on red bases, thousands in number, but so slender as to recall the most delicate carving in ivory or the fairy architecture of some Gothic cathedral; yet many, perhaps most, were over five hundred feet in height, and thickly set in a narrow belt or series some miles in length. Their appearance was so strange and beautiful as to call out exclamations of delight from all our party."

From a view point 1,200 feet above the confluence of the two rivers, Dr. Newberry wrote, "The great cañon of the Lower Colorado (the Grand Canyon), with its cliffs a mile in height, affords grander and more impressive scenes, but those having far less variety and beauty of detail than this. From the pinnacle on which we stood the eye swept over an area some fifty miles in diameter, everywhere marked by features of more than ordinary interest: lofty lines of massive mesas rising in successive steps to form the frame of the picture; the interval between them more than 2,000 feet below their summits. A great basin or sunken plain lay stretched out before us as on a map. Not a particle of vegetation was anywhere discernible; nothing but bare and barren rocks of rich and varied colors shimmering in the sunlight. Scattered over the plain were thousands of domes, towers, columns, spires, of every conceivable form and size. Among these, by far the most remarkable was the forest of Gothic spires [the Needles], first and imperfectly seen as we issued from the mouth of the Cañon Colorado. Nothing I can say will give an adequate idea of the singular and surprising appearance which they presented from this new and advantageous point of view. Singly, or in groups, they extend like a belt of timber for a distance of several miles. Nothing in nature or in art offers a parallel to these singular objects, but some idea of their appearance may be gained by imagining the island of New York thickly set with spires like that of Trinity Church, but many of them full twice its height. Scarcely less striking features in the landscape were the innumerable cañons by which the plain is cut. In every direction they ran and ramified deep, dark, and ragged, impassable to everything but the winged bird."

It is interesting to note that Captain Macomb's enthusiasm for the grandeur of canyonlands was much different from that of Dr. Newberry. Macomb wrote, "I cannot conceive of a more worthless and impracticable region than the one we now found ourselves in."

Ten years later, in 1869, Major John Wesley Powell made the first documented journey down the Green and Colorado Rivers. Although he had lost his right arm in the Civil War at the Battle of Shiloh seven years before, at the confluence of the two rivers Powell made the strenuous ascent to the rim rock and took detailed notes of what he saw. He then travelled down Cataract Canyon, and named it, before continuing through the Grand Canyon.

Major Powell again descended the Colorado River in 1871, naming and mapping the land he traversed. Other explorers followed. Prospectors penetrated deeper into canyonlands looking for gold, silver, or copper but finding little. Cowboys and sheepherders entered seeking the sparse grassland and the few permanent creeks and water seeps located mostly at the fringe of the canyon country. Meager pockets of gas and oil were discovered in later years, but it was not until the early 1950s during the uranium boom days that widespread exploration of the land was to occur. The ore was much in demand for use in the making of atomic bombs, and more recently, to fuel atomic power plants. During the decade to follow, the equivalent of a modern-day gold fever prompted prospectors to systematically search the land by air or extensively by four-wheel-drive vehicles. The widespread exploration taking place during the fortune-seeking mania of the day produced nearly all the roads that now give access to the parkland and surrounding terrain. Massive mineral surveys and detailed geologic maps were produced by both federal and state agencies, and knowledge of canyonlands was greatly increased.

The canyonlands territory was the last in the continental United States to be explored. As more people visited the area it became increasingly known that this isolated sector of the country held a magic to be found nowhere else. Former Secretary of the Interior, Stewart Udall, upon touring the canyon country stated, "Acre for acre, the canyonlands of Utah are the most spectacular in the world." But even before the access gained by the uranium days, as early as the 1930s, Park Service recreational planner Paul V. Brown, in a report to park planner George W. Olcott wrote, "Do you recall that first terrifying revolt of our physical bodies at being subjected to such overwhelming and unaccustomed scale of landscape as we looked down, down, down into the abyss of that writhing cataclysm? Back in normal surroundings, it is easy to smile in recollection of the violent denial that rose within us as the shock of that scene pounded through our veins, as if the once too insolent flesh was protesting over this sudden dwarfing comparison of its puniness to the mighty forces of nature."

Visitor Center

Maps   One of the most useful maps for Canyonlands National Park is the large USGS topographic quadrangle titled "Canyonlands National Park and Vicinity." This large (3'8"-by-4'10") map was compiled in 1969 from 1:62 500-scale maps dated 1951 to 1968 and from aerial photographs taken in 1968. Although this map is dated, it gives a complete overview of the three districts of the park along with the proximity of surrounding areas, including Moab, Canyon Rims Recreation Area (the region bordering the park to the east, not named since it had not yet been designated when the map was made), Indian Creek, and the Glen Canyon National Recreation Area (bordering the park to the west). The map is for sale for an unbelievable $4 through the non-profit Canyonlands Natural History Association at Arches and Canyonlands National Parks, Natural Bridges National Monument and the Moab Information Center. One may purchase membership to the Natural History Association for $20 per year ($10 for renewal) and receive a 20% discount on merchandise sold at their sales areas.

Also useful (although of lesser value for relationships to surrounding areas) is the "Trails Illustrated" series to the parks of the Colorado Plateau. These maps were updated in late 1980s and early 1990s, and as a result include names (such as Moses and Zeus Towers in Taylor Canyon) that were not named at the time the large USGS map was compiled.

The Trails Illustrated series maps are printed on 100% plastic tearproof and water resistant material but are subject to damage by petroleum products like camp fuel and sunscreen.

Geology and geography

Wingate Sandstone is the predominate rock upon which climbs are established throughout Canyonlands, including Castleton Tower, Moses and the walls of Indian Creek. Unique in that it erodes slowly, fracturing along straight vertical planes, Wingate is very angular in appearance, often with chimneys and crack systems remaining the same size for a hundred feet or more.

Wingate rock is someitmes confused with Navajo Sandstone when its Kayenta cap rock has eroded away and its form has changed from a rush color to lighter-colored rounded domes. Examples of this effect are The Bride, near Moab, and the Coke Ovens in Colorado National Monument. Where this has happened the rock will be extremely soft and nearly impossible to place belay or rappel anchors on.

Above the cross-bedded Kayenta (atop the Wingate) is Navajo Sandstone. Most routes of this relatively softer rock are found throughout Zion National Park and along Wall Street near Moab. Like the Wingate, it is of aeolian (wind deposited) deposition, fine grained and of whiteish color.

Below the Wingate in descending order of age is the slope-forming Chinle (no climbs established) and the red-to-maroon-colored Moenkopi of mudflat deposition. The Moenkopi is the most recognizable stratum of rock on the desert. It resembles a chocolate layer cake and often appears with thin horizontal bands of light green (organic deposition). At the time of deposition, the Moenkopi Formation was a 200-mile (322km) flat, level flood plain which stretched from present day western Colorado to western Utah. Few climbs exist on the Moenkopi although it is the cap rock of the Fisher Towers.

The Rivers One of Major John Wesley Powell's men christened the Colorado River "The Dragon." Above the confluence it sleeps, but south of the confluence it is formidable, roaring ferociously through Cataract Canyon, a challenging and sometimes deadly stretch.

As the Green and Colorado carved the canyonlands, it is the rivers which will inevitably return them to level land. The rivers rasp their way through layer after layer of rock by carving a gorge no wider than the river itself. Canyon walls are undercut and succumb to the laws of gravity. Big rocks are reduced to little rocks and little rocks to particles of sand washed to the Gulf of California in Mexico. Canyons are formed from the original river gorge aided by a complicated network of tributaries. The system resembles branches of a tree smaller and more numerous as they move further from the main trunk. Occasional flash floods contribute enormously to endless erosion, sweeping debris from the higher land to the river. Geologists estimate that the river washes away three cubic miles of rock each century.

From the town of Green River, the Green glides at the base of deep canyon walls through Labyrinth and Stillwater canyons to confluence with the Colorado River 120 miles (193km) below. The Colorado River runs for 64 miles (103km) from Moab to the confluence (47 miles, 75.6km, from Potash).

Above the confluence of the Green and Colorado Rivers, layers of rock dip slightly northward, so that the rivers flows against the texture of the rock. Consequently they are breaked and glide at gentle grades. The Green drops less than a foot per mile (1.6km) through Labyrinth and Stillwater Canyons, and the Colorado meanders smoothly through its canyons at a similar rate. The flow is so lazy that the Green makes a double loop at Bowknot Bend and the Colorado slides back upon itself in a great circle at The Goose Neck (below Dead Horse Point) and further downstream at the Loop.

Below the confluence the river flows with the texture of the rock. The grade steepens dramatically to a point where, through Cataract Canyon, it drops an average of 8 feet (2.4m) per mile, exceeding the gradient in the Grand Canyon. At The Big Drop, the river plunges thirty feet (9m) in one mile (1.6km). There were 52 rapids before Lake Powell inundated lower Cataract Canyon in the early 1960s, now only 26 remain. No dams restrict the flow of the Green and Colorado Rivers for hundreds of miles upstream from Cataract Canyon, and since the flow of the lower Colorado beyond this point is programmed from Glen Canyon Dam, Cataract Canyon is a unique remnant of the untamed river of Major Powell's day.

Flora and fauna

Potholes, whether dry or filled with rain water, are vulnerable to degradation by the unknowing visitor. Although potholes appear to be lifeless, they are home to a variety of organisms which may be destroyed by pollution from human contact (sunscreen, sweat, insect repellents, pets, and other foreign materials). Numerous creatures have adapted to the desert's wet and dry cycle including crustaceans, insects, tadpoles, frogs, and snails. Many creatures aestivate, hibernate, or are dormant during dry periods and awaken to intense life when moisture returns. It is important for the health of the desert that we do not disturb these fragile islands of life. Unless it is a medical emergency, it is unconscionable to bathe, swim, or trample wet or dry potholes. Please be a responsible visitor in this very special land.

Climate

Throughout the Colorado Plateau, spring and autumn are the most pleasant months for visits. During the latter part of April and the first week or two of May, desert wildflowers are in dramatic display. In the Spring relentless winds are common. Thundershowers can be expected Spring, Summer, and Fall. Although Canyonlands summer temperatures during June, July, and August are often in the 100-degree range, days are much less unpleasant than in humid areas. There have been a number of deaths from lightning strikes throughout the years. Summer thunder storms are especially dangerous. A few precautions if lightning occurs: avoid high ground, moist regions such as alcoves or drainages, tall trees; natural lightning rods include mountain bikes and climbing hardware. If possible, stay in your vehicle until the storm passes, or crouch on the ground, preferably on something to insulate the body. Do not become a lightning rod by bunching together with your comrades.

Flash floods are another real hazard. They can appear from nowhere and are frequently powerful enough to dislodge large boulders, uproot trees, and tumble vehicles like weightless toys. Avoid washes and dry arroyos, even though a storm seems distant. On the positive side, summer thunderstorms produce spectacular waterfalls cascading from slickrock canyon rims. Locals frequently jam the River Road (State 128 east of Moab) during cloudbursts to view more than a dozen major waterfalls within the first mile (1.6km).

Precautions and regulations

Many of the following regulations and prohibitions are from the January 1995, Canyonlands National Park backcountry management plan.

A permit is not required for climbing in Canyonlands National Park. However, if the climbing stay is overnight, a backcountry use permit is required and climbers are subject to all provisions for minimum impact camping. Some formations may be closed to climbing at various times, thus climbers should always check at park headquarters or a ranger station before making their intended ascent. Overnight permits may be obtained in Moab at Canyonlands National Park headquarters, 2282 South West Resource Boulevard (801 259-3911), or at any ranger station. To save the delicate cryptobiotic soil, please remember to walk on slickrock, in drainages, or on paths whenever possible while approaching climbs.

Climbing within the park is limited to free climbing or clean aid climbing. No new climbing hardware may be left in a fixed location; however, if an existing bolt or other hardware item is unsafe, it may be replaced. This limits all climbing to existing routes or new routes not requiring placement of fixed anchors. Protection may not be placed with the use of a hammer except to replace existing belay and rappel anchors and bolts on existing routes, or for emergency self-rescue. Software left in place must match the rock surface in color. The intentional removal of lichen or plants from rock is prohibited. The physical altering of rock faces, such as by chiseling, glue reinforcement of existing holds, and gluing of new holds is prohibited. The use of motorized power drills is prohibited. Technical rock climbing is prohibited in the Salt Creek Archeological District of the Needles, the detached Horseshoe Canyon Unit of the Maze District, and on any arch or natural bridge named on the United States Geological Survey 1:62,500 topographic map of Canyonlands National Park and Vicinity, with the exception of Washer Woman Arch. Climbing, ascending, descending, or traversing an archeological site or cultural resource is also prohibited.

Note: Although only clean aid climbing is legal within Canyonlands National Park, a number of classic aid climbs have been included in this section with the anticipation that many will be climbed clean and thus come within the scope of the new backcountry management regulations.

Wood fires are not allowed in the park. One may only have charcoal fires in designated camp sites with the use of a firepan (not furnished by the park), and ashes must be packed out. Water is not available at the Island-in-the-Sky or the Maze visitor centers. Recommended minimum per day per person is one gallon and should be doubled for those involved in strenuous activities such as mountain biking or climbing. Pets are not allowed on back country trails and must be on a leash at parking areas. If you plan to climb in the park your pet should be left at home or boarded with a kennel located through a phone directory in Moab.

Toilets and Human Waste Toilets are provided along backcountry roads at heavily used day use locations as well as at designated campsites in the Island-in-the-Sky and Needles districts. They are not provided in the Maze because of the difficulty of pumper-truck access. Campers at vehicle campsites in the Maze are required to carry out solid human waste in a portable toilet system. Toilet systems are available through boating and RV supply stores and may be rented from some tour companies. Where toilets are not provided and carry out is not required, solid human waste should be buried in "catholes." A cathole is a small hole excavated 6 to 8 inches (15 to 20cm) deep, at least 300 feet (91m) from water sources (including seeps, potholes, springs, streams, and the Green and Colorado Rivers), potential water sources (arroyos or dry washes), archeological or historical sites, alcoves or rock shelters, and campsites. Used toilet paper, feminine hygiene products, diapers, or any other paper product must be carried out of the park in a sanitary manner, such as self-sealing plastic bags. Burning toilet paper is prohibited.

Maintained backcountry toilets in The Needles and Island-in-the-Sky districts may be phased out in the future and portable toilets to be carried by campers will probably be required.

Emergencies If climbing in the White Rim or Taylor Canyon areas, report problems to the Island visitor center, or dial 911 at the telephone near the building. If an emergency occurs after visitor center hours, rangers may be notified at their residence behind the visitor center.

Paraphernalia

A standard desert climbing rack for free climbs includes two sets of Friends, one set of TCUs, one set of stoppers and quickdraws with 24" slings for multiple pitch climbs.

Order of climbs

Routes begin left to right along the Green River at the northwestern border of the park, followed by Taylor Canyon, then climbs located downriver. Island-in-the-Sky, in the northern sector of the park, is followed by The White Rim Area, then south to The Needles District in the southeast area of Canyonlands. The final section covers climbs in the remote Maze District in the southwest area of the park.

Photo: Jeff Widen

Dale Tower

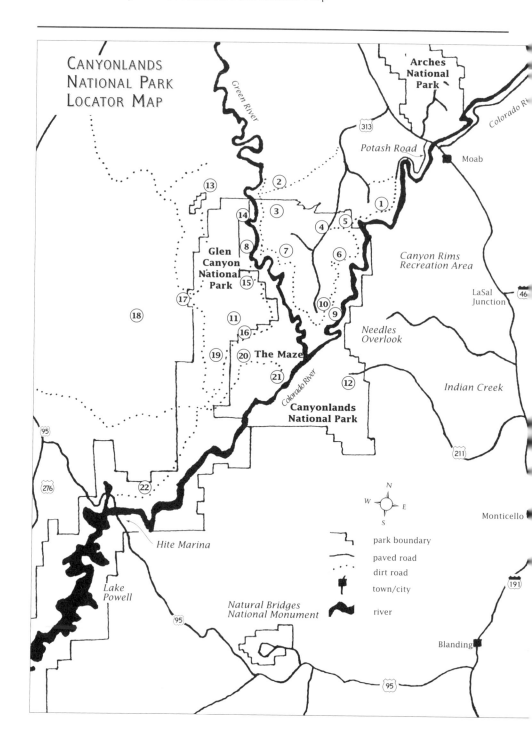

1. Dead Horse Point State Park

2. Horsethief Road

3. Taylor Canyon:
   Moses and Zeus

4. Island-In-The-Sky Visitor Center

5. Shaefer Road

6. Washer Woman, Monster Tower:
   Airport Tower

7. Willow Flats Campground
   Green River Overlook

8. Candlestick Tower

9. Monument Basin

10. Grand Viewpoint

11. Cleopatra's Chair

12. Squaw Flat Campground:
    The Needles

13. Horseshoe Canyon:
    Antelope Tower

14. Turks Head

15. Buttes of The Cross

16. Ekker Butte

17. Hans Flat Ranger Station

18. The Pinnacles

19. Bagpipe Butte

20. Elaterite Butte

21. Standing Rock, The Maze

22. The Sewing Machine Needle,
    The Middle Finger

Seoul Games

Photo: Eric Bjørnstad

Green River Area

Climbs in this area are on Wingate walls bordering the Green River within the park boundaries, before (north) reaching Taylor Canyon and below (south of) Taylor Canyon. The routes *Smokin' Deal*, *Marlboro Cig*, and *Seoul Games* are included in this chapter for their geographic location a few tenths of a mile north of the park boundary. To approach, drive 9 miles (14.5km) north of Moab on U.S. 191. Turn left (west) on State 313 where a sign will read "Island-in-the-Sky District of Canyonlands National Park and Dead Horse Point State Park." Just before Mile Post 10 (12.3 miles, 19.8km, from U.S. 191) turn right (west) onto the dirt Horsethief Trail: 13.2 miles (21.2km) further, the trail descends 2000 feet (610m) in 1.5 miles (2.4km) via spectacular switchbacks to Horsethief Bottom at the Green River. This is the western beginning of the White Rim Road. Turn left (downriver) and drive to the park boundary signs (3.9 miles, 6.2km).

SMOKIN' DEAL I, 5.10, 1 pitch, 60 feet (18m)

First Ascent: Gary Olsen, Bret Ruckman, September 1988.

Location and Access: *Smokin' Deal* is located at Point Bottom just north of the park boundary. The area is identified by a 50-yard-long (46m) pullout on the left which is an old road cut. Two lone cottonwood trees are visible 0.1 mile (0.16km) ahead of this point. The route is located 100 feet (30m) left of *Marlboro Cig*. Begin up an offwidth and climb to a tight handcrack in a face to a double-bolt anchor.

Paraphernalia: Standard desert rack, including six-inch crack protection.

Descent: Rappel the route.

MARLBORO CIG I, 5.9+, 1 pitch, 80 feet (24m), ★

First Ascent: Bret Ruckman, Gary Olsen, September 1988.

Location and Access: The route is located 600 feet (183m) left of *Seoul Games* and 100 feet (30m) right of *Smokin' Deal*. The route climbs a left-facing crack system. Slings are visible from below.

Paraphernalia: Friends (1) #2.5, #3.5.

Descent: Rappel from a single bolt.

SEOUL GAMES I, 5.11–, 1 pitch, 165 feet (50m), ★★★

First Ascent: Bret Ruckman, Gary Olsen, September 1988.

Location and Access: The route is located 600 feet (183m) right of *Marlboro Cig* and climbs a prominent right-facing dihedral identified by a large leaning boulder at its base. Lieback up and out of a hole, then stand atop the leaning boulder. Continue up a lieback corner. Slings are visible from the parking area. Photo on page 176.

Paraphernalia: Friends (4) #1, (5) #1.5, (5) #2, (5) #2.5, (2) #3.

Descent: Rappel the route from a two-bolt rappel point.

GLAD TO BE A TRAD I, 5.13a, 1 pitch, 165 feet (50m), ★★★★★

First Ascent: Steve Hong, Steve Carruthers.

Location and Access: The route is located right of *Seoul Games* and climbs a right-facing dihedral to a thin crack on the upper face.

Paraphernalia: Friends #2; TCUs; quickdraws.

Descent: Rappel the route.

Boundary Wall Area

These routes are located on the Wingate wall above or near the park boundary sign 3.9 miles (6.2km) downriver from the "Y" at the bottom of the Horsethief Trail switchbacks which is the beginning of the White Rim Road west.

KINDER AND GENTLER II, 5.11–, 1 pitch, ★

First Ascent: Bret Ruckman, Marco Cornacchione, May 1989.
Location and Access: The route is located left of *Circle of Quiet*, Begin up a right-facing dihedral. Photo on page 179.
Paraphernalia: Standard desert rack.
Descent: Rappel the route.

A CIRCLE OF QUIET II, 5.11d, 2 pitch, 150 feet (46m), ★★★★★

First Ascent: Bret Ruckman, Marco Cornacchione, May 1988. First Free Ascent: Bret Ruckman, Stuart Ruckman, May 1991.
Location and Access: The climb is just left of *Marco My Word*. The route begins at an area of stacked blocks on the right side of the wall above the boundary sign. Halfway up the route is a ledge and an optional belay. Slings are visible from below. Photo on page 179.
Paraphernalia: Friends (1) #1, (3) #1.5, (5) #2, (6) #2.5, (2) #3; TCUs (1), #.4, #.5, #.75.
Descent: Rappel the route.

MARCO MY WORD II, 5.10d, 1 pitch, 100 feet (30m), ★★

First Ascent: Marco Cornacchione, Bret Ruckman, May 1988.
Location and Access: The route is located just right of *A Circle of Quiet*. Slings are visible from below.
Paraphernalia: Friends (3) #4.
Descent: Rappel the route.

SHADOW CHASER I, 5.10+, 1 pitch, 65 feet (20m)

First Ascent: Bret Ruckman, Marco Cornacchione, May 1988.
Location and Access: The route is located 400 feet (122m) right of *Marco My Word*, on the south side of the same formation. Climb a right-facing corner with a funky start.
Paraphernalia: Unknown.
Descent: Rappel the route.

B.F.E. I, 5.11, 1 pitch, 165 feet (50m), ★★★★★

First Ascent: Bret Ruckman, Gary Olsen, September 1988.
Location and Access: *B.F.E.* is located above Saddle Horse Bottom. The route climbs the Wingate wall above an old wooden horse corral, obvious on the left 0.6 mile (0.9km) beyond the park boundary sign. To view the climb drive 0.1 mile (0.16km) beyond the corral, where the route with rappel slings becomes visible. *B.F.E.* climbs halfway up the wall and is located below the leftmost obvious deep chimney just inside the left profile of Wingate wall. Ascend a west-facing shallow eight-inch (20cm) dihedral, right-facing for 165 feet (50m). Begin behind a large pillar right of the dihedral and shuffle left atop a flake to a rest on its top. Continue up the dihedral past a pod and a small roof on the right, then one on the left. Photo on page 180.
Paraphernalia: Friends (3) #.5, (4) #.75, (5) #1, (5) #1.5, (3) #2, (5) #2.5, (3) #3.
Descent: Rappel the route from double-bolt anchors.

Photo: Eric Bjørnstad

From left to right: Kinder and Gentler, Circle of Quiet and Marco My Word

Photo: Eric Bjørnstad

B.F.E.

Horsethief Tower

Horsethief Tower is located above Saddle Horse Bottom across the Green River from the boundary sign to the park at the mouth of Horsethief Canyon in the Glen Canyon National Recreation Area (identified on the large USGS map "Canyonlands National Park and Vicinity"). It is included in this chapter due to its geographic proximity to the climbs at the park's northwest border. The tower is obvious directly ahead on the west side of the Green River, 2.7 miles (4.3km) from the "Y" at the bottom of the Horsethief Trail switchbacks.

To reach from Mineral Bottom, drive south to the boundary sign and cross the swift water of the Green by inner tube, canoe or raft.

RIVER PIRATES III, 5.10, 3 pitches, 300 feet (91m)

First Ascent: Ken Trout, Rusty Kirkpatrick, Kirk Miller, Ron Olevsky, 1984.
Location and Access: Approach the tower from the far right side of the northeast face.
Pitch 1: From the right side of the northeast face, chimney up to the right side of an obvious saddle, 5.8.
Pitch 2: Continue up a wide crack for 75 feet (23m), past a protection bolt, to a ledge.
Pitch 3: After moving up and right, spiral around the tower to the left. A large Tri-cam protects the crux, 100 feet (30m).
Paraphernalia: Standard desert rack, with extra #3.5, #4 Friends; a large Tri-cam for the crux.
Descent: Two double-rope rappels down the route, the first to the top of Pitch 2, the next to the ground.

Charlie Horse Needle

Charlie Horse Needle comes into view 1.2 miles (1.9km) downriver from the park boundary sign.

CHARLIE HORSE NEEDLE III, 5.11c, 3 pitches, 250 feet (76m)

First Ascent: Ron Olevsky, Joy Ungritch (5.7, A2), 2 May 1985.
Location and Access: The route ascends via aid up the crack system on the north face of the tower. Only the free *Sims-Hesse Variation* is now legal according to park regulations, thus further detail is not included in this description.

SIMS–HESSE VARIATION III, 5.11c, 3 pitches

First Accent: Ken Sims, Mark Hesse, Maura Hanning.
Location and Access: This was the first free ascent of the tower. The route climbs a crack system on the north face joining the original route at the second pitch, 5.10b. Pitch 2 is climbed at 5.10b and Pitch 3 at 5.11c.
Paraphernalia: Two sets of Friends, including half sizes; (1) #4, #7 Tri-cam; (12) nuts.
Descent: Rappel the route.

XX

hands

5.10 fist

5.10+

belay #1
in chimney
no fixed anchors

5.10 fist

Photo: Eric Bjørnstad

Backcountry Management Crack

Taylor Canyon

Taylor Canyon and Moses and Zeus Towers are identified on the Trails Illustrated maps of the park. Only Taylor Canyon is identified on the large USGS map of Canyonlands National Park and Vicinity.

Taylor Canyon drains west into the Green River. It is marked by a sign pointing to Moses and Zeus 2.5 miles (4km) downriver (south) from the park boundary sign. This location is at the extreme northwestern boundary of Canyonlands National Park. A chemical toilet is located at the entrance to the canyon.

Moses and its neighboring towers first come into view 2.3 miles (3.7km) up the Taylor Canyon road from the canyon's entrance.

The road up the canyon is generally passable by two-wheel drive vehicles with high clearance, but conditions will vary from season to season. Five miles (8km) up the canyon from the Green River the road ends at a primitive campsite with a chemical toilet. A permit is required for all overnight stays within the park, obtainable at the Island-in-the-Sky visitor center a short distance beyond the Horsethief Trail turn off on State Highway 313.

HAND OVER FIST I, 5.11d, 1 pitch, 160 feet (49m), ★★★

First Ascent: Bret Ruckman, Stuart Ruckman, 22 May 1991.

Location and Access: The route is located at the mouth of Taylor Canyon on a south-facing wall just right of an obvious arête. The climb has a very arduous approach due to the Moenkopi/Chinle cliff bands. Begin fist and climb over an overhang past two pods to double anchors.

Paraphernalia: Friends (3) #4, (2) #3, (1) #2.5, (2) #2.

Descent: Rappel the route.

BACKCOUNTRY MANAGEMENT CRACK (aka Slugfest) III, 5.10+, 2 pitches, 160 feet (49m)

First Ascent: Dave Medara, Lorne Glick, 6 November 1994.

Location and Access: This two-pitch route is located on a buttress above an old sheep camp 3.6 miles (5.8km) up Taylor Canyon. The route, with slings visible, is in view straight ahead of the road at a point three miles (4.8km) from the entrance to Taylor Canyon. The route is identified by its right-facing dihedral just left of a smooth wall reaching from bottom to top of the Wingate. The old sheepherders' camp from which *Backcountry Management Crack* is approached is formed by a split boulder and is covered with much graffiti. To approach the route hike to the base of the cliff and traverse left around the obvious prow of the buttress to its northwest facing side. The large right-facing corner will be obvious above. The route can be climbed in one pitch if one has enough big gear. Photo on page 182.

Paraphernalia: Two #3, many #3.5 and #4 Friends; smaller gear to belay at mid-height.

Descent: Rappel the route.

Left Canyon Crack and Seven-Up Crack

These climbs are located approximately 200 feet (61m) apart on the left side of the first canyon branching to the north (left) from Taylor Canyon.

LEFT CANYON CRACK I, 5.10, A2, 1 pitch, 150 feet (46m)

First Ascent: Steve Walker, Bert Stolp.

Location and Access: The route is located about 200 feet (61m) left of *Seven-up Crack* at a point where the wall is offset at the bottom, making the crack appear offwidth. Begin 5.9 hands, then 5.10 fingers that lead to A2 nailing and a hanging belay from (3) anchors. The route is legal only if it can be climbed with clean aid.

Paraphernalia: Standard desert rack.

Descent: Rappel the route.

Warning: Park regulations require all aid climbing on this route be clean aid. Traditional hammer aid is prohibited.

SEVEN-UP CRACK I, 5.10–, 1 pitch, 120 feet (37m)

First Ascent: Chris Begue, Kent Wheeler, Chuck Grossman, April 1986.

Location and Access: *Seven-up Crack* is located on the left side of the wall to the right of *Left Canyon Crack*. Ascend a hands/fistcrack to rappel anchors.

Paraphernalia: One set of Friends with extra #3, #4.

Descent: Rappel the route.

Photo: Jeff Widen

Moses Group

Moses

The five-mile (8km) Taylor Canyon road ends at a primitive camp with a chemical toilet. A designated trail leads in 1 mile (1.6km) to the base of Moses. The National Park Service encourages climbers to use minimum impact practices when visiting Taylor Canyon and other park areas. Please help preserve this fragile desert environment by staying on existing roads and trails, on slickrock or in drainages.

Moses has for some time been the second most popular desert tower climb (Castleton Tower first in popularity). Among the numerous ascents up its five routes, of note is the climb in 1991 by Alan Lester and Dave "Mr. Spider Mitt" Crawford of the *Primrose Dihedrals*, *Pale Fire*, and the *Dunn Route* in one exhaustive 12-hour day.

PALE FIRE (North Face Route) IV, 5.12, 4 pitches, 600 feet (183m)

First Ascent: Fred Beckey, Eric Bjørnstad, Jim Galvin, Tom Nephew, Gregory Markov (V, 5.8, A3, 6 pitches), 21-25 October 1972. First free ascent: *Pale Fire* is the free version of the North Face route. First ascent of *Pale Fire* was by Chip Chace, Charlie Fowler, May 1981. First solo ascent: Ron Olevsky, with aid, Fall 1982. The route is generally climbed in four pitches with a 198-foot rope (60m).

Location and Access: *Pale Fire* follows an obvious crack system on the north profile of the tower as one approaches from Taylor Canyon. This is a point left of the *Dunn Route*.

Pitch 1: Climb a thin flaring fingercrack at 5.12 (the crux). Ascend handcracks with bolts for protection, 5.10, 180 feet (60m).

Pitch 2: Continue up the handcrack, 5.10, 100 feet (30m).

Pitch 3: Climb a slab at 5.10+, 100 feet (30m).

Pitch 4: Continue to the summit, 5.8, 80 feet (24m).

Paraphernalia: Three sets of Friends #1 through #3, with (2) extra #2, (1) extra #1, #1.5, #2.5; (2) each #0, #1 TCUs; (1) set of wires; many quickdraws.

Descent: Rappel the *Diretissima Route*.

DUNN ROUTE IV, 5.11, 5 pitches, 600 feet (183m)

First Ascent: Jimmy Dunn, Stewart Green, Doug Snively, Kurt Rasmusson IV, 5.9, A4 1973. First free ascent: Jeff Achey, Glenn Randall, 1982.

Location and Access: This climb, the second ascent of Moses, is up the northwest edge of the landform right of *Pale Fire*.

Pitch 1: Begin with 5.9 face climbing to cracks to a hanging belay.

Pitch 2: Continue via 5.10- stemming cracks which trend right to a 5.9 chimney, or trend left into a broken 5.9 crack system. The left variation requires a 55-meter rope or a mid-point belay.

Pitch 3: Climb up then left to a belay below an overhanging handcrack, 5.8.

Pitch 4: Climb an overhanging 3.5" (9cm) handcrack (5.11) past fixed pitons then continue up a 5.9 chimney or if small enough burrow (5.8) up to belay bolts.

Pitch 5: Face climb to the summit, 5.8.

Paraphernalia: Two sets of Friends with extra #3.5 and #4; (2) #4 Camalots; (1) set of wires.

Descent: Rappel the *Diretissima Route*.

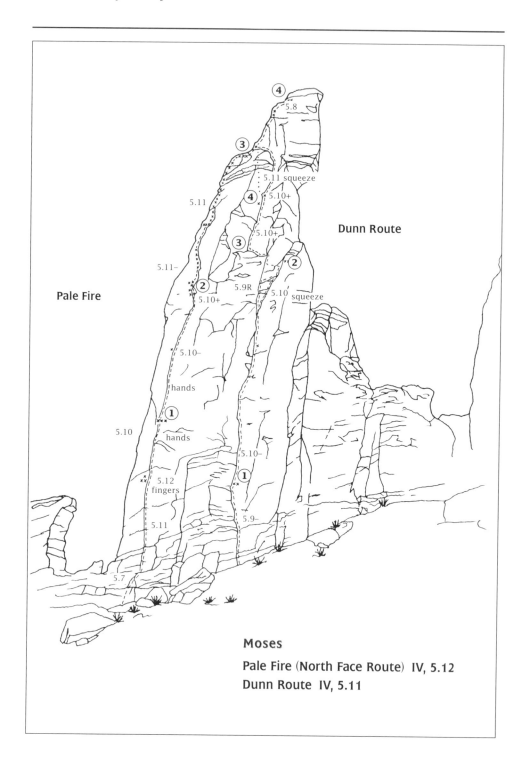

Dunn Route

Pale Fire

Moses
Pale Fire (North Face Route) IV, **5.12**
Dunn Route IV, **5.11**

PRIMROSE DIHEDRALS IV, 5.11+, 7 pitches, 565 feet (172m),
★★★★★

First Ascent: Ed Webster, solo, April 1979, (5.8, A3). First free ascent: Ed Webster, Steve Hong, October 1979.

Location and Access: *Primrose Dihedrals* climbs the southeast face of the tower.

Pitch 1: Chimney up a shallow inverted V-slot. Exit on the right side and continue to a good belay ledge, 5.11+, 60 feet (18m). Or traverse in from the notch to the right, 5.8.

Pitch 2: Climb a left-facing corner, 5.10 hands, then 5.9 lieback, to a stance beneath a small roof. Bypass the roof to the right, 5.10, to a stance (and bolt) and continue on 5.10 fingers, then follow a 5.9 lieback to a belay beneath a roof on the left.

Pitch 3: After clipping into a pin, downclimb 5.8 approximately 40 feet (12m) to 5.8 flakes on the left which lead 5.10- to a good belay ledge (with a bolt anchor). This is about 145 feet (44m) above the belay at the end of Pitch 1.

Pitch 4: Climb 5.9 fingers then around a small 5.10 roof. Continue via a long 5.10 dihedral, hand and fist, to a semi-hanging belay beneath "The Ear," an overhanging flake with a six-inch crack behind it.

Pitch 5: Climb 5.9 wedged blocks to The Ear.

Pitch 6: Climb The Ear via 5.11+ offwidth (eight-inch, using a bolt ladder for protection). A transition is made to a few lieback moves which widen to a tight squeeze chimney then a sloping belay ledge (with a bolt anchor). It is approximately 130 feet (40m) from the third to the sixth belay, 5.11+.

Pitch 7: Continue up a 5.8 chimney then face climb to the summit.

Paraphernalia: Friends (2) each #1, #2, #2.5, (3) each #1.5, #3, #3.5, additional #1, #1.5, #2, would be useful; (1) set of wires; many runners.

Descent: Rappel the *Diretissima Route*.

THE PROMISED LAND V, 5.10+, A3+, 6 pitches, 460 feet (140m)

First Ascent: Charlie Fowler, Sue Wint, May 1988.

Location and Access: The route climbs fracture lines directly up to the chin of Moses, then out the chin to the summit.

Pitch 1: The route begins offwidth with six thin pitons and climbs to the top of a pillar, 5.10.

Pitch 2: Face climb to a grove, then up and right, 5.10+.

Pitch 3: Climb via thin nailing to a ledge, A2.

Pitch 4: Continue to a good ledge, A2+.

Pitch 5: The crux is climbed with thin nailing (A3+) to the base of the chin. Continue out the chin (A2+) to a hanging belay.

Pitch 6: Climb to the summit via fixed bolts.

Paraphernalia: Two sets of Friends; (2) sets TCUs; #1 through #7 Tri-cams; (1) set of Rocks; (5) knifeblades; Lost Arrows; (6-8) Leepers; (2) ½", (2) ⅝", (5) ¾", (2) 1", (1) 1¼" angles; a wrench and keyhole hangers.

Descent: Rappel the *Diretissima Route*.

Warning: Park regulations require all aid climbing on this route be clean aid. Traditional hammer aid is prohibited.

SOUTH FACE DIRETISSIMA IV, 5.11a, A3, 6 pitches, 630 feet (192m)

First Ascent: Jim Beyer, solo (1½ days), 1990.

Location and Access: The climb is located between *Primrose Dihedrals* and *The Promised Land*. The first ascent used no bolts and was the fifth route established on the tower. The route begins 45 feet (14m) left of *Primrose Dihedrals*.

Pitch 1: Climb 5.10+ crack to a hanging belay.

Pitch 2: Traverse left, then up, to a belay ledge, 5.9, A2, 120 feet (37m).

Pitch 3: Climb a broken crack system to a hanging belay, 5.8, A2+, 130 feet (40m).

Pitch 4: Continue up the crack system which widens from fingers to five inches, 5.10+, 120 feet (37m).

Pitch 5: Climb a 5.6 chimney with a 5.8 exit move to a belay, 130 feet (37m).

Pitch 6: Reach the summit via 5.8 face climbing.

Paraphernalia: Friends (1) #3, #4; (2) sets of TCUs; #3 Camalot; 5", 6" tube chalks; wired nuts; (1) Birdbeak; (5) knifeblades; (8) Lost Arrows; (4) each angles to ¾"; (5) Leepers.

Descent: Rappel the route.

Warning: Park regulations require all aid climbing on this route be clean aid. Traditional hammer aid is prohibited.

DIRETISSIMA DIRECT START

This A3, 100-foot (30m) direct start was established by Ed Webster during the second ascent of the route, during which three bolt anchors were placed at each belay station. Begin directly below the crack system of *Diretissima* where a belay bolt is in place and two bolts on the overhang above.

Zeus

Zeus is the thin spire just east of (behind) Moses.

NORTHEAST FACE II, 5.7, A0, 2 pitches, 300 feet (91m)

First Ascent: Fred Beckey, Eric Bjørnstad, September 1970.

Location and Access: Bolts placed on the historic first ascent were chopped by an unknown party playing God, leaving behind the graffiti of bolt-hole scars.

SISYPHUS (aka South Face Dihedrals) III, 5.11+S, 4 pitches, 270 feet (82m), ★★★★★

First Ascent: Jimmy Dunn, Doug Snively, 1973. First free ascent: Chip Chace, Jeff Achey, October 1981.

Location and Access: The route climbs obvious dihedrals on the south face of the tower. There is a drilled-angle piton on the first pitch above the original bolt at the pod. The bulge on the third pitch is the crux climbed at 5.11+.

Paraphernalia: Friends (1) #3.5, #4, (2) each #1.5, #2, #2.5, #3; (3) each #1, (4) #.5, (2) each #0 TCUs; (1) set of wires.

Descent: Rappel the northeast face 75 feet (23m) then 150 feet (46m) to the ground.

Thracian Mare

Thracian Mare is the tower immediately west (in front) of Moses.

NORTH FACE III, 5.8, A3, 3 pitches, 250 feet (76m)

First Ascent: Ron Olevsky, solo, 1983.

Location and Access: Begin on the left side of the north face.

Pitch 1: Climb a strenuous left-facing dihedral, 5.8, 90 feet (27m).

Pitch 2: Continue up a varnished crack capped by a roof to a 5.8 chimney, 100 feet (30m).

Pitch 3: Ascend over the roof at the top of the chimney (A3) and climb to the northeast shoulder, then third class to the summit, 60 feet (18m).

Paraphernalia: Two sets of Friends with extra #1.5, #2, #2.5, #3; (2) #4 Camalots; (1) set of wires; (2) ½" angle piton, (1) ⅝", ¾" angle piton.

Descent: Rappel the route.

Warning: Park regulations require all aid climbing on this route be clean aid. Traditional hammer aid is prohibited.

THRACIAN KNIGHTMARE III, 5.11, 3 pitches, 250 (76m)

First Ascent: Chuck Grossman, Kent Wheeler, April 1986.

Location and Access: The route climbs a large right-facing flake near the right side of the west face, then ascends an obvious crack system to the summit.

Paraphernalia: Standard desert rack.

Descent: Rappel *North Face*.

WEST FACE III, 5.8, A3+, 250 feet (76m)

First Ascent: Davin Lindy, James Funsten, February 1992.

Location and Access: The route climbs a curving seam on the narrow west face of the landform.

Paraphernalia: Standard desert rack.

Descent: Rappel *North Face*.

Warning: Park regulations require all aid climbing on this route be clean aid. Traditional hammer aid is prohibited.

The Ark

Between Moses and Zeus.

FADED DREAM I, 5.10, 2 pitches, 150 feet (46m)

First Ascent: James Garrett, Dave Anderson, Will Gilmer, October 1988.

Location and Access: The route ascends the north face of the landform.

Pitch 1: Begin at a crack system in line with a point slightly left of the highest rock of the tower. Climb a prominent right-facing chimney of the large evident flake that abutts the tower, 5.7.

Pitch 2: Standing atop the middle of the flake, climb straight up a finger/handcrack passing two bolts below the summit, 5.10.

Paraphernalia: Standard desert rack.

Descent: Due to the poor quality of the summit rock, the first ascent team placed a single ⅜"-by-3½" bolt on top and lowered to the two bolts on the ridge where they then rappelled from solid rock.

Photo: Eric Bjørnstad

Zeus and Aphrodite

Aphrodite

Aphrodite is located next to the rimrock behind (east) of Moses and Zeus.

SWEDISH–AMERICAN ROUTE III, 5.9+ R, A2, 6 pitches, 400 feet (122m), ★★★

First Ascent: Ed Webster, Anders Bergwall, Anders Swensson, 3-5 November 1991.

Location and Access: There are two possible starts to the climb. The original start begins up the prominent left-facing dihedral on the west (left) end of the tower's south face. But it is easier to follow the arête itself along its entire length, starting near Zeus.

Pitch 1: Jam and lieback up the left-facing corner at the left end of Aphrodite's south face (5.9+) to a ledge 60 feet (18m) up. Continue up the wider crack in the prominent dihedral above (#4 Friend), liebacking with some face moves, up onto the main horizontal ridge, 5.9+,125 feet (38m).

Pitch 1a: Start at the extreme western end of the arête. Overcome an initial block, then walk along the ridge to a thin vertical crack on the right which splits a narrow fin. Jam the crack (5.9) and hike east along the spectacular ridge to the top of the Pitch 1 dihedral, 5.9, 150 feet (46m).

Pitch 2: Easy climbing leads to the right along the ridge, then step down and move across a narrow exposed ledge to a drilled piton belay anchor, 5.0, 20 feet (37m).

Pitch 3: Face climb (5.9+), then follow a steep but easy A1 bolt ladder to a big belay ledge on the arête, 5.9+, A1, 90 feet (27m).

Pitch 4: Follow A1 drilled angles out right across a face into the base or upper groove, a main feature of the route. Free (5.9+) and aid (A2) up the V groove to a belay ledge on the right, 5.9+, A2, 110 feet (34m).

Pitch 5: Avoid loose-looking blocks in the main crack above by climbing the right handcrack, then tensioning left into the final chimney and exposed handcrack. Jam up this (5.9), great moves, to a good ledge below the final capstone. Aid on 4 bolts (A1) up a blank wall to a large ledge, 5.9, A1, 130 feet (40m).

Pitch 6: Climb up easily, chimney behind a huge detached block, step left, and make an unprotected 5.9 face move to the summit, 5.9R, 80 feet (24m).

Paraphernalia: Standard desert rack including (2) #4 Friends; Lost Arrows and knifeblades (Pitch 4).

Descent: Rappel *East Ridge*.

Warning: Park regulations require all aid climbing on this route be clean aid. Traditional hammer aid is prohibited.

GRAVESTONED IV, 5.8 R, A3+, 3 pitches, 280 feet (85m)

First Ascent: James Funsten, Davin Lindy, February 1992.

Location and Access: *Gravestoned* climbs the narrow west face of Aphrodite.

Pitch 1: Begin up the best-looking line of a double crack system, 5.8, A1, 100 feet (30m).

Pitch 2: Ascend a seam past bolts and continue over a lip to a belay station, A3=, 140 feet (43m).

Pitch 3: Face clim to the summit, 5.8R, 40 feet (12m).

Paraphernalia: One #4 Friend; (2) sets of cams #.4, #3.5; (1) set of Rocks; Lost Arrows (3-4) #5,#6, (1-2) #7.

Descent: Scramble to the east side of the landform to rappel anchors. One short and one long rappel.

Warning: Park regulations require all aid climbing on this route be clean aid. Traditional hammer aid is prohibited.

THE WAFER III, 5.10c, 4 pitches, 400 (122m)

First Ascent: Ed Webster, Chester Dreiman, 4 November 1983.

Location and Access: The route climbs the east ridge of Aphrodite. Traverse around the south side of the tower to the crack system facing the rimrock wall.

Paraphernalia: One set of Friends.

Descent: From the summit, rappel to the ledge at the beginning of Pitch 3. Continue to the detached block at the beginning of Pitch 2, then rappel to the ground.

THE ROTOR III, 5.10, A4, 4 pitches

First Ascent: Doug Hall, Mike Pennings, November 1994.

Location and Access: The route climbs the direct south fact.

Paraphernalia: Thin pieces to a #4 Camalot.

Descent: Rappel the east edge.

Warning: Park regulations require all aid climbing on this route be clean aid. Traditional hammer aid is prohibited.

Saddle Tower Buttress

Saddle Tower Buttress is located approximately 0.5 mile (0.8km) northwest of Point 5735 on the large USGS map "Canyonlands National Park and Vicinity," at the head of Rough Canyon which is named on the park map. Rough Canyon is the first offshoot from Taylor Canyon as one hikes right (east) of Moses. Rough Canyon and Point 5735 are also identified on the two Trails Illustrated maps, "Arches and Canyonlands National Parks" and "The Needles, and the Island-in-the-Sky of Canyonlands National Park" map.

SADDLE TOWER BUTTRESS IV, 5.11–, A2, 4 pitches, 500 feet (152m), ★★★★

First Ascent: Tom Thomas, Dan Mathews, March 1986.

Location and Access: The route begins at the west corner via hand-and-fist cracks. A classic sit-down chimney is climbed in the middle of the tower for two pitches, then cracks are followed up and around to the south side of the monolith. Continue (scramble) around to the east side, over the saddle. An aid pitch is then followed to a large ledge via a south side crack, to the final summit block. From the ledge a nut placement is possible in a solution pocket. The summit is reached by a few bouldering moves. It is hoped future parties will not place bolts but climb the summit block in the same high style as the first ascent party.

Paraphernalia: Standard desert rack; extra #2.5, #4 Friends; (1) set of stoppers; small selection of pitons were used on the first ascent.

Descent: One rappel off the summit to the saddle, then rappels off the west side of the tower.

Warning: Park regulations require all aid climbing on this route be clean aid. Traditional hammer aid is prohibited.

Outlaw Spire

Outlaw Spire is also know as Hardscrabble Spire. Twelve miles (19.3km) downriver from Taylor Canyon the White Rim Road becomes passable only to four-wheel-drive vehicles as it climbs steeply up Hardscrabble Hill (identified on the large USGS map "Canyonlands National Park and Vicinity" and the Trails Illustrated series). Outlaw Spire is clearly in view on the Wingate walls above.

SOUTH–SOUTHWEST FACE III, 5.10–, A3, 4 pitches, 300 feet (91m)

First Ascent: Bill Ellwood, Bryan Ferguson, 14 May 1993.

Location and Access: The route climbs the south-southwest face via many bolts.

Paraphernalia: Unknown.

Descent: Rappel *Direct Erection* to the north.

Warning: Park regulations require all aid climbing on this route be clean aid. Traditional hammer aid is prohibited.

DIRECT ERECTION III, 5.10, A3, 4 pitches, 300 feet (91m)

First Ascent: Chris Sircello, James Funsten, 17-18 May 1993.

Location and Access: *Direct Erection* was established during the second ascent of the tower. Pitches 1 and 2 ascend the south face to a notch. Pitches 3 and 4 continue to the summit via the north face.

Paraphernalia: Two sets of cams #.4, #4; #4 Camalot; (1) set of nuts; (5) Birdbeaks; (1) Fish Hook; (3) RURPs; (15) knifeblades and Bugaboos; (10) long Lost Arrows; (3) Leepers.

Descent: Rappel the route to the north.

Warning: Park regulations require all aid climbing on this route be clean aid. Traditional hammer aid is prohibited.

The Turks Head

The Turks Head is located on the west side of the Green River in the northwestern section of Canyonlands National Park, across the river (south) from Tuxedo Bottom. It is identified on the large USGS map "Canyonlands National Park and Vicinity" and the Trails Illustrated series. To reach from the Horsethief Trail, continue downriver from Taylor Canyon on the White Rim Road. The road requires four-wheel-drive 12 miles (19.3km) beyond Taylor Canyon at Hardscrabble Hill. Rappel to the bank of the river (leaving a fixed rope for the return) at a point across from The Turks Head. An inner tube or boat of some kind will be necessary to cross the river to the landform. The river is both deep and swift, and caution is essential. The original ascent parties made the climbs while on a rafting trip down the Green.

TURKS HEAD ONE II, 5.8, A2, 1 pitch, 160 feet (49m)

First Ascent: Bego Gerhart, Jim Deane, Lady Ote, October 1973.

Location and Access: From an upriver viewing, the route is located a few feet left of the extreme right profile of the landform.

Paraphernalia: One set of Friends.

Descent: Rappel the route.

Warning: Park regulations require all aid climbing on this route be clean aid. Traditional hammer aid is prohibited.

REEPICHEEP II, 5.9, A2, 1 pitch, 160 feet (49m)

First Ascent: Bego Gerhart, Tom Clawson, Lady Ote, September 1974.

Location and Access: The route begins a few feet right of *Turks Head One*.

Paraphernalia: One set of Friends.

Descent: Rappel the route.

Warning: Park regulations require all aid climbing on this route be clean aid. Traditional hammer aid is prohibited.

Island-In-The-Sky White Rim Area

The Island-in-the-Sky is the northern region of the park and is reached from U.S. 191, 9 miles (14.4km) north of Moab. Turn west and drive about 22 miles (35km) via State Highway 313. The

White Rim circles the Island-in-the-Sky via a broad bench 1200 feet (366m) below the mesa top and 1000 feet (305m) above the Colorado River to the east and the Green River to the west.

To reach the White Rim east region, descend the Shafer Road which begins just north of the Island visitor center or continue down the Potash Road (State 279) located four miles (6.4km) north of Moab (1 mile, 1.6km, south of the entrance to Arches National Park).

To reach the western region of the White Rim drive to the Island-in-the-Sky and turn right (west) onto the Horsethief Trail just before Mile Marker 10 and descend the steep switchbacks to Mineral Bottom (passable by two-wheel drive) where a left (south) turn begins the White Rim Road west.

The Grand Blast

The Grand Blast is located on the west prow at Grand View Point. To reach, hike three-fourths of the way south to Junction Butte Viewpoint and bear left. An old unofficial trail known as the Government Trail, descends steeply and precariously to the White Rim 1200 feet (366m) below. The trail follows large ledges and at times is very exposed. Once at the base of the cliff work left several hundred yards to the west prow. From the base of the Wingate, the route is the most striking line on the west prow.

THE GRAND BLAST III, 5.11–, 3 pitches, 450 feet (137m)

First Ascent: Katy Cassidy, Earl Wiggins, March 1988.
Location and Access: The route faces west and tops out at the tip of the Island-in-the-Sky peninsula, directly across from Junction Butte (to the south).
Pitch 1: Climb a straight in four-inch (10cm) crack just left of a shallow chimney for 50 feet (15m). This leads into a flared dihedral that continues for another 100 feet (30m) to a semi-hanging belay under the first large roof, 5.10+, 160 feet (49m).
Pitch 2: Climb over the first roof and on to the second roof. After the second roof continue up the handcrack in the headwall to the Wingate slab above. Face climb up the slab and belay at the top of it below the final headwall, 5.11–, 150 feet (46m).
Pitch 3: Go left around the corner and angle up into a dihedral and on to the top, 5.9, 140 feet (43m).
Paraphernalia: Three sets of Friends.
Descent: Walk on the trail back to Grand View Point parking lot.

Candlestick Tower

Candlestick Tower is named on the large USGS map "Canyonlands National Park and Vicinity," and the Trails Illustrated series.

The spire is located on the west side of the Island-in-the-Sky on the White Rim Plateau above the Green River. Its location is at a point of land projecting west from the Island at an area south of Holeman Basin and north of Soda Springs Basin. It may be viewed from the Island-in-the-Sky Road 1 mile (1.6km) south from the Grand View Point and Upheaval Dome junction (looking west from a gravel pullout). This is also a point 7 miles (11km) south of the Island visitor center on the park road to Grand View Point. The first ascent party reached the tower by rappelling 400 feet (122m) from the mesa via a gully located northwest of the Willow Flat Campground and then hiking about 2 miles (3.2km) cross-country to the tower.

From the White Rim Road approach from a wash on the east side of the tower located 4 miles (6km) east of the Candlestick campsite.

TWO WORLDS ROUTE III, 5.7, A4, 4 pitches, 450 feet (137m)

First Ascent: Jimmy Dunn, Doug Snively, Larry Hamilton, Dick Byrd, March 1974.

Location and Access: The route ascends a crack system on the west edge of the landform.

Paraphernalia: One set of Friends; (1) set of wires.

Descent: Rappel the east face from the east end of the summit plateau.

Warning: Park regulations require all aid climbing on this route be clean aid. Traditional hammer aid is prohibited.

SOUTHWEST CORNER III, 5.10, 4 pitches (2 roped, 2 third class), 450 feet (137m)

First Ascent: Scott Gilbert, Jim Newberry, John Pearson, Bob Dickerson, Ernie Ulibarni, and Paul Nabors, March 1976.

Location and Access: The route climbs the southwest buttress of the tower. Approach up the east slope of the landform, then traverse to the north and finally the southwest corner of the tower. Pitch 1 and 4 are third class.

Pitch 1: Third class up the southwest buttress, behind a large flake-like boulder to the right (east of the base of a vertical crack which ascends over a small roof).

Pitch 2: Continue (stemming and jamming) over a 5.10 roof and up a squeeze chimney to a belay ledge.

Pitch 3: Ascend straight up and over a chockstone then left and up the face to where two separate flakes come horizontally out from the wall. Belay from the ledge above.

Pitch 4: Move left (west) third class and continue to the summit.

Paraphernalia: Two sets of Friends, extra #2; (1) set of wires.

Descent: Rappel the east face beginning at the top of Pitch 3. This is a point located at the east end of the summit plateau.

EAST FACE III, 5.10, 6 pitches, 450 feet (137m)

First Ascent: Kent Lugbill, Glenn Randall, October 1982.

Location and Access: The route ascends left of the pillar at the notch end of the east face and climbs to the lowest point in the skyline. It then continues up the ridge to the summit. There are no hanging belays.

Pitch 1: Begin up a rotten and poorly protected pitch–past a 5.10 handcrack–toward the prominent skyline notch.

Pitch 2: Climb a wide 5.10 handcrack up the steepening wall.

Pitch 3: Climb up and right to the base of an offwidth.

Pitch 4: Continue up the offwidth to the notch, 5.9+.

Pitch 5: A 5.9 handcrack leads out of the notch and over bands of dangerous third class ledges.

Pitch 6: Continue up an easy chimney which splits the summit block.

Paraphernalia: One set of Friends; (1) set of wires.

Descent: Rappel the east face from the east end of the summit plateau.

Chip and Dale Towers. Chip Tower is on right.

Chip and Dale Towers

Chip and Dale Towers are located down the White Rim Road 4 miles (6.4km) from the junction of Shafer Canyon and the White Rim Road. The spires are obvious, high on the rimrock walls to the west of Musselman Arch. Chip is the outside (lower) tower, Dale the higher and closer landform to the rimrock.

CHIP TOWER—STUFFIN' NUTS III, 5.9, A2/3, 4 pitches, 240 feet (73m)

First Ascent: Jeff Widen, Jeff Singer, October 1993.

Location and Access: The first ascent approach was from the White Rim where the tower was climbed via its south face.

Paraphernalia: Friends (1) #1, (5) #1.5, (4) #2, (4) #2.5, (4) #3, (3) #3.5, (3) #4; (1-2) sets of TCUs; (1) hook; (2) knifeblades; (2) Lost Arrows; (1) baby angle; (1) ¾" angle; long slings for rappels.

Descent: Three rappels from the summit to notch, to the ground on the south side of the spire.

Warning: Park regulations require all aid climbing on this route be clean aid. Traditional hammer aid is prohibited.

DALE TOWER—BOYS NIGHT OUT III, 5.9, A1, 3 pitches, 330 feet (100m)

First Ascent: Jeff Widen, Jeff Singer, Cameron Burns, 2 October 1994.

Location and Access: The landform was approached from the White Rim Road. Boys Night Out climbs the tower from the north via the notch between the tower and the wall behind, two pitches. A final pitch reaches the summit. Photo on page 173.

Paraphernalia: Two sets of Friends; (1) #4 Camalot; (2) sets of TCUs; (2) 6" pieces; (1) 8" piece (optional); (3) ½" angles for drilled holes; (2) knifeblades; extra webbing.

Descent: Rappel to the notch then the route to the base of the spire.

Warning: Park regulations require all aid climbing on this route be clean aid. Traditional hammer aid is prohibited.

Tiki Tower

Tiki Tower is a thin obvious spire north (upriver) of Monster Tower/Washer Woman Arch. This is a point south of the turn to Lathrop Canyon, above the Airport Tower campsites, between Airport Tower and the rimrock behind it (west).

BRAVE LITTLE TOASTER III, 5.9, A1, 3 pitches, 260 feet (79m)

First Ascent: Jeff Widen, Mitch Allen, November 1991. Paul Frank and Fred Lifton worked with Jeff Widen and Mitch Allen on Pitch 1.

Location and Access: Begin on the right side of the south face and climb to a prominent notch then left to the tower itself.

Paraphernalia: Three sets of TCUs; Camalots (2) #1, (3) #1.5, (3) #2, (2) #2.5, (1) #3, (2) #3.5, (2) #4.

Descent: Rappel the route.

Warning: Park regulations require all aid climbing on this route be clean aid. Traditional hammer aid is prohibited.

Chip Tower

Stuffin' Nuts III, 5.9, A2/3

40'

A2/3

5.9

130'

chimney 5.8

3/4"

A1

2" to 3"

A1

110'

1 1/4"

70'

5.8 loose

Dale Tower

Boys Night Out III, 5.9, A1

③ 120'

A0

5.9 squeeze

A1

5.9 ow 6"

5.8

hands

②

90'

5.8

① 120'

5.8

5.6

5.8 hands

5.9 squeeze

A1

5.9

Airport Tower

Airport Tower is the prominent butte on the White Rim located west of Lathrop Canyon. It is erroneously identified as Washer Woman on the large USGS map "Canyonlands National Park and Vicinity." It is correctly identified on the Trails Illustrated map of the park. The tower is closed 1 January to 30 June.

WIND SHEAR III, 5.11, A1, 5 pitches, 460 feet (140m)

First Ascent: Galen Howell, Sonja Paspal, Steve Swanke, July 1994.

Location and Access: Approach from the Airport Tower campsites. Hike up an old road/wash until under the far end of the north face, then up the talus slope. The route is located 35 feet (11m) right of *Sky Pilot*.

Pitch 1: 5.10, 130 feet (40m).

Pitch 2: 5.11, 100 feet (30m).

Pitch 3: 5.10, A1, 130 feet (40m).

Pitch 4: 5.9, 100 feet (30m).

Pitch 5: Fourth class.

Paraphernalia: Three sets of Friends with extra #1, #3, #3.5; (1) set of stoppers; (2) #4 Camalot.

Descent: Rappel the route.

Warning: Park regulations require all aid climbing on this route be clean aid. Traditional hammer aid is prohibited.

SKY PILOT III, 5.10, A3, 6 pitches, 460 feet (140m)

First Ascent: Mike Baker, Leslie Henderson, 16 September 1995.

Location and Access: The route climbs the northwest face beginning 35 feet (11m) left (east) of *Wind Shear*. Hike up to the Lathrop trail (to the north) and continue up an old road/wash until under the far end of the north face, then hike up the talus to the route. *Sky Pilot* is the farthest right-hand line that goes from bottom to top. High on the route is a 200-foot (61m) perfect five-inch (23cm) splitter crack. It is believed the route will go free in the future at about 5.11.

Pitch 1: 80 feet (24m), A2.

Pitch 2: 150 feet (46m) 5.10, A3.

Pitch 3: 85 feet (26m), A1.

Pitch 4: 60 feet (18m), A1.

Pitch 5: 50 feet (15m) 5.8, A1.

Pitch 6: Fourth class to the summit

Paraphernalia: One each TCUs; (1) each #.75 to #3 Camalots, (3) or more #4 Camalots for the splitter crack; stoppers. The first ascent party used five pitons but they will not be necessary when the route is climbed clean.

Descent: Four double-rope rappels down *Wind Shear*.

Warning: Park regulations require all aid climbing on this route be clean aid. Traditional hammer aid is prohibited.

Monster Tower, Washer Woman Arch, Sandcastle

Washer Woman Arch's location is erroneously identified on the large USGS map of Canyonlands National Park and Vicinity. It and Monster Tower are correctly identified on the Trails Illustrated map series. Washer Woman Arch is the only arch in the park that is NOT off-limits to climbing.

If approaching via the Potash Road, the junction of Shafer Canyon and the White Rim Road will be reached about 14.5 miles (23km) beyond the Potash Mine at the end of State Highway 279. At this junction there is a restroom. A sign points to Shafer Canyon and Moab to the north, and to the Shafer Road switchbacks to the west (which end 4 miles, 6km, at the paved Highway 313 atop the Island-in-the-Sky). From the Highway 313 junction with the Shafer Road, the Island-in-the-Sky visitor center is about 1 mile (1.6km) south. The Potash approach is very scenic but may require high-clearance and/or four-wheel-drive after thunderstorms have eroded the road. From the junction of the White Rim Road, 13 miles (21km) south (down the White Rim Road) the towers come into view as one loops around the head of Buck Canyon.

Monster Tower

Approach up the south-facing talus slope.

KOR-DALKE–SCHAFER IV, 5.11, 7 pitches, 650 feet (197m)

First Ascent: Layton Kor, Larry Dalke, Cub Schafer, 26 December 1963. Second ascent: Glenn Randall, Charlie Fowler, November 1982. This was the third overall ascent of the tower.

Location and Access: Scramble to the beginning of the climb at the tower's northeast corner, then ascend the east side to a ledge system. There is less rope drag if Pitch 1 is divided into two pitches. It then traverses to the west and continues on the west face to the summit. The only aid on this first ascent of the tower was three moves on the summit block.

Paraphernalia: Standard desert rack; (1) set of TCUS with (3) #1.5, (2) #2, (1-2) #2.5, (2) #3, (2) #3.5, (1) #4; medium stoppers; #10 hex; (2) #4 Camalots if doing the offwidth on Pitch 3.

Descent: Rappel *North Ridge*.

KOR–DALKE–SCHAFER VARIATION

This is a variation by Evelyn Lees and Rick Wyatt which begins left of Pitch 1 and in two pitches joins the original route at the beginning of Pitch 3, 5.10.

HARRISON–SMITH VARIATION

This variation climbs the face past two bolts, ten feet (3m) left of the summit pitch, 5.11. It was first accomplished by Richard Harrison and Jay Smith in November 1982 (fourth overall ascent of the tower) followed three days later by Ed Webster and Chester Dreiman on their fifth overall ascent of the tower.

Photo: Tom Cotter

Jim Bodenhamer on first pitch of **North Ridge**, *Monster Tower*

MONSTER OF ROCK III, 5.11, 7 pitches, 650 feet (198m)

First Ascent: Ed Webster, Chester Dreiman, 3 November 1982.
Location and Access: The route climbs the south face of the tower, 5.10, finishing with the *Harrison-Smith* 5.11 finish up the north ridge. This was the second overall ascent of the tower.

LOS BANDITOS III, 5.9, A3, 5 pitches, 650 feet (198m)

First Ascent: Stan Mish, Mimi De Gravila, June 1983.
Location and Access: The route ascends the tower from the northeast, left of the original route. This was the sixth overall ascent of Monster Tower.
Paraphernalia: Two sets of Friends with extra #4; (6) baby angles; a selection of Lost Arrows; short and long knifeblades and Bugaboos.
Descent: Rappel the *Kor-Dalke-Schafer.*
Warning: Park regulations require all aid climbing on this route be clean aid. Traditional hammer aid is prohibited.

NORTH RIDGE III, 5.11a, 7 pitches, 650 feet (198m), ★★★★

First Ascent: Ken Trout, Kirk Miller, May 1981.
Location and Access: The route begins up the northeast corner of the landform. The 5.11 climbing on the fifth pitch follows the *Harrison-Smith Variation* to the original route on the summit blocks. On Pitch 3, one may climb offwidth and chimney to the left or a loose variation obvious to the right. The route may be approached from the saddle on the north side of the tower.
Pitch 1: Climb a left-facing corner to a pedestal and belay bolts, 5.9.
Pitch 2: Continue up a crack system to a belay ledge, 5.10+.
Pitch 3: Climb an easy offwidth to a ledge with belay bolts, 5.9.
Pitch 4: Climb a corner to an offwidth and a belay ledge with bolts, 5.11a.
Pitch 5: Continue up shattered rock to a belay ledge, 5.9.
Pitch 6: Climb up a corner, then out a roof.
Pitch 7: Face climb left to the summit, 5.11.
Paraphernalia: Two sets of Friends with extra #1, #3, #3.5; (1) set of stoppers; (1) #4 Camalot.
Descent: Rappel the route.

Washer Woman Arch

Approach up the south-facing talus slope. See front cover credit on page ii.

WEST FACE IV 5.8, A3, 8 pitches, 400 feet (122m)

First Ascent: Rick Horn, John Horn, Pete Carmen, April 1967.
Location and Access: The route climbs an obvious line on the west face beginning below the arch formed by the arms of The Washer Woman.
Pitch 1: Scramble to the saddle and work down and across to a point below a big chimney directly under the arch.
Pitch 2: Climb 100 feet (30m) to the right of the chimney and traverse back toward it by squeezing behind a small flake.

Pitch 3: Climb the chimney free to a ledge 30 feet (9m) below a large chockstone jutting over the chimney and belay station. Below are smaller rocks wedged at various angles.

Pitch 4: Climb the large chockstone to a slot about five feet (1.5m) wide with two vertical cracks in a right angle corner. Belay from bolt anchors.

Pitch 5: Move left and climb a wide crack past an overhang, then traverse left below the second overhang.

Pitch 6: Continue to the knifedge ridge above the overhang and belay.

Pitch 7: Climb to a flat belay station above the arch.

Pitch 8: The summit pitch climbs the center of the face (past three bolts) to the top c. the Washer Woman's head.

Paraphernalia: Standard desert rack; selection of pitons.

Descent: One rappel leads to the top of the arch, two more lead to the windowsill, then two more lead to the ground.

Warning: Park regulations require all aid climbing on this route be clean aid. Traditional hammer aid is prohibited.

IN SEARCH OF SUDS III, 5.10+, 5 pitches, 400 feet (122m),
★★★★★

First Ascent: Glenn Randall, Charlie Fowler, November 1982.

Location and Access: The route climbs a crack system on the right side of the southwest face. Approach via the south slope.

Pitch 1: Climb a crack hands-to-bigger-than-fist which ends just below the window (arch) that cuts through the tower (The Eye of the Needle). Belay below The Eye, 5.10, 150 feet (46m). The window is not visible from the start of the climb.

Pitch 2: Climb a 5.7 chimney which cuts the left wall of The Eye. Belay from a ledge below the ridge, 5.9.

Pitch 3: Climb a bulge to the ridge and belay, 5.10.

Pitch 4: Traverse along the ridge and climb up the arch, which is easy except for a 5.9 headwall. Belay at the final headwall.

Pitch 5: Climb the headwall at 5.10+ and ascend the summit blocks.

Paraphernalia: Two sets of Friends with extra #3; (1) set of TCUs; (1) set of wires.

Descent: Rappel the west face.

THROUGH THE LOOKING GLASS III, 5.11, 4 pitches, 400 feet (122m)

First Ascent: Robert Warren, Steve Wood, Jeff Webb, late 1980s.

Location and Access: The route begins on the east face (the opposite side of the tower from *In Search of Suds*). Pitch 1 climbs a 5.11 offwidth. Pitch 2 continues up and through "The Eye of the Needle," a 10-by-40-foot (3m-by-12m) high notch, then pass through The Eye and continue up the *In Search of Suds* route to the summit.

Paraphernalia: One set of Friends; (1) set of nuts.

Descent: Rappel *West Face*.

Sandcastle

The tower is located in Buck Canyon beside Washer Woman Arch and Monster Tower. It is the obvious smaller tower nearest the Island-in-the-Sky rimrock.

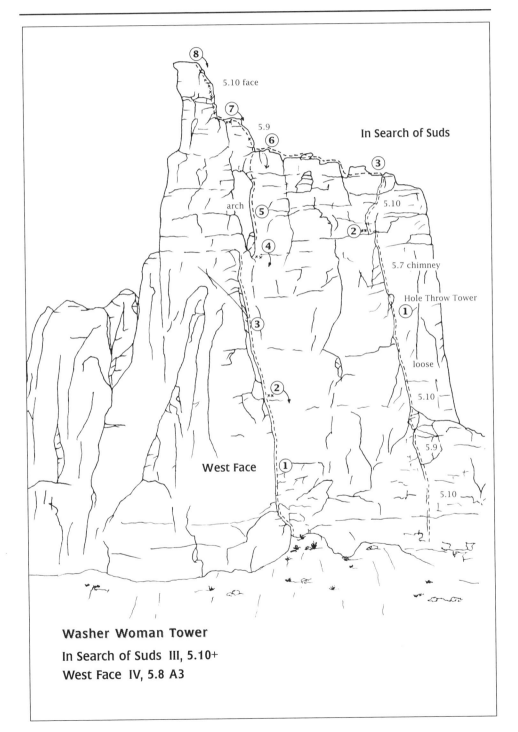

In Search of Suds

8

7

5.10 face

5.9

6

5

arch

4

3

2

5.10

5.7 chimney

Hole Throw Tower

1

loose

5.10

5.9

5.10

3

2

1

West Face

Washer Woman Tower

In Search of Suds III, 5.10+

West Face IV, 5.8 A3

CRYPTO-BIOTIC TIDE IV, 5.8, A3, 4 pitches, 400 feet (122m)

First Ascent: Mike Wood, James Funsten, March 1992.

Location and Access: The route starts up the southwest side and climbs to the notch between the Island and the spire before continuing up the northern prow.

Pitch 1: Climb to the col between the spire and the Island-in-the-Sky Mesa, 5.8, A1.

Pitch 2: Move right to the spire and ascend the northern-west prow to a belay ledge, 5.8, A1.

Pitch 3: Continue up overhanging rock to a good belay ledge with triple anchors. Leave a rope fixed for the return, A3.

Pitch 4: A couple of free moves takes one to A2 climbing and the summit anchors.

Paraphernalia: One #5 Tri-cam; (2) Birdbeaks; (15) knifeblades; (15) long Lost Arrows; (3) Leepers; angles 1¼"; (2) sets of cams; (1) set of Rocks.

Descent: Rappel the route.

Warning: Park regulations require all aid climbing on this route be clean aid. Traditional hammer aid is prohibited.

WAVES IV, 5.10–, A3, 5 pitches, 350 feet (107m), ★★★★

First Ascent: Jim Bodenhamer, Al Torrisi, 14 April 1993.

Location and Access: *Waves* was the second ascent of Sandcastle. The route climbs the south side of the landform.

Pitch 1: Begin near the left side of the east face and climb 5.10- to a double-anchor belay.

Pitch 2: Continue 5.9 then A1 to a belay below a huge flake.

Pitch 3: Tension traverse left to an A3 crack system which climbs above the flake 5.6 to a double-anchor belay.

Pitch 4: Climb up and right at 5.9 then A2/A3 to belay ledge.

Pitch 5: Continue up and right to the summit, 5.8, A2.

Paraphernalia: Standard desert rack; (2) #4 Camalots; (4) knifeblades; (4) Lost Arrows; (3) baby angles; (3) ⅜" angles.

Descent: Rappel the route. All rappel stations have baby angles in ⅜" holes with the exception of the fourth belay point which has soft rock. It has been rappelled with a 1½" piton in a ⅜" hole.

Warning: Park regulations require all aid climbing on this route be clean aid. Traditional hammer aid is prohibited.

Islet-in-the-Sky and Blocktop

These thin pinnacles are located high off the mesa of Island-in-the-Sky about 5 miles (8km) downriver from Monster Tower/Washer Woman Arch along the White Rim Road. They are exceedingly difficult to locate from the rim, and horrendous to hike to from the White Rim Road. Blocktop is the taller and stouter of the two formations and is located closer to the rim than Islet-in-the-Sky.

Both towers are located above the Buck Canyon drainage which is identified at a point immediately south of Monster Tower/Washer Woman Arch on the large USGS "Canyonlands National Park and Vicinity" map and the Trails Illustrated series.

Photo: Jim Bodenhamer

Islet-in-the-Sky and Blocktop

Islet-in-the-Sky

To reach Islet-in-the-Sky, rappel from the Island-in-the-Sky from at a point about two miles (3.2km) south of the junction of the Grand View Point and Upheaval Dome road (8 miles, 12.8km south of the visitor center).

ISLET-IN-THE-SKY IV, 5.10+, A3, 6 pitches, 400 feet (122m),
★★★★★

First Ascent: Ken Trout, Bruce Lella, 1976. Second ascent: Bill Ellwood, Bruce Hunter, Greg Doubek, Brian Hansen, 1983.

Location and Access: The route climbs a handcrack to the notch, then continues via thin nailing and hanging belays to the summit. If approach is from the mesa top, leave fixed ropes for the return. Photo on page 162.

Paraphernalia: One set of Friends; selection of knifeblades and Lost Arrows.

Descent: Double-rope rappel back down the route. If approach was from mesa top, ascend fixed ropes.

Warning: Park regulations require all aid climbing on this route be clean aid. Traditional hammer aid is prohibited.

Blocktop

See approach for Islet-in-the-Sky.

BLOCKTOP IV, 5.10, A0, 5 pitches, 415 feet (127m)

First Ascent: Bryan Ferguson, Bill Ellwood, Greg Doubek, 11-12 October 1985. Second ascent: James Funsten, Jeff Hollenbaugh, 10 September 1992.

Location and Access: The tower is climbed from its north side and is expected to go free at some point in the future. Leave fixed ropes when appropriate for return.

Paraphernalia: Two sets of Friends size #1 to #2.5; (1) set of TCUs up to ¾"; several large pieces (#4s).

Descent: Rappel the route, then ascend fixed ropes to mesa top.

Warning: Park regulations require all aid climbing on this route be clean aid. Traditional hammer aid is prohibited.

Monument Basin

Monument Basin is named on the large USGS map "Canyonlands National Park and Vicinity" and the Trails Illustrated maps "Arches/Canyonlands National Parks," and "The Needles and Island-in-the-Sky of Canyonlands National Park."

Monument Basin may be viewed from Grand View Point 12 miles (19km) south of the Island-in-the-Sky visitor center. To reach, descend the Shafer Road to the White Rim Road and continue south about 14.5 miles (23km). See approach for Monster Tower on page 201. To descend into Monument Basin one must either rappel from the White Rim or scramble down an old sheep trail reached from the northeast side of the basin. See locator map.

An alternate approach into Monument Basin is to hike in a northeast direction from the southwest edge of the basin. (The old road at the point is now closed to vehicle passage and mountain bikes.) A descent is possible via a gully marked with cairns at the end of the closed road.

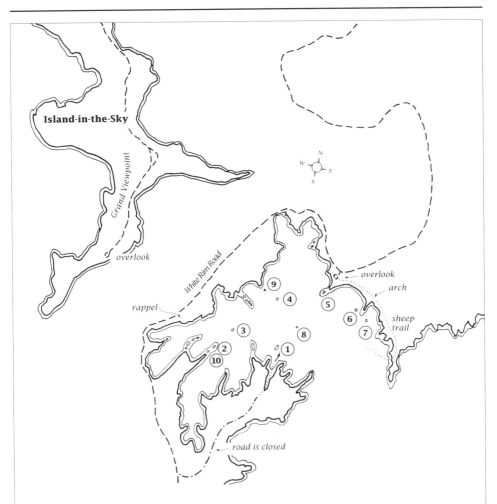

MONUMENT BASIN LOCATOR MAP

(1) The Mock Turtle   (6) The Enigmatic Syringe

(2) Shark's Fin   (7) The Deathalonian Spire

(3) Standing Rock   (8) Mars Tower

(4) Staggering Rock   (9) Unknown Tower

(5) The Meemohive   (10) Bruce Smith Tower

Standing Rock

Standing Rock is the tallest and thinnest tower when viewing from Monument Basin at Grand View Point. It is noted on the Monument Basin engraved plaque as The Totem Pole.

STANDING ROCK (aka The Totem Pole) III, 5.11– (or C2), 4 pitches, 305 feet (93m), ★★★★★

First Ascent: Layton Kor, Huntley Ingalls, with Steve Komito working on the lower pitches, 3 days, 13-15 October 1962, (IV, 5.7, A4). First solo ascent: John Middendorf (8 hours), June 1991. First free ascent: Keith Reynolds, Walt Shipley (40th overall ascent), 26 October 1993.

Location and Access: Begin on the east side of the spire. There are spacious ledges atop Pitches 2 and 3. Mike Baker suggests (on his 33rd overall ascent on 9 April 1993) that the spire is a six-hour climb (8½ hours car-to-car). Photo on page 219.

Pitch 1: Climb a large corner system, then traverse right under a roof. Continue up a wide crack past a bolt, then up to a bolted belay, 5.10.

Pitch 2: Traverse out right on an easy ledge, then up a right-facing corner to a steep thin crack. Continue up and right to a belay, 5.10+/5.11.

Pitch 3: Climb up and left out bulges (crux) past fixed gear, then continue up to a left-facing corner and flake system to a belay on the right, 5.11–.

Pitch 4: Continue up and right on easy ground to the summit, 5.6.

Paraphernalia: Friends (2) sets; (2) #4 Camalot; Tri-cams (2) #5 through #7; TCUs (2) sets of wires; (10) medium to large wired nuts; quickdraws.

Descent: One may make two double-rope rappels down the route or rappel 90 feet (27m) to the top of Pitch 2, then 100 feet (30m) to the top of Pitch 1 and finally 115 feet (35m) to the ground.

EASTER BUNNY III, 5.8, A4, 3 pitches, 305 feet (93m)

First Ascent: Barry McLane, Simon Peck, 20-21 April 1992.

Location and Access: The route climbs the obvious crack system on the east face for two pitches before traversing right to finish on the north face. Begin on the opposite side from the first ascent route. *Easter Bunny* was established during the 32nd ascent of the tower.

Pitch 1: The pitch finishes at a sling belay consisting of two drilled and epoxied angles.

Pitch 2: Continue straight off the belay to a large horizontal bedding seam. Traverse the seam (5.7) to the crack system on the right side of the east face. Climb the crack until it peters out, then continue on hooks (A4) to the bedding seam and move right to an A1 corner. The pitch ends at the corner of a ledge with two more drilled and glued angles.

Pitch 3: Ascend a short knifeblade crack on the left of the belay to reach the bedding seam then traverse the seam on hooks (A4) to a ledge. Climb the right-hand of two thin cracks (A3) to another ledge. Make a move right under an overhang to reach an A1 crack leading to the summit

Paraphernalia: Standard desert rack; (2) Fish Hooks.

Descent: Rappel the original route.

Warning: Park regulations require all aid climbing on this route be clean aid. Traditional hammer aid is prohibited.

Shark's Fin

Shark's Fin is located two land forms northeast of The Totem Pole.

SHARK'S FIN IV, A4, 4 pitches, 250 feet (76m)

First Ascent: Katy Cassidy, Earl Wiggins, Art Wiggins, 1986.
Location and Access: The route follows the east ridge.
Paraphernalia: Standard desert rack.
Descent: Rappel *Fetish Arête.*
Warning: Park regulations require all aid climbing on this route be clean aid.
Traditional hammer aid is prohibited.

FETISH ARETE IV, 5.10, A2, 4 pitches, 250 feet (76m), ★★★★★

First Ascent: Rob Slater, Bruce Hunter, Jim Bodenhamer, Tom Cotter, May 1992.
Location and Access: The route climbs the southwest ridge of the tower. Pitch 1 was named "Flat Chested Potatoe Fetish Head," 5.10, A1. Pitch 2 "Long Leg Fetish," 5.9, A2. Pitch 3 "Gold Nose Ring Fetish," 5.10. Pitch 4 "Blonde Pony Tail Fetish," 5.10. The climb was the third overall ascent of the tower and the second route established.
Paraphernalia: Standard desert rack; (2) pitons.
Descent: Three rappels back down the route, beginning with a rappel from a shaky boulder.
Warning: Park regulations require all aid climbing on this route be clean aid.
Traditional hammer aid is prohibited.

The Mock Turtle

The Mock Turtle is the largest free standing and only tower in Monument Basin which has a White Rim sandstone summit making it taller than Standing Rock. The climb is located 0.25 mile (0.4km) northeast of Standing Rock.

MUD WRESTLING IV, 5.10, 5 pitches, 320 feet (98m), ★★★★

First Ascent: Steve "Crusher" Bartlett, Roger "Strappo" Hughes, 27 October 1990.
Location and Access: *Mud Wrestling* climbs the northeast side of the tower.
Paraphernalia: Friends #6, #7; Camalots #3, #4; wires for the top pitch.
Descent: Rappel the route.

The Enigmatic Syringe

The tower is located approximately 1 mile (1.6km) east of Standing Rock. Approach from the Monument Basin Overlook. Follow the rim east (left-facing out) for an easy 0.25 mile (0.4km) to where the tower is visible. Sling rappel from a #4 Camalot/#3 Friend and a bush back-up. A 150-foot (46m) airy rappel over a large ceiling leads to the talus where a short five-minute hike brings one to the base of the tower.

ALTERED SANITY III, A3, 2 pitches, 250 feet (76m)

First Ascent: Roger "Strappo" Hughes, solo, 14-15 May 1990.
Location and Access: The route ascends the main trunk of The Enigmatic Syringe via the southwest face (Standing Rock side). The second pitch ascends the slender

"syringe" directly off a platform. All fixed anchors are drilled pitons (no bolts). Pitch 1 begins up the left side of a column and climbs A3 then wide to a ledge at the base of the syringe, 160 feet (49m). Strappo suggest it is large enough for a 16-person bivy. Pitch 2 climbs the syringe to its summit, 90 feet (27m).

Paraphernalia: Friends #6, #7; Camalots #3, #4; wires for the top pitch; a selection of thin to wide aid placements.

Descent: Rappel the route.

Warning: Park regulations require all aid climbing on this route be clean aid. Traditional hammer aid is prohibited.

Staggering Rock

This tower is a thin spire northeast of Standing Rock.

STAGGERING ROCK IV, 5.9, A3, 2 pitches, 200 feet (61m)

First Ascent: Steve "Crusher" Bartlett, Roger "Strappo" Hughes, 22 May 1991.

Location and Access: The tower is climbed via its north side.

Paraphernalia: Two to three sets of Friends plus (1) #5.5; up to a #4 Camalot; TCUs; medium to large stoppers; small selection of Lost Arrows and baby angles; (1) Leeper.

Descent: Rappel 150 feet (46m) down the route to a ledge halfway up Pitch 1, then 40 feet (12m) to the ground.

Warning: Park regulations require all aid climbing on this route be clean aid. Traditional hammer aid is prohibited.

The Meemohive

The Meemohive is located 0.5 mile (0.8km) northwest of The Enigmatic Syringe. See The Enigmatic Syringe on page 211 for approach details.

THE MEEMOHIVE IV, 5.9+, A2, 4 pitches, 300 feet (91m), ★★★

First Ascent: Steve "Crusher" Bartlett, solo, 1 June 1991.

Location and Access: The route climbs the northwest face of the tower. The climb has only four placements of aid at a ten-foot (3m) section. The summit pitch climbs an eight-foot (2m) roof via a 5.9+ handcrack, then face climbs to avoid loose blocks in a crack. A traverse left to pockets avoids a final overhang and crumbly mantle.

Paraphernalia: Three sets of Friends; TCUs; a few nuts; (2) standard angles; (2) Leepers; (2) Long Dongs.

Descent: Rappel the route.

Warning: Park regulations require all aid climbing on this route be clean aid. Traditional hammer aid is prohibited.

The Deathalonian Spire

The spire is located southeast of The Enigmatic Syringe. See Enigmatic Syringe on page 211 for details.

THE DEATHALONIAN SPIRE III, 5.10, A3+, 2 pitches, 200 feet (61m)

First Ascent: Frosty Weller, Keen Butterworth, 20 October 1990.

Location and Access: The spire is located southeast of The Enigmatic Syringe. It is reached off the east end of the White Rim peninsula encircling Monument Basin.

Photo: Steve "Crusher" Bartlett

The Meemohive north face

The spire is climbed via its west face. Begin in a muddy groove on the north side. Nail and free climb up the groove about 40 feet (12m), then free climb up and left to a one-inch (2.5cm) crack. Aid the crack and climb back right to a belay ledge on the west shoulder, 5.10, A3, 80 feet (24m). Continue up a corner and nail a thin crack up and left under a short overhang to a ledge. Climb via free and aid to a five-foot (1.5m) headwall. A couple of aid moves using stacked pitons in solution pockets brings one to a ledge just below the summit and an easy move to the top, 5.8, A3+, 80 feet (24m).

Paraphernalia: Standard desert rack; (8) knifeblades and Bugaboos; (6) Lost Arrows; (2) Leepers; (3) ½", ¾", 1¼", (2) 1½", 2".

Descent: The first ascent party rappelled the west face 165 feet (50m) to the base of the climb from 40 feet (12m) of 9mm rope tied around the summit.

Warning: Park regulations require all aid climbing on this route be clean aid. Traditional hammer aid is prohibited.

Mars Tower, Unknown Tower, Bruce Smith Tower

See the locator map on page 209.

MARS LANDER III, 5.9, A3, 400 feet (122m), 7 pitches

First Ascent: David Goldstein, Douglad MacDonald, 1995.

Location and Access: The route ascends the northwest face of Mars Tower, up an obvious crack system that leads to the saddle below the highest point (far right) of the tower. The route is expected to go hammerless in the future. First ascent party used the hammer fewer than 12 times.

Paraphernalia: Tiny pieces to #5 Camalot; Birdbeaks.

Descent: Rappel to the saddle, then to anchors at the base of a wide crack (about 120 feet–37m).

Warning: Park regulations require all aid climbing on this route be clean aid. Traditional hammer aid is prohibited.

UNKNOWN TOWER rating unknown

First Ascent: Unknown.

Location and Access: Slings are visible from below, no further inforamtion is known.

BRUCE SMITH TOWER—SACK DANCE III, 5.11a R, 5 pitches, 225 feet (69m)

First Ascent: David Goldstein, Douglad MacDonald, 1995.

Location and Access: The formation is the second tower right of Mock Turtle, in the middle of the basin. The route climbs the northwest face, mostly on the left side of an obvious "boot" and "leg."

Pitch 1: "Bad Things, Man" pitch. Climb rotten rock with no protection to a right-facing corner with some gear, then step right to an unprotected mantle (the "Swell the Shoe" move). Traverse left 20 feet (6m) to a good ledge, 5.9R.

Pitch 2: Climb corners on good steep rock to the top of the "Bad Knee," a detached pillar, then traverse left and p a short fingertip lieback to a hanging belay, the "Three Point Stance," 5.10.

Pitch 3: Climb loose rock to an alcove, 5.9+.

Pitch 4: Undercling and jam a bulge, then dirty cracks and a difficult mantle; more flaky cracks to a belay on the "Shoulder Pad," 5.11a.

Pitch 5: Improbable face climbing over three bulges to "The Helmet," a huge baguette balanced on dirt. The first ascent team reports "desperate mantle and worse downclimb on and off the summit...wild and classic pitch, protected with Tri-cams and small TCUs in pods."

Paraphernalia: Camalost (1) #4; small TCUs; wires.

Descent: Downclimb to the shoulder then rappel to the gound with 55m ropes.

The Needles District

The Needles District is a complicated and remote area located at the extreme southeastern edge of the park. It is particularly advisable to visit with a park ranger at the Needles visitor center to gain information on current road and trail conditions and to obtain a good maps of the region. It is identified on the large USGS map "Canyonlands National Park and Vicinity" and the Trails Illustrated series.

To reach, drive from Moab 40 miles (64km) south on U.S. 191 and turn west (right) on State Highway 211. Signs will direct you to Newspaper Rock, through Indian Creek and 31 miles (50km) to the Needles visitor center. Just beyond is the Squaw Flat campground, and the difficult four-wheel-drive Elephant Hill, a popular gateway to the interior region of the Needles.

Gilbey's Tower

Gilbey's Tower is located in a 960-acre (65 square mile) grassy meadow known as Chesler Park. It is approached with difficult four-wheel-drive over Elephant Hill toward Butler Flat. Turn east (left) to the Joint Trail parking area and hike about 1 mile (1.6km) to the northeast part of Chesler Park. Of a group of three spires, Gilbey's Tower will be the first "climbable" on the right (west). An alternate three-mile (5km) approach is to drive via two-wheel drive to Elephant Hill and park, then hike the trail toward Druid Arch. At the sign to Chesler Park turn right.

GILBEY'S TOWER III, 5.10, 4 pitches, 300 feet (91m)

First Ascent: Scott Gilbert, John Pearson, Bob Dickerson, Jim Newberry, March 1976. Second ascent: Jim Newberry, Chuck Grossman, John Pearson, 1981.

Pitch 1: Climb a crack and chimney system up the southeast buttress to a small blocky ledge, 5.7+, loose.

Pitch 2: Traverse 45 feet (13.7m) left (west) on a darker band of red sandstone. The traverse goes across small hand- and footholds to a good flake belay at the start of an offwidth and chimney system that leads to the summit block, 5.9, poor protection.

Pitch 3: Ascend up overhanging offwidth to a chimney and then more offwidth to a stance below the summit, 5.10, loose and difficult to protect.

Pitch 4: Continue up and right, face climbing to a short steep crack that leads to the top, 5.8.

Paraphernalia: A small rack plus larger hex's. Several rock-colored slings are required to tie off the summit blocks for rappel.

Descent: Rappel down the west face to the flake belay at the top of Pitch 2, then to the ground.

Manky Pin

Manky Pin is located 2.5 miles (4km) from the junction of Beef Basin Road #104 and Bobby's Hole Road. To approach from Squaw Flat Campground, go to Chesler Park and take the Beef Basin Road #104 southwest to the Bobby's Hole Road. Continue up Pappy's Pasture between Point 6480 and the house on the USGS Park map. The features described in this approach are identified on the large USGS map of Canyonlands National Park and Vicinity.

MANKY PIN I, 5.8, 1 pitch, 90 feet (27m)

First Ascent: Jake Tratiak, Robber Alledrege, 12 December 1987.

Location and Access: The route ascends the north face of the right-most landform when viewed from the north. Climb up through a broken area, then angle left past a left-facing dihedral to a ledge and on to the summit.

Paraphernalia: Friends #3 to #3.5.

Descent: Walk off the east side of the landform.

Crack of Many Colors

Crack of Many Colors is a tower located about 200 yards (183m) due west of a signpost located 4.9 miles (7.8km) from the trailhead at Squaw Flat campground. The sign reads "Devil's Kitchen campground 2.6 miles." *Crack of Many Colors* ascends an obvious chimney on the south corner of the landform. Two bolts are visible about 140 feet (42.6m) from the base of the route.

CRACK OF MANY COLORS I, 5.9, 2 pitches, 140 feet (43m)

First Ascent: Robert A. Kooken, Al Hymer, February 1988.

Location and Access: Begin up the chimney/crack system at 5.7, then move onto the face around a difficult point in the chimney, 5.9. The chimney/crack can be climbed as two pitches, with the first pitch ending at about 90 feet (27m) in a slot. The second pitch is approximately 50 feet (15m) long, and is rated 5.8. The crack/chimney ends at about 140 feet (42.6m) up at rappel slings visible from below.

Paraphernalia: Two sets of Friends; hexes #10, #11. There are two ⅜" bolts at the top of the route.

Descent: One 130-foot (40m) rappel off the southwest side of the landform.

The Maze District

The Maze is the southwest sector of Canyonlands National Park. It is a complicated area of canyons south and west of the confluence of the Green and Colorado Rivers. From Moab the approach to this remote land requires a full day of travel with a high-clearance four-wheel-drive vehicle. (There was no vehicle access to The Maze until 1957 when mineral exploration blazed trails into this remote region.) Overnight stays require a permit, and a portable toilet system must be carried to designated campsites.

There is a spectacular overview of The Maze from Green River Overlook on the Island-in-the-Sky district of the park. An information kiosk with an engraved plate depicts the view south

Photo: Chris Renegade Meyer

The Maze

and includes the Land of Standing Rocks, Elaterite Butte, Ekker Butte, Turks Head, and Cleopatra's Chair.

Approach to The Maze is from State Highway 24, 34 miles (55km) northeast of Hanksville, 24 miles (39km) south of I-70 east of the town of Green River. Turn east on a dirt road 0.5 mile (0.8km) south of the marked turn to Goblin Valley State Park. The road is impassable if wet. The sign at the turn from Utah 24 reads "Hans Flat 32 miles, Park Ranger 46 miles, Flint Trail 60 miles, The Maze 80 miles, Utah 95 100 miles." It is 133 miles (214km) from the Hans Flat Ranger Station to Moab. At the Hans Flat Ranger Station, permits, maps and updated road conditions may be obtained.

An alternate approach is via a four-wheel-drive road north of Hite Marina. To reach, drive a short distance north from the marina on State Highway 95. Turn right on the only dirt road located between the Colorado and Dirty Devil Rivers. Follow the main tracks in a general northeast direction. The Middle Finger, a hoodoo east of the road, will be obvious as well as the striking Sewing Machine Needle (visible from Hite Marina). Both approaches to The Maze are long. Since road conditions change with each summer thundershower, it is best to get an updated condition report from the Hans Flat ranger station. This may be done in person or by telephone. Call the main park office in Moab (801)259-3911 for the current Hans Flat number. A mountain bike is very useful for approach when the four-wheel-drive track becomes non-negotiable, but note that mountain bikes must stay on vehicle roads.

A number of routes in this section are outside The Maze District of the park in the bordering Glen Canyon National Recreation Area and are included because of their approach from four-wheel-drive roads located within The Maze District. Some climbs in the remote Maze may also be approached from a float trip down the Green River. See page 165 for more information on Glen Canyon National Recreation Area.

Cleopatra's Chair
Located at the end of the North Point Road 10 miles (16km) past the Hans Flat Ranger Station in the Glen Canyon National Recreation Area.

CLEOPATRA'S CHAIR II, 5.6, 500 feet (152m), ★★★★

First Ascent: Carl Diedrich, Julie Calhoun, Andy Pitas, Wendy Pitas, 9 November 1994.

Location and Access: The first ascent team calls the climb one of the best easy routes in the desert and the best view in all of Utah. The first ascent was done with a rope, although no gear was placed. Begin up a corner/ramp on the west face at 5.6. Continue inside an easy chimney. Use a shoulder stand to exit the chimney onto the shoulder of the landform. From there it is an easy 340-foot (104m) scramble up the south shoulder to the top with many variations possible.

Paraphernalia: Pitch 1 can be protected with #2.5 to #3 Friends.

Descent: Downclimb to the beginning of the shoulder, then make a free-hanging double-rope rappel 160 feet (49m) off the south wall from one drilled angle and a solid bush.

The Sewing Machine Needle (aka The Man Behind The Rock)
The Sewing Machine Needle is the spectacularly thin spire in the butte visible from Hite Marina on Lake Powell, when looking to the north. It is located just outside the Glen Canyon National Recreation Area. The tower is named on the Browns Rim USGS quadrangle and the Trails Illustrated map "Canyonlands Maze District and Northeast Glen Canyon." To reach, turn left (north) from Hite Marina onto State Highway 95. Turn right (east) on the only dirt road located between the Colorado and the Dirty Devil Rivers. Follow the main tracks toward The Needle which in places may require road building or four-wheel-drive. The Sewing Machine Needle will be reached in about 25 miles (40km).

THE TREADLE III, 5.8, A2, 2 pitches, 275 feet (84m)

First Ascent: Fred Beckey, Eric Bjørnstad, Lou Dawson, Reid Condiff, May 1975. Second ascent: Lou Dawson and party. Third ascent: Frosty Weller, Jonathan Auerbach, Randall Weekley, 25 October 1994.

Location and Access: Climb the best looking crack at the base of the southwest face to a belay below the vertical shaft of the needle. Continue, mostly on fixed anchors, to the summit.

Paraphernalia: One set of Friends.

Descent: Rappel the route.

Photo: Charlie Fowler

Kyle Copeland on Standing Rock, Monument Basin

The Middle Finger Tower

The Middle Finger Tower is a hoodoo located to the right of the road to The Sewing Machine Needle in the Glen Canyon National Recreation Area.

THE MIDDLE FINGER TOWER I, 5.9, A3–, 3 pitches, 130 feet (40m)

First Ascent: Steve Anderton, Bill Duncan, 9 March 1992.

Location and Access: The route climbs the south face of the landform.

Pitch 1: Climb a left-facing dihedral to a large ledge, 5.9, 30 feet (9m).

Pitch 2: Continue to the top of a large block (A2+/A3-). Follow thin cracks up and left to an easy chimney, 5.6. Follow the chimney to a ledge, 75 feet (23m).

Pitch 3: Follow a seam to a small ledge then move left to easy ledges and the summit, A3-, 25 feet (8m).

Paraphernalia: One set of Friends up to 4"; (1) set of stoppers; (1) Birdbeak; (1) knifeblade; (3) Lost Arrows; (3) ½", ¾" angles.

Descent: Rappel the route.

Standing Rock

Standing Rock appears on some topographic maps as Candlestick Spire but should not be confused with the Candlestick Spire located on the White Rim off the west side of the Island-in-the-Sky district of the park. It is correctly identified on the large USGS map of "Canyonlands National Park and Vicinity." Standing Rock, in The Maze District of the park, is located in the Land of Standing Rocks which is a plateau in an area north of a region known as Ernies Country. From the Hans Flat Ranger Station drive south down Gordon Flats to an eventual left (east) turn and a long four-wheel-drive trail to the Land of the Standing Rocks. The road will pass just south of the tower. Approach takes five hours from the ranger station. The landform is also identified (along with Standing Rock Camp) on the Trails Illustrated map series. Camping permit and updated approach information should be obtained from the Hans Flat Ranger Station. Since the climb is literally in the Standing Rock Camp, it should only be climbed when the campsite has been reserved by the ascent party.

STANDING ROCK ONE

First ascent circa 1970s, further information is unknown. Rappel slings are visible on the south side of the tower.

CHORTLER'S JOY II, 5.9, A1, 3 pitches, 145 feet (44m)

First Ascent: Jon Burnham, Bill Duncan, 18 October 1994.

Location and Access: The route faces west then north. Pitch 1 begins on the west face and climbs 5.9 ending up an A1 seam to a belay ledge. Pitch 2 traverses left along the belay ledge to the north edge of the tower. Pitch 3 climbs to the summit via offwidth, hands, and then 5.9 fingers.

Paraphernalia: Standard desert rack; a selection of knifeblades.

Descent: Rappel to the west from fixed anchors.

Warning: Park regulations require all aid climbing on this route be clean aid. Traditional hammer aid is prohibited.

Ekker Butte

The Butte is identified on the large USGS map "Canyonlands National Park and Vicinity," and the Trails Illustrated map series. Directions are best obtained from the Maze Ranger Station where an update on regulations and current road conditions may be obtained.

Ekker Butte is located south of the Milland Canyon Benches, east of the Orange Cliffs, and just north of Horse Canyon, in the Glen Canyon National Recreation Area. This is a location just less than 1 mile (1.6km) north of the zigzagging Canyonlands National Park boundary.

SOUTH TOWER II, 5.10b, 3 pitches, 300 feet (91m), ★★★

First Ascent: Tom Thomas, Dan Mathews, January 1987.

Location and Access: The south tower of the landform is lower in elevation than the main butte. The route climbs southeast to southwest. Begin up a loose chimney on the southeast ridge of the tower and climb to a belay ledge, 5.8. Continue up 5.9+ to a 5.10b handcrack which is located on the face of the tower rather than in the corner. From a good belay ledge continue up a right-facing corner with a four-inch (10cm) offwidth for 40 feet (12m), which leads to the summit via 5.9+ climbing (protect with the #4 Friends).

Paraphernalia: Friends (1) #1.5, (2) sets #2 through #3.5, (3) #4; medium to large nuts.

Descent: Rappel the route to the ledge above Pitch 1, then directly to the ground.

Bagpipe Butte

Bagpipe Butte located in the Glen Canyon National Recreation Area. This is a point just north of the Wayne County southern border. Approach is from the Hans Flat Ranger Station via the dirt track which descends south through Gordon Flats. The Butte may be reached by climbing the rock east of the road and hiking about 1 mile (1.6km) further east to the landform.

An alternate approach and easier hike to the butte is by continuing south to the four-wheel-drive Flint Trail and following it east, then northeast toward Big Water Canyon and Elaterite Basin. Before reaching these destinations Bagpipe Butte will be obvious to the west of the four-wheel-drive road.

BAGPIPE BUTTE II, 5.10, A3, 2 pitches, 150 feet (46m)

First Ascent: Tom Thomas, solo, January 1987.

Location and Access: The base of the north (highest) summit block is reached by an easy chimney on the west side of the north face. It was also climbed via twin handcracks on the east side of the north face. These routes bring one to the base of the 40 foot (12m) true north face which was aided (A3) by the first ascent party.

Paraphernalia: One set of Friends with extra #1.5, #2, #3.

Descent: Rappel the route.

Bathtub Butte

The landform is located on BLM land just outside (west of) Glen Canyon National Recreation Area (which is west of the national park boundary), 1.5 miles (2.4km) due east of Fiddler

Butte. It is identified as Point 6229 on the large USGS map of "Canyonlands National Park and Vicinity," at a location just east of the named Fiddler Butte. The same designations are identified on the Fiddler Butte USGS quadrangle.

GUNSIGHT PINNACLE III, 5.11–, A2, 5 pitches, 360 feet (110m)

First Ascent: Tom Thomas, Gil McCormick, Dan Mathews, October 1987.

Location and Access: Gunsight Pinnacle rises about 100 feet (30m) above the notch between the Pinnacle and the north and south summits of Bathtub Butte. Begin left of an obvious 20-foot (6m) fingercrack on the west face of the landform (below the northern notch).

Paraphernalia: Standard desert rack.

Descent: Rappel the route.

NORTH SUMMIT III, 5.11, A2, 4 pitches, 360 feet (110m)

First Ascent: Tom Thomas, Gil McCormick, October 1987.

Location and Access: The north summit is reached via an obvious crack on the south face of the landform. The route follows *Gunsight Pinnacle* to the notch. Continue another 50 feet (15m). The route eventually leads to a pedestal on the north side of the tower.

Paraphernalia: Two sets of Friends; (3-4) knifeblades; (2) pieces 4" to 5".

Descent: Rappel the route.

The Pinnacles

The Pinnacles are located in Happy Canyon west of the Glen Canyon Recreation Area. This is a point just south of the Garfield County line on the map. The formation is identified as "The Pinnacle" on the Fiddler Butte USGS topographic quadrangle. The landform is a collapsing butte (geologically speaking) which is a composite of many towers up to 200 feet (61m) in height. At each end of the butte towers are separated by large chimneys.

To reach, descend south from the Hans Flat Ranger Station down Gordon Flat and then west up The Big Ridge area to Two Pipe Springs, then hike north to Happy Canyon and east where a rappel into the canyon is necessary before continuing the hike west to The Pinnacles. The rappel point is just south of a peninsula of The Big Ridge and just north of an obvious Navajo Sandstone knob. This is a very remote region west of the park, east of the Dirty Devil River. Considerable route finding will be required over a long day of four-wheel and high-clearance driving. Expect an epic desert approach.

There is a spring near the bottom of the rappel point which issues from the base of the Wingate and gave about two quarts of water every five minutes during the 1987 first ascent approach. It is identified by tall grass growing under the drip and white lime deposits appearing about 20 feet (6m) up the wall from the top of the talus.

Once on top of the east and west towers of The Pinnacles it is possible to hop across deep chimneys from one tower to another, similar to the Walking Rocks region of the White Rim in the northeast region of Canyonlands National Park.

NORTH TOWER I, 5.11, 1 pitch, 100 feet (30m)

First Ascent: Tom Thomas, Gil McCormick, October 1987.

Location and Access: The northernmost tower is climbed via an obvious crack system on the south face. The ascent from the notch is up a four-inch (10cm) crack for one pitch of hard 5.11, 60 feet (18m). Begin up the west face, below the northern notch. This is a point left of an obvious 20-foot (6m) fingercrack where there are two corners which face one another 30 feet (9m) up the rock. The route eventually leads to a pedestal on the north side of the tower.

Paraphernalia: Standard desert rack.

Descent: Rappel the route.

WAITING FOR KENNEDY II, 5.10+, 4 pitches

First Ascent: Pete Gallagher, John Catto, Fall 1992.

Location and Access: The route climbs the center of the east face via a corner crack system. Climb through a hole (visible from below) located below the overhanging caprock and finish on the west face 50 feet (15m) left of the regular route.

Paraphernalia: Standard desert rack.

Descent: Rappel the southwest original route.

EAST TOWER I, 5.11–, 2 pitches, 200 feet (61m)

First Ascent: Tom Thomas, Gil McCormick, October 1987.

Location and Access: The east tower is climbed via a crack system inside a chimney which widens from a full arms-length to fingertips at the top.

Paraphernalia: Standard desert rack.

Descent: Rappel the route.

WEST TOWER I, 5.11–, 2 pitches, 130 feet (40m)

First Ascent: Tom Thomas, Gil McCormick, October 1987.

Location and Access: The west tower is climbed beginning with a blocky hand jam pitch of 75 feet (23m) on the south face. The beginning of the route is located behind minor towers which do not lead to the higher summit.

Paraphernalia: Standard desert rack.

Descent: Rappel the route.

THE LITTLE TOE I, 5.11–, 2 pitches, 130 feet (40m)

First Ascent: Tom Thomas, Gil McCormick, October 1987.

Location and Access: The Little Toe is the central, free-standing tower of The Pinnacles group. The first ascent route climbs 60 feet (18m) up the spire to its summit via a west-facing arête.

Paraphernalia: Standard desert rack.

Descent: Rappel the route.

Buttes of The Cross

The Buttes of The Cross are located in the Glen Canyon National Recreation Area just south and east of The Maze district of the park. The approach is via State Highway 24 northeast of Hanksville, Utah. Turn east and follow signs to Hans Flat Ranger Station (four-wheel-drive recommended). The rough road beyond the ranger station eventually passes to within a few hundred yards of the Buttes of The Cross. Topo maps and a visit at the ranger station on the way in will do much to ensure success in making this full-day approach. No pitons or bolts were used on the first ascent; please repeat the climb in the same good style. The landform is split by a gap that has a large chockstone (visible for miles) wedged at its top.

An alternate approach is from a float trip down the Green River to Anderson Bottom where the Buttes of The Cross may be approached via a two-mile (3.2km) hike due west. The Buttes of The Cross landform is named on the large USGS map "Canyonlands National Park and Vicinity" and the Trails Illustrated series.

WEST CHIMNEYS III, 5.9, 5 pitches, 350 feet (107m)

First Ascent: Paul Horton, Lynn Watson, 25 May 1987.

Location and Access: No pitons or bolts were used on the first ascent. The route starts on the west side of the butte in the chimney that ascends to the chockstone of the cross. After two-and-a-half pitches a short lieback leads left out of the main chimney and into a smaller chimney that leads to the summit ledges.

Paraphernalia: Standard desert rack.

Descent: Downclimb to the top of Pitch 4, then rappel to a point just above the top of Pitch 2. Downclimb to the top of Pitch 2 and rappel to the top of Pitch 1, then to the ground.

THE EPICUREAN III, 5.10c, 6 pitches, 550 feet (168m)

First Ascent: John Rosholt, Keen Butterworth, 12 May 1990.

Location and Access: The route climbs an obvious crack system on the north face. Pitch 1 climbs loose 5.10 rock to a belay stance. Pitch 2 ascends the crux (5.10c) protected by #3 Friends, ending at a belay stance. Continue up to a belay (below a heinous looking chimney), Pitch 4 traverses left past a dirt groove to a more reasonable chimney and a belay for Pitch 5 which is climbed 5.9+, finishing on the ridge at 5.4. Pitch 6 is easy fifth class to the summit.

Paraphernalia: Two sets of Friends with several #3, #3.5; (1) set of nuts.

Descent: Three double-rope rappels from anchors at the top of Pitch 5.

Antelope Tower

Antelope Tower is located on BLM land just outside the boundary of the Horseshoe Canyon satellite region of Canyonlands National Park, in a deep canyon adjacent to Horseshoe Canyon. It is approached from Utah 24 north of the Hans Flat Ranger Station. Approach as for Horseshoe Canyon and walk down the canyon (Barrier Creek) until the Wingate rock rises and falls on the side walls. The tower is hidden in the canyon. It is weathered from the Navajo formation (above the Wingate) and located about 2 miles (3.2km) south-southeast of the Antelope Valley Reservoir No. #3 as noted on the large USGS map "Canyonlands National Park and Vicinity." Considerable route finding may be required to locate the tower.

An alternate approach is to hike up the canyon from a float trip down the Green River. The mouth of Barrier Creek is covered with a forrest of tamarisk growth, but once beyond the entrance the canyon walls steepen and become very spectacular, offering a lifetime of potential climbing routes.

HIDDEN IN THE CANYON I, 5.10, A2, 3 pitches

First Ascent: Tom Thomas, Tony Moats, November 1986.

Location and Access: The route is on a west-southwest face and climbs a large chimney. Once inside the view is open to the south. The climb is unique in that one climbs out of a deep narrow canyon and up to the level of the surrounding land.

Paraphernalia: One set of Friends with protection up to six inches and a small selection of pitons.

Descent: Rappel the route.

Wherever we look there is but a wilderness of rocks, deep gorges where the rivers are lost below cliffs and towers and pinnacles and ten thousand strangely carved forms in every direction, and beyond them mountains blending with the clouds.

John Wesley Powell

...At daybreak, I am the sole owner of all the acres I can walk over. It is not only boundaries that disappear, but also the thought of being bounded.

Aldo Leopold

ERIC BJØRNSTAD
A CLIMBING LIFE

Eric Bjørnstad is perhaps best known as a pioneer of desert towers during the incredible early years when those phenomenal spires were first being climbed. Indeed, many of us climbing his routes today would shudder at the idea of doing them in the 1960s and early '70s with the available gear and lack of information. Certainly Eric's name is indelibly etched in the rich lore of desert climbing. But a broader look also reveals a life of great variety and interest, both within and outside the climbing world.

From the start, Eric engaged himself in a wide range of endeavors. Raised in California, his early passions included poetry writing, chess, speed typing, classical music, and played both the piano and oboe. He also sought physical challenges such as boxing, in which he excelled. Eric began camping early, with numerous trips to the High Sierra, and like many climbers then and now, a great love of high places was kindled.

Eric's first job was as a Gandy Dancer on the narrow gauge railroad near Lone Pine, California. This began a working life of incredible variety; over the years he worked as a draftsman, piano salesman, photo processor, gardener, bartender, dump truck driver, tree topper, and

handyman at a sorority traded for a place to live, to name only a sampling. His life apart from work was no less interesting. He married three times (to a Hungarian beauty queen, an art student, and the daughter of a major American business mogul), divorced three times, and fathered four children (David, Heather, Mara, and Eigerwand). He practiced Theravada Buddhism in Berkeley in the '50s, partied with the likes of Alan Watts, Jack Kerouac, and Ferlinghetti and took up spelunking. In the late 1950s he moved to Seattle and began a long career in alpine mountaineering. He amassed an impressive list of climbs and first ascents: Zodiac Wall, the first grade VI on the Squamish Chief, the North Face of Mount Howser in the Bugaboos, first winter ascent of Mt. Robson, first ascent of the North Face of Mt. Slesse, seventh ascent of Liberty Ridge on Mt. Rainier, Mt. Seattle in the St. Elias Range in Alaska, second ascent of the West Peak of the Moose's Tooth, and many others. He also taught climbing for the Seattle Mountaineers, served on the Seattle Mountain Rescue team for eight years, and represented American climbers during the Seattle World's Fair French-American climbing week. It was also during this time that Eric began to write about climbing, in both magazines and books. He co-authored the *Climber's Guide to Leavenworth Climbing Areas* with Fred Beckey and wrote the "Pitoncraft" chapter for the second edition of the classic text *Mountaineering, Freedom of the Hills.*

From the 1960s on, Eric moved often and lived in cities across the country. He added weaving and three dimensional stained glass to his professional repertoire, as well as proprietorships of five restaurants/coffee houses. He also developed a passion for climbing in the mysterious landscape of the Southwest desert. The routes that he and other desert pioneers established on these spooky towers tested the limits of existing equipment and techniques as well as their nerves. First ascents in the '60s included Echo Tower in the Fisher Towers, the Beckey Buttress on Shiprock (20 days), Middle Sister and Jacobs Ladder in Monument Valley, Chinle Spire, and the 574th overall ascent of Devil's Tower when he and Fred Beckey put up the popular *El Matador* route.

During these years, Eric climbed with such well-known figures as Ed Cooper, Alex Bertulis, Don Claunch, Harvey T. Carter, Yvon Chouinard and Galen Rowell. He also developed an intense relationship with Fred Beckey–the two would share many first ascents over the years.

In the 1970s he began a ten year period as a researcher investigating the effects of air pollution on lung health for the Harvard School of Public Health, which kept him traveling extensively. He returned to the desert time and again during this period, establishing first ascents such as Eagle Rock Spire in Monument Valley (another 16-day marathon), and Zeus and Moses in Canyonlands. He also did the 5th ascent of the incredible Totem Pole in Monument Valley, during the making of the film *The Eiger Sanction.*

In 1985 Eric finally made Moab his permanent home. He opened his famous Teahouse Tamarisk (24 page menu), made the 600th ascent of Castleton Tower, the first ascent of the 1000 foot El Piñon Blanca in Mexico, and participated in the first ascents of such well-known climbs as *Zenyata Entrada* in Arches. He also undertook the phenomenal researching and writing task of authoring *Desert Rock*, the only comprehensive guide to desert climbs.

Eric now guides hikes in Arches, works with Canyonlands Natural History Association, drives four-wheel desert tours, produces and sells Desert Glass Light Catchers, etched glass window hangings of anasazi rock art, and is completing an expanded four-volume guide to technical rock climbs on the sandstone walls of the southwest desert, the only comprehensive climbing guide to the Colorado Plateau.

Eric has truly lived a climbing life–in the high mountains, on rock walls, and in the desert Southwest. He has lived a well rounded life as well, full of rich and enviable experiences. He loves the company of climbers, and will spend hours telling and listening to stories or pressing for information. His home is like a climbing museum. Yet, just as easily, he will revel in an opera or classical orchestral piece, or spend an evening preparing a fine dinner.

These guides are a tribute to Eric's life as a climber–and to his love for this desert land.

Jeff Widen
November 1995